D0907273

BEING LA DOMINICANA

DISSIDENT FEMINISMS

Elora Halim Chowdhury, Editor

A list of books in the series appears at the end of this book.

Being La Dominicana

Race and Identity in the
Visual Culture of Santo Domingo

RACHEL AFI QUINN

UNIVERSITY OF
ILLINOIS PRESS
Urbana, Chicago, and Springfield

Publication of this book was supported in part by funding from
the University of Houston's Women's, Gender & Sexuality Studies
Program and the UH Friends of Women's Studies.

© 2021 by the Board of Trustees
of the University of Illinois
All rights reserved
1 2 3 4 5 C P 5 4 3 2 1
⊗ This book is printed on acid-free paper.

Library of Congress Cataloging-in-Publication Data
Names: Quinn, Rachel Afi, author.
Title: Being la Dominicana : race and identity in the visual
    culture of Santo Domingo / Rachel Afi Quinn.
Description: Urbana : University of Illinois Press, [2021] | Series:
    Dissident feminisms | Includes bibliographical references and
    index.
Identifiers: LCCN 2021010536 (print) | LCCN 2021010537 (ebook)
    | ISBN 9780252043819 (hardcover) | ISBN 9780252085802
    (paperback) | ISBN 9780252052712 (ebook)
Subjects: LCSH: Women—Dominican Republic. | Feminism—
    Dominican Republic. | Dominicans (Dominican Republic)
    —Race identity.
Classification: LCC HQ1514 .Q85 2021 (print) | LCC HQ1514 (ebook)
    | DDC 305.4097293 —dc23
LC record available at https://lccn.loc.gov/2021010536
LC ebook record available at https://lccn.loc.gov/2021010537

Contents

Acknowledgments

When I first visited my father in Ghana at age seventeen, his mother, Sarah Doe Kpetigo Glover ("Nano"), gave me the Ewe name Ametolesi, meaning roughly "many people stand behind you." This could not be more true! I have marveled at my good fortune to have such wealth of loved ones near and far. This book is based on research from a decade and a half of travel to the Dominican Republic and time spent living there. Many transnational communities have sustained me over the years, and I recognize how all of them have had some influence on me as I crafted this book. As someone who thrives on the energy and inspiration of others, over the last decade I have had the opportunity to connect with more people who have helped make this book a reality than I can possibly remember and name here—but I will give it a try.

Thank you to the numerous scholars I had the pleasure of working closely with at University of Michigan while in the Program in American Culture: Evelyn Azeeza Alsultany, who deftly guided me through my graduate studies; María Cotera, Jesse Hoffnung-Garskof, and Lori Brooks, who each in their own way helped me find my way with a first iteration of this project; many thanks to Nadine Naber, Ruth Behar, and Magdalena Zabarowska in this regard as well. I am particularly appreciative of the ever-thoughtful mentorship and steady calm of Tiya Miles. Thank you also to Brandi Hughes, who made sure I would find somewhere to land. The solidarity of so many sustained me throughout graduate school: special thanks to Patricia Moonsammy, Afia Ofori-Mensah, Roxana Galusca, Laura Wernick, Kanika Harris, and Vanessa Díaz, with a big a shout-out to Shana Weaver.

I would not have been prepared to do this project, or had a way to approach the work without the training I received for just two weeks at Cornell as part of the Future of Minority Studies (FMS) summer institute led by Chandra Talpade Mohanty and Beverly Guy-Sheftall in 2009. The FMS community has been foundational to my work as a transnational feminist scholar and the relationships forged there have inspired and fortified me on this long journey. I am thankful to have found peer mentorship and friendship with Sylvanna Falcón, Tania Triana, Azza Basarudin, Sharmila Lodhia, Michelle Telles, Shareen Roshanravan, Edwin Hill, Moya Bailey, Arica Coleman and many other dear FMSers. I have also been fortunate to join the fold of the National Women Studies Association (NWSA), which has offered beloved community. The NWSA's Transnational Feminisms caucus—born out of the Thinking Transnational Feminisms summer institute at Ohio State University of which I was fortunate to be a part—continues to inspire my work. Funding for this project began with the University of Michigan's Global Transformations Fellowship that got me to the Dominican Republic for the first time. Since, the University of Houston has been a tremendous supporter of this research over the years. I was able to complete this project through the gift of time and intellectual community provided by a Woodrow Wilson Career Enhancement Fellowship, while comradery and funding from the UH Underrepresented Women of Color Coalition helped get me to the finish line—with special thanks to Erika Henderson and Andrea Georgsson for investing in my success.

Of course, this book is only possible thanks to the generosity of strangers willing to share with me about their lives—and translate the details. Many brilliant and talented friends in Santo Domingo contributed to my understanding of and love for the Dominican Republic over the years. Most especially, I am thankful for the friendship and generosity of Yaneris González Gómez, Diana Pérez, Nathaly Ramos, Alejandra Prido, Michelle Ricardo, Dulcina Abreu, Xiomara Fortuna, Isabel Spencer, Aurora Martínez, Glaem Parls, Marcos Morales, Laura Bretón Despredal, Jeannette Tineo Durán, as well as Princess Jiménez, Merlyn Cornelio, Inda George, and numerous other kind souls who are not named in my work. I truly would not know the Dominican Republic the way I do without my longstanding relationship with la familia García, in particular Marta, Mercedes, Criselda, Patricia, and la doña Merida Reynosa de García ("Palina"), and all that I have learned from their health clinic FUVICREF serving women and girls in their hometown of Sabana Grande de Boyá. In my neighborhood of Los Jardines del Norte, I was welcomed by Suni Rosario Batista and her children Liberman, Darlyng,

Carlos, Jerilee, and Ana Celia, and their extended family. It has also been a pleasure to know Nairobi Acosta and Edwin Pérez and their daughter, Genesis, since she was very small. I am also lucky to have overlapped in my time in Santo Domingo with Erika Martínez—who taught me much about the processes of writing and friendship—and friends Meg Hendrickson and Roberto Obando, Sarah Adler-Milstein, and Julio Gonzalez Ruíz. Julio's passion for life, and for the Dominican Republic, will remain an inspiration to all of us who knew him. Much gratitude goes to my humble friend Lucía Mendez Rivas for sharing her beautiful artwork for the cover image and to photographers Lorena Espinoza Peña and Fran Afonso, along with Penelope Callado and Cindy Galán. Ana Francisca Acevedo has been a patient and enthusiastic friend and language teacher over the years and was critical to my research success, as was Lisa Borchetta in the early stages of this project. I am also grateful to Tertúlia Feminista Magaly Pineda under the leadership of Esther Hernández-Medina and Yildalina Tatem Brache and all who have welcomed me into that space. Many more scholars and activists whom I have encountered in Santo Domingo have kindly encouraged me in this journey, namely Quisqueya Lora, Frank Moya Pons, Sergia Galván Ortega, and the late Magaly Pineda and Tony de Moya. I have felt fortunate to join a tremendous network of Dominican studies scholars, who have supported my intellectual growth and trusted in my work, in particular Lorgia García Peña, Raj Chetty, Maja Horn, April Mayes, Elizabeth Manley, Sharina Mailla-Pozo, Zaida Coroniel, and Jacqueline Jiménez Polanco.

My sincere thanks go out to the team of scholars who were willing to workshop my manuscript and provide feedback necessary to propel it forward: Roberto Tejada, Keith McNeal, Christina Sisk, and Elizabeth Gregory, with Ana S. Q. Liberato. Thanks also to Trevor Boffone, Sarah Luna, Julie Tolliver, Kavita Singh, and Maria Gonzalez who offered thoughtful comments on an early chapter; to Sandra Zalman who welcomed my thoughts on Surrealism, and to the UH Caribbean studies working group including Mabel Cuesta, who made possible my first publication in Spanish. Historian friends Marcia Walker-McWilliams and Leandra Zarnow also modeled for me the care and rigor with which I might write the stories of women. This book would not exist without the patient guidance of editor Dawn Durante during her time at University of Illinois Press, where my work met with kind and enthusiastic reviewers. Neither would there be a book without the calm and skillful guidance of copyeditor Jordan Beltrán Gonzales. Not least of all, I am extremely grateful to Elora Halim Chowdhury for her mentorship and ability to see this book when I could not.

Houston is an incredible place to live and work. I am fortunate to have landed in yet another expansive community of creatives who have influenced my thinking, including my co-conspirators Rubén Durán, Donna Pinnick, and Michael Brims, with whom I had the pleasure of making the documentary film *Cimarrón Spirit* (2015). I also draw much inspiration from mentoring relationships with Rikki Bettinger, Sylvia Fernández, Robyn Lyn, Monica Lugo, Sylvia Mendoza, Adrienne Perry, and Jess Waggoner, all now cherished friends. Endless gratitude goes out to my clever friend and online writing partner of so many years Jillian Báez; and to members of my most recent writing community Derria Byrd, LaShonda Sullivan, and Lanice Avery, guided briefly yet profoundly by Meredith Gadsby. I also know I would not have made it over the finish line without cheerleaders like Abigail Lapin Dardashti, Mariola Alvarez, Julia Jordan-Zachary, Mai-Lin Hong, and Santhi Periasamy.

Both of my parents, Naomi Robin Quinn and Bernard Kwesi Glover, passed away in the years that I have been writing this first book and professionalizing as a scholar. I do not have the pleasure of putting a copy of it into their hands, but certainly their encouragement led me down this path and I trust they would be proud. I am also grateful to have had as adopted family Davi Ruby Dey (who gave me sisters Aseye, Nayram, and Emefa) and Kweku Garbrah while they were on this earth. Andrea Yeager, Ronny Quevedo, Ayanna McCloud (and my godson Zahir Jones), Bryant Holsenbeck, Mig Little Hayes, Sara Mayer, Cornelius Moore, Rahdi Taylor, and Barrie McClune are family to me and I could not have known I could write a book without their great confidence in me over so many years.

Not least of all in this endeavor, I happily thank my number-one cheerleader and most thoughtful reader, Eesha Pandit, for being a true inspiration in my feminist scholarship and with whom I am grateful to have made a life in Houston, Texas. Eesha's brilliance and emotional intelligence continue to inspire me—as does her feminist rage.

BEING LA DOMINICANA

Introduction

Transnational Feminist Cultural Studies, Visual Culture, and the Ethnographic Project

Tens of thousands of faceless ceramic dolls of varying shapes, sizes, and colors line the dusty shelves of gift shops throughout Santo Domingo. To purchase a *muñeca sin rostro* (doll without a face) is to choose among the many for sale throughout the capital: in the supermarket La Sirena, in tourist boutiques along the pedestrian mall El Conde, or even in the city's Barrio Chino. The muñecas sin rostros become Mother's Day gifts, souvenirs of tourists' visits to the Dominican Republic, or presents carried off into the diaspora by soon-to-be houseguests or relatives making holiday visits, like the ubiquitous oil paintings of the frizzy orange *framboyan* trees or the colonial architecture and cobblestone streets of the capital city. The doll is crafted with a long bell-shaped dress and high collar reminiscent of a bygone colonial era; she is clasping a bouquet of flowers at her waist. Made from the clay of different regions of the country, her skin tone is determined by the color of the earth. Close inspection reveals that each is unique in form and paint. Beneath her wide-brimmed hat and floral embellishments, every doll's face is blank.[1]

Ask any Dominican why the muñeca sin rostro looks the way that she does and they will tell you it is because "we are a mix of everything, we are Spanish, we are indigenous, we have African roots. Our features cannot be represented in any one form." In a society in which the vast majority of its members are racially mixed, this explanation refers to the Latin American ideology of *mestizaje* in which racial mixture between Europeans and Indigenous peoples is celebrated; it became social policy in Latin America due to Mexican philosopher José Vasconcelos's vision of "La Raza Cósmica" (The Cosmic Race). Yet the story of the muñeca sin rostro told today seems to also imply that Dominican women have no one single identity; rather, you can see in them whatever you wish to see—they are interchangeable, easily reproduced, anonymous pawns in a larger economy. The muñeca sin rostro is one of several symbols integral to the visual discourse of contemporary Santo Domingo that I have chosen to gather, curate, and examine in this text. It joins a vast collection of ethnographic moments and visual illustrations that I juxtapose in ways that they might speak to one another.

Taking a transnational feminist cultural studies approach to reading contemporary Dominican society and popular culture, *Being La Dominicana* examines the importance of everyday visual culture in the lives of Dominican women growing up in Santo Domingo, from social media's vernacular images to Dominican theater productions, to Dominican-made music videos and films. I ask, how do Dominican women theorize their own experiences of race and color within the dominant visual discourse of the Caribbean? I build on the insights of Krista Thompson, who draws from the culture of the region to argue that black people's performance for the camera is an act of self-making.[2] In particular, I contend that the manner and process of self-making within the visual economy of the Dominican Republic, and the performance of race and gender among young Dominican women in Santo Domingo, relies on their capacity for racial transformation—a racial logic that serves the demands of digital visual capital in the contemporary moment. I interpret contemporary Dominican cultural productions through a diversity of Dominican symbols of the everyday. Looking at Dominican visual culture in this way, I take into account a legacy of Surrealism that emerges within the contemporary moment in Santo Domingo and I look at several decidedly surrealist contemporary texts.

Like other Caribbean nations, the Dominican Republic has always existed as a transnational space. Long before the country's formation as a nation-state, the island of Saint Domingue existed as a transnational and trans-cultural space.[3] In the past, technologies such as the sailing ship produced these Caribbean networks.[4] But today, other technologies assist in the flow of people, goods, ideas, capital, and culture in and out of these spaces, and digital technologies, in particular, facilitate the rapid flow of beliefs, images, meanings, and emotions. As nations desperately try to define and determine the bounds of their territories, national borders are increasingly porous, and Dominican transnational identity and experiences do not require physical travel abroad. The term "globalization" was utilized by scholars of Latin America and the Caribbean in the 1990s, but more recently "transnational" has been a key term of analysis in contemporary cultural studies to highlight cultural "connectivities" or linkages among nation-states.[5] As historian

Elizabeth Manley has shown, Dominican women under dictatorship in the twentieth century "found and expanded spaces of global and transnational activism that advanced basic political rights and paved the way for the feminist movement."[6] Transnational connectivities were a part of producing and sustaining Dominican women's feminist projects.

According to Dominican historian Frank Moya Pons, many politicians in the United States and the Dominican Republic have "understood the Dominican Republic as a satellite of the US in the Caribbean Region. It has for decades remained under US supervision, in a way, through US economic reliance and thus US control, for the sheer fear of having 'another Cuba' in the Caribbean."[7] Amalia Cabezas has described the Dominican Republic as having "long been a quasi-colony of the United States," and until the 1990s, it was viewed as "emblematic of the problems that could beset Cuba, troubles such as child prostitution, gambling, casinos, widespread social inequities, and the pervasive lack of a social safety net for its citizens."[8] The United States occupied the Dominican Republic through military intervention from 1916 to 1924 and invaded the country again in 1965—on both occasions with the explicit aim of influencing political outcomes and "making the world safe for capitalism" in the years before and during the Cold War.[9]

Today, one can plainly see a US cultural occupation of the Dominican Republic, though it is not the only country with influence there.[10] Being Dominican in Santo Domingo now means watching American-made TV shows on your smartphone as much as it means viewing Latin American *telenovelas* with the family; it means immediately adopting new fashions, foods, values, and language from abroad, celebrating Thanksgiving and Halloween, and sustaining a connection to relatives overseas via social media twenty-four hours a day. The neoliberalization of Dominican women's lives—including the increased privatization of daily life, the nation-state's investment in a global tourism industry, and the broad influence of US popular culture and cultural values—is legible throughout Dominican society and visual culture, and central to the culture of Santo Domingo.

"Ya somos americanizadas [We are already Americanized]," asserts a friend (via Facebook chat) who grew up in Santo Domingo, where countless new condo towers, a massive Ikea, and a rapidly expanding Metro rail system reflect in the city's landscape how Dominicans understand themselves as "transnational subjects" of the contemporary age.[11] An entire generation of Dominicans are forming their identities within a nation that has changed dramatically under neoliberal development schemes; they are significantly assimilating to US culture without ever leaving the island.[12] English slang like "chillin'" and hybrid phrases like *vamos al* party," "*que hay de* new," and "*tomar un* chance" turn up in conversation. Dominicanisms capture a fluid use of language from *afuera* (outside the island). As Carlos Andújar Persinal writes of Dominican Spanish, "Of course we are not speaking an academic Spanish, but a typical Spanish from the street, the colloquial, that is cultural Spanish and that is social Spanish that represents the history and culture of American peoples."[13] Linguistic shifts are ongoing, as Dominican youth on the street in Santo Domingo, or on Facebook in diaspora, can tell you. Shifts in the meaning of the visual in Santo Domingo—including racial meanings—are equally important.

In her essay in the *Black Scholar*, Lorgia García Peña effectively theorizes the deep roots of an ever-shifting notion of blackness among Dominicans. To understand how Dominican blackness might be misinterpreted and misunderstood by many, suggests García Peña, it is necessary to understand that it is continually produced through a sort of ebb and flow, or "*vaivén*" as she calls it, that reflects "translations and negotiations of racial ideology across markets and nations."[14] García Peña is clear that "Dominican blackness is an embodied concept that is performed, and inscribed on the flesh of national subjects through social processes that are very much linked to the political and economic realities of the nation in its relationship to the history and persisten[t] presence of colonial (Spain) and imperial (US) impositions."[15] While her examination of Dominican blackness and its flows points to markets, the ways that I theorize experiences of race and mixed race among Dominican women explore how they internalize these colonial and imperial impositions.

The See/Saw of Mixed Race

My interdisciplinary analysis of the significance of mixed-race bodies is informed by an understanding of race as a social construct that, like gender, is inherently performative. While I do not necessarily apply a performance studies methodology to my readings of visual culture and ethnography throughout this text, I recognize that "blackness and performance are two discourses whose histories converge at the site of otherness."[16] Because mixed-race people of African descent are often signifying and/or performing race in multiple ways as we move across space and time, we have insights into the ways that race is being performed and a heightened awareness of the details of difference to which, on any given day, we may fail to measure up. When shifting to represent different identities (e.g., black while in Europe, not black while in the Dominican Republic), Dominican women are often required to perform race and gender in ways that lead to insight and interiority. As E. Patrick Johnson affirms, "Self-reflexivity is usually a by-product of cultural performance, and this is particularly true for the performer who performs the Other."[17] A self-conscious awareness drawn from the experience of identifying as black, yet being fair enough in color to pass as white, is an emergent theme in literature of women of the African diaspora.[18]

An awareness of one's subjectivity, argues feminist filmmaker and cultural theorist Trinh T. Minh-ha, is essential to understanding the world outside of one's self: "The moment the insider steps out from the inside she's no longer a mere insider. She necessarily looks in from the outside while also looking out from the inside. Not quite the same, not quite the other, she stands in that undetermined threshold place where she constantly drifts in and out."[19] This theory speaks to my own experience of assimilating into Dominican culture as an outsider and the ways that this text provides at some points an auto-ethnography of my time in Santo Domingo. However, it also provides a useful way to understand the experience of racial malleability that for myself and the women I write about is one of being "not quite the same, not quite other" in our families and our communities. In other words, our racial identities may be experienced as a constant drifting. Many anthropologists have observed this experience of being at the same time both inside and outside when asked to write about their own communities by serving as "native informants." Jill Olumide refers to this epistemic knowledge of being racially ambiguous as the "mixed race condition."[20]

Throughout *Being La Dominicana*, I demonstrate the ways that Dominican women's mixed-race identities are not only in constant movement but also that they "see/saw" in relation to others on a hierarchical scale of power. I use the term *see/saw*, then, to convey this feeling of drifting up and down, and to point to the fact that the movement is relational: the act of see-sawing up and down requires that there be another body against which to balance one's self in that moment. See/sawing thus requires that for one person to rise, another must sink: a highly relational construction of racial meaning. As I show throughout this text, Dominican women's identities are constantly recalibrated through relational interactions that reproduce hierarchies of color, class, gender, sexuality, and more, thus revealing power dynamics, specifically in relation to blackness. In part due to their racial ambiguity, they can see/saw up and down in a racial hierarchy in any given moment, because the racial meaning of their body is only fixed at the moment of interaction. The form I use in constructing this term with a forward slash is also influenced by the critical theoretical work of Dominican scholar Lorgia García Peña, whose concept of contra*diction* employs italics in order to effectively demonstrate her theory of the changing nature of *dominicanidad* across space and time as it is produced through language. She necessarily exerts force on a word in English, so that it can adequately capture the ways dominicanidad is always contested and negotiated.[21]

My own use of a forward slash within the concept see/saw serves three unique purposes: 1) it reminds us of the act of visual engagement in structures of power around race by demarcating two different forms of the verb "to see"; 2) it acknowledges the possibility of seeing one thing racially in one way and then looking back on it at a different moment only to understand it another way. This is repeatedly the case in my study of race, gender, and sexuality in Dominican society: I am constantly reevaluating what I see and what I once saw in the archive of cultural productions, digital media, and ethnographic moments that I have gathered. And, finally, 3) the line between the two words captures a sort of cleaving and separation from others that occurs when one is forced to see the world in new ways. The line between the two acts of seeing—past and present—marks for us a process of fragmentation that is integral to the production of subjectivity that I explore among Dominican women. It is a production of self that occurs through a weaving together of visual images and navigating representations in visual culture.

Within the complex category of "the Americas," the Dominican Republic's intimacy with the United States is noteworthy. A hemispheric orientation to my analysis illuminates the many connections across the region.[22] As many families in Santo Domingo squeeze into tiny cinderblock apartments that lack consistently running water or electricity, US cable television with subtitles translates the MTV reality shows and Atlanta local news that flows into their homes. High-end malls and US fast-food chains respond to and cultivate a desire on the part of Dominicans in the capital city to live like those outside the country. Writes Diana Taylor, "The Americas, I have been taught to believe, are one—and I still believe it. Produced and organized through mutually constitutive scenarios, acts, transactions, migrations, and social systems, our hemisphere proves a contested and entangled space."[23] Across this text, I explore how transnational subjects are produced within the Dominican Republic and the many ways, as Taylor states, "the First World is in the Third World just as the Third World lives in the First."[24] For, while the Dominican neighborhood of Washington Heights in Upper Manhattan exists as an ethnic enclave where you can live out your days speaking only Dominican Spanish and eating *asopao* and *tostones con salami*, a corresponding reality holds true for North American expats who enjoy English-speaking upper-class lives in Santo Domingo; upscale supermarkets across the Dominican Republic offer a wide array of specialty foods for foreign palates (and paychecks).

Cultural histories of contemporary life in Santo Domingo are few and far between.[25] Past presidents Rafael Trujillo, Joaquin Balaguer, and Juan Bosch were all prolific writers and publishers on the history of the nation; they were also notorious for scripting the story of events only in ways they wanted their actions remembered. Academic discourse that informs scholarly perceptions of the Dominican Republic frequently omits the dynamic realities of contemporary life and gendered experiences.[26] Yet women of color have a distinct view within the workings of neoliberalism and its contradictions in daily life, and this book reflects that. Women of color feminism as a theoretical approach is at the center of my work. It is an epistemology essential to drawing meaning from the cultural productions of women of African descent because it places personal narrative at the fore, positioning the experiences of other women of color as epistemic knowledge that counters colonialist and imperialist narratives about who Dominican women are. Furthermore, when M. Jacqui Alexander calls for "pedagogies of the sacred" as part of our work as black feminist, transnational, women scholars, she is urging us to reclaim embodied knowledges, valuing beliefs and practices that have so often be dismissed. As a praxis, women of color feminism challenges accepted norms and cultural constructions such as heteronormativity and heteropatriarchy.[27] Women of color worldwide demanded of the feminism of the 1970s and 1980s this level of self-reflexivity in which white women might recognize their own privilege and complicity within a hegemonic structure from which they benefit.

Applying transnational feminist theory as a paradigmatic approach to my research has meant locating myself in solidarity with the many Dominican women who inform how I tell this story. They are themselves activists and artists connected to elaborate transnational feminist networks; they regularly cross borders and are shaped by these experiences. Transnational feminism also demands that I be conscientious about depicting the inherent inequalities that come up each time women of color sit together (even metaphorically) at the same table and it reminds me of the urgency of the work to be done among us.[28] Ultimately, my transnational feminist analysis is informed by *their* insights about globalizing systems of uneven development, and the postcolonial narratives of race and gender that they navigate daily.[29] I have sought out feminist alliances with women of color for whom my presence and engagement in their lives is a benefit and with whom I share a critique of capitalism and globalization across gender, class, race, and nation. Many of the women I write about feel exploited as workers in industries that cross borders—some work at call centers or are earning degrees in tourism to work in hotels.

By using the term *transnational* I seek to highlight their experiences of neoliberal globalization and its fluid movement on many societal registers. I claim a transnational feminist research methodology because of the conversations I have engaged in that have shaped my approach to the work at this moment in time. Furthermore, I wrestle with the imperialist model of "knowledge extraction" as I seek a collaborative methodology through which Dominican women's voices in my scholarship are foregrounded.[30] Transnational feminist studies is not fully formed as a field, as Richa Nagar and Amanda Locke Swarr have argued, and as my scholarship shows, it does require greater self-critical examination if it is to suggest that inherent power dynamics might be disrupted through unorthodox ethnography.[31] I disrupt by sharing my work with the community I write about as I write, and by including their full names in the text when they have chosen to be identifiable.[32] And a transnational feminist approach to this project has offered me a way of theorizing my own experiences of the insider-outsider ebbs and flows of African diaspora solidarities in the Dominican Republic. And it has provided me a better lens through which to bear witness in spaces in which cultural production as knowledge production occurs among women in Santo Domingo.

Out from Underneath the Imagery of the "Picturesque"

To tell this story about the lives and experiences of Dominican women, I am certain I must tell it with and *through* visual culture and account for how photographs make visible Dominican women's mixed-race bodies within a specific racial schema. Writes Gloria Anzaldúa, "Images are more direct, more immediate than words, and closer to the unconscious. Picture language precedes thinking in words; the metaphorical mind precedes analytical consciousness."[33] The photograph has been used to both humanize and dehumanize in the tropics and has been employed with great consistency to create spectacle. The Caribbean has a long history tied to the "picturesque," a space of tropical flora, fauna, and the desirable native Other. As Hazel Carby argues, it is through the technology of photography that these images serve to "fix the colonies in a pre-modern moment."[34] Moreover, photography was developed alongside tourism, serving in part as a way to collect and bring back a piece of a place that one visited. And as Thompson writes, "colonial representations were frequently not just reflective of colonial views but became constitutive and iconic parts of the colonies' landscape."[35] Photography was and is a part of constituting the native Other in these spaces. For instance, Greg Grandin reminds us, "Photography's close association with travel writing, naturalism, medicine, and anthropology coincided with the extension of nineteen-century European imperialism, providing visual confirmation of ascendant pseudoscientific and rationalized discourses of civilization, nation, and race."[36] Furthermore, photographs can at times racialize or deracialize bodies. Highlighting contrasts between who is perceived as "modern" and who is perceived as "savage," is a tactic of imperialism past and present that has consistently been used to justify colonial intervention.[37]

Photographs hanging on the wall of a Dominican home today echo a time in which households obligatorily hung portraits of dictator Rafael Trujillo as a sign of their allegiance to the nation. His image served as a reminder that he was always watching over them, both as a patriarch in the home and as an agent policing how they performed their Dominicanness. Studio portraits of two teenage girls hang on the wall above the dining table of their family's Santo Domingo apartment. Their hair blows in the artificial breeze of a portrait studio. It only falls straight down past their shoulders or flutters in the breeze because it has been chemically straightened and pressed. The studio photographs work to confirm the racial status of each of the young women by demonstrating that they have "pelo liso" or "good hair," thus positioning them within the Dominican racial category *morena* (brown) or even *morenita* (a little brown), and thereby distancing them from blackness. How these portraits are placed—centrally, alongside graduation photos—in this working-class household tells a story of status attainment; the omission of a dark-skinned family member on the photo wall reinforces other values.

When I look at family photographs of others, I find myself obsessively reading for "family resemblances," trying to see who looks most like whom. This viewing habit comes from being told as a black child that I did not look like my white mother. When one has to look beyond color, one must learn other phenotypic details on which to measure similarity and difference and relationship: the way that the people in the photo are sitting together, the setting and space that surrounds them. There is information for the viewer about the subjects' relationships to one another and their intimacies, more so when viewing a family photo in which each family member is a different shade. Photographic images capture social hierarchies as well as gradations of color, differences that are named in Dominican speech, like *negra, morena, india* (with gender indicated by the last letter of the word), and many other terms that articulate gradations of difference. The term *morena* may be employed by Dominicans to refer to a woman who is dark in color, but in a more socially acceptable way, thereby avoiding use of the term *negra* or black, which is so often used in the Dominican Republic to refer to Haitians.[38] Details of difference are commonsense observations and visual code for those who live in racially mixed communities. Details of phenotype that produce racial categories are critical to how systems of race are sustained, not only on an individual basis but as a larger social system.

Women in the Caribbean have for centuries learned to use their bodies and their sexuality to access power and wealth.[39] The images that *dominicanas* circulate online of themselves in Santo Domingo today emerge and exist within a visual economy in which their raced and sexualized bodies are valued for drawing capital to the region. Moreover, a visual economy built on what outsiders are eager to believe about the Dominican Republic influences the aesthetic decisions made online by Dominican women tied to their association with blackness. As Thompson writes in *Shine: The Visual Economy of Light in African Diasporic Aesthetic Practice*: "Photographic forms . . . not only circulate particular iconographies and represent specific geographies, but the shared genres inform a sense of connection between diasporic groups, encouraging similar approaches to posing in public, to a photographic self-fashioning. They also offer the possibility of recognition by one's peers and diasporic counterparts as co-participants, with different level of power and visibility in visual cultural expressions."[40]

When represented online as beauty pageant contestants, fashion models, and film stars, globally disseminated media narratives make Dominican women out to be little more than landscape or goods to be consumed in a global marketplace.[41] "Tropicalization," which Frances R. Aparicio and Susana Chavelez-Silverman use to describe the application of a Latin American exoticized ethnic identity, is inextricable from the context in which Dominican women in Santo Domingo live their lives. Their bodies are "tropicalized" by their location and their identities are understood through a racialized narrative that gives them a particular value, namely one that involves positioning them as part of an exotic temptation narrative for foreigners.[42] The transnational economy of media and popular culture that Dominican women engage with is infiltrated by the hegemonic discourses that hypersexualize their bodies and prize them as being of greatest value to foreigners.

Whose Narrative Eye in the Caribbean?

In popular discourse we are familiar with the common phrase "seeing is believing" to suggest that to see something with one's own eyes is to know it to be true. Yet in reality, the "visual eye," or how one sees in the physical world, draws on a great deal of sociocultural bias. This becomes most evident when we begin to talk about what we see when we see mixed race. Seeing the racial identity of others requires not only visual cues but also narratives that inform our recognition of those visual cues.[43] Across this text, I consider the ways that a "narrative eye," or what we already believe to be true about race, informs how we *see* Dominican women—and how they see one another. Quite often, race is destabilized through its production and reproduction within mass media; the internet, for example, provides a proliferation of photographic images that inform racial meaning. Meanings attributed to visual representation of a Dominican body by the viewer are in constant flux, not unlike the ways that representations of Latinas in Hollywood film have shifted across decades.[44] Dominican women's bodies are often racially ambiguous in such a way that the subtleties of phenotype are perceived differently depending on surrounding information. Understanding that the visual eye is informed by cultural beliefs is crucial to reading the meaning of mixed race in the Dominican Republic.

Drawing on their own words and cultural productions, I explore how Dominican women understand their transnational identities and experiences of mixed race in Santo Domingo today. I argue throughout that hierarchies of color, the possibility for racial fluidity, and a malleable racial imaginary enable unique neoliberal processes of identity formation for Dominican women. Experiences of malleable racial identity, along with gender and sexuality, reveal the intersections of dynamics of power that Dominican women navigate in Santo Domingo in the contemporary moment, particularly when there is a social value placed on being able to transform one's self in terms of identities we have long presumed fixed. I heed Siobhan Somerville's challenge "to recognize the instability of multiple categories of difference simultaneously rather than assume the fixity of one to establish the complexity of another."[45]

Through ethnography and visual culture analysis I question the types of transnational identities that Dominican women in Santo Domingo forge within this cultural context. How do they fare beneath the weight of a culture of neoliberal policy and global development? How do they imagine themselves within an economy that relies on their labor in and out of the public sphere, or their availability as consumable goods?[46] And how do we imagine Dominican women within a Caribbean economy that relies so much on the outsider's consumption of the visual? By highlighting social media throughout, and its centrality to Dominican identity and experience, I am able to account for the ways that a hypervisual culture is critical to Dominican women's processes of self-making in Santo Domingo. My investigation aligns with Michael Omi and Howard Winant's assertion that "The effort must be made to understand race as *an unstable and 'decentered' complex of social meanings constantly being transformed by political struggle* [emphasis in original]."[47]

Being La Dominicana explores three fundamental aspects of contemporary Dominican society that are shaping the lives and identities of Dominican women in a neoliberal Santo Domingo: the hypervisuality of popular culture, the commodification of mixed-race bodies of African descent (in particular racially ambiguous Dominican women's bodies), and the ubiquity of violence against women and girls. I argue that it is necessary to foreground visual discourse as central to Dominican society where hierarchies of color inevitably factor into the production of other categories of identity. By exploring how Dominican women are characterized in advertising, murals, billboards, and Dominican films and videos, and how they represent themselves in their own cultural productions, I confront the enduring (mixed) race and gender stereotypes that young Dominican women navigate. At the same time, I am attentive to the constant destabilization of Dominican women's identities as they move transnationally and how their identities are recalibrated through relational interactions that reproduce hierarchies of color, class, gender, and sexuality, thus revealing fundamental power dynamics. Dominican women, I contend, navigate the world shaped by the possibility of bodily transformation, and whether intentional or not, this epistemic knowledge relies on a nonbinary framework of understanding racial identity in relationship to blackness.

In addition to engaging in both ethnographic practices and auto-ethnography, drawing on visual culture studies and mixed-race studies, *Being La Dominicana* also applies a queer lens of analysis to numerous aspects of Dominican popular culture that resist heteronormative interpretation. By exploring a broad range of Dominican women's perspectives and their lived experiences—from Marxist students fighting for environmentalism, education, and LGBTQ+ rights, to Metalheads, Hare Krishnas, slam poets, and black lesbian feminists pushing back against a conservative culture—I counter existing stereotypes of Dominican womanhood that are embedded in extensive cultural histories of slavery, colonialism, and decades of dictatorship. These stereotypes appear to combine essentializing representations of Black women and Latinas in the United States. For example, the saintly and reliable Dominican mother, lauded as the "*ama de casa* (female head of household)," is also seen as a self-sacrificing and hardworking "*luchadora* (fighter)," and at times the figure seems to echo the "mammy" archetype prominent in the United States who is dedicated to her family and asexual. In contrast, the curvaceous and narrow-waisted hypersexual mistress/girlfriend represents a costly sex object that every Dominican man is expected to have. Although light-skinned, this "megadiva" echoes the Jezebel archetype of African American lore, while doing double duty as the "fiery Latina." The many young women I interviewed readily describe these stereotypes and how they negotiate these limiting gendered expectations daily, along with expectations of a traditionally conservative culture, shaped by Catholicism. The ubiquitous juxtaposition of the Virgin (the good daughter) and the Whore (the hypersexualized girlfriend), along with the self-sacrificing Dominican mother, become further entrenched under the weight of a neoliberal economy and the uneven development of Santo Domingo. Another often overlooked archetype of *la dominicana* that emerges in this text is that of the respectable, well-educated Dominican woman, often portrayed as the striving student, as with the studious rebel Minerva Mirabal, famously depicted by Julia Álvarez in her 1994 novel *In the Time of the Butterflies*.

Being La Dominicana draws on an extensive archive of works produced by artists and activists including print and online publications, documented live performances, photographic images, and online discourse via Facebook in particular, essential to broadening US scholarly perspectives on Dominican identity. Facebook is brimming with images of Caribbean destinations, vacation photos in which locals themselves participate in the production of visual portrayals of an exoticized space. Today, one's family album is online—always already in the palm of any smartphone user's hand—and the curated wall of images is a digital one. Selfies and Facebook photos within an economy of the picturesque inform the ways that Dominican women learn about themselves through streams of transnational media. As Susan Sontag recognized, with the technology of twentieth-century photography, "We learn to see ourselves photographically."[48] Meanwhile, images of brown-skinned Dominican women's bodies that circulate widely online do so with similar consequences to that of black women's bodies elsewhere: they are understood as commodities.[49] There is no way to view them outside of such a racialized and gendered historical interpretation and it is equally difficult for the women to view themselves outside of this framework. As Norman Bryson explains,

"When I learn to speak, I am inserted into systems of discourse that were there before I was, and will remain after I am gone. Similarly, when I learn to see socially, that is, when I begin to articulate my retinal experience with the codes of recognition that come to me from my social milieu(s), I am inserted into systems of visual discourse that saw the world before I did, and will go on seeing after I see no longer."[50] Dominican women learn to see and be seen in racial terms within a dynamic cultural context that is informed by global media.

The social media archive I have gathered for this text serves as a time capsule, or a window into life in Santo Domingo. Early photography altered our sense of what it means to know something about the world by having "seen it with our own eyes"; how we see ourselves was also changed by technology.[51] Images on social media have had an equally profound impact on how we view ourselves. How Dominican women interpret and curate images online has much to tell us about race and gender in Dominican society. For this reason, I joined my Dominican friends and interviewees in engaging in the media-saturated cultural moment; a cultural analysis of race and mixed race done through ethnography alone would have been incomplete. I read Facebook as a dynamic archive through which to see how Dominican women are invested in representing themselves. Today's digitally circulated vernacular images, I argue, are an essential part of how Dominican women produce and reproduce contemporary ideas about racial ambiguity, gender, and sexuality in Santo Domingo. These aspects of their identity are already rooted in existing "scopic regimes" under which they learn to see themselves.[52]

Immersed in Dominican culture I ask, How are our eyes constantly conditioned to read race and color within a Dominican scopic regime? How differently do my eyes read race from how Dominicans might? Cuban artist and scholar Coco Fusco writes in her introduction to *Only Skin Deep*, "Americans consume an astounding amount and variety of racial imagery and fantasy in music, literature, film, television, pornography, tourism, advertising, fashion, and beauty products. Sensationalized racial conflicts that accentuate racial polarities and enforce stereotypes are just as popular grist for the media mill as the prospect of eliminating, accentuating, or transforming racial characteristics through miracle treatments and morphing machines."[53] In fact, in our globalized popular media of today, an acceptable "brownness" has replaced blackness in representations of the female ethnic Other, priming brown and ambiguous bodies for transnational consumption.[54] Thus, the possibility of adapting one's racial identity through symbols of race and class—being able to alter physical attributes to embrace or at other moments distance oneself from blackness—is pivotal to many Dominican women's lives.

Writing transnational cultural studies at this moment in time, when the transmission of information via the internet is nearly instantaneous, is simultaneously terrifying and exhilarating. Conversations take place about images online when users respond with other images evolving and reinforcing the social meaning and significance of each image deployed. Visual referents easily cross linguistic divides, signifying universal meanings as communities receive widely circulated advertising from abroad. The racial essentialism of modernity now appears to have been traded in for the "assemblage"—like music mash-ups in which an old song is revitalized by being blended with a new one.[55] Popular culture from the United States takes on new life as Dominicans repurpose for their own use aspects of the culture they claim. Michael Jackson's 1991 hit song "Remember the Time" acquired new cultural significance when it was remixed and transformed into merengue dance music by Dominican artist Omega. A form of transnational cultural pastiche, mash-ups are inherently part of Dominican life, equally evident in street foods that riff on American fast food to *música raíz*, a Dominican form that blends several different styles of music—and in visual culture online and off. Like elsewhere in the world, visual culture in Dominican society is deployed to transmit national ideologies, battle sexism, resist government corruption, and challenge neoliberal imperialism. From cellphone videos and digital snapshots shared among peers, to music videos circulated across worldwide networks, Dominicans in Santo Domingo today utilize digitized visual discourse that constantly engages social hierarchies of race, gender, and color. In the work of award-winning Dominican writer Rita Indiana Hernández, for example, one can see that she joins together pieces of transnational media to produce cultural productions that are highly legible among Dominicans.

"We're watching *Rocky III* again cuz it looks like, along with *Dirty Dancing*, it's the only thing playing this summer," writes Hernández in her novel *Papi*, as she expertly conveys the cultural continuity between the United States and the Dominican Republic in the 1980s. Through her adolescent protagonists, Hernández portrays what Maja Horn argues are the subjectivities of a disenchanted generation of Dominicans who grew into their identities in the shadow of Rafael Trujillo's dictatorship (1931–1960), while living under the presidency of Joaquín Balaguer.[56] *Papi* focuses on life in Santo Domingo under the presidency of Leonel Fernández (2004–2012), a president committed to modernization that came in the form of construction and technological infrastructure, more recently Danilo Medina (2012–2020) carried this forward. Both represent the Partido de la Liberación Dominicana, or PLD, and were viewed by those on the political left as a continuation of the same political trajectory as the dictatorship.

When in his first term as president in 1996, Fernández vowed that he would make Santo Domingo into a "little New York" (the place of his childhood), he was mobilizing an ideology of contemporary Dominican identity—as modern, connected to New York City, invested in notions of progress—and hinting at major construction projects to come.[57] This notion of progress was a tried-and-true formula of dictator Rafael Trujillo before him. During his three terms in office, "Leonel," as he was known, funded the construction of bridges, parks, tunnels, and a shiny new Metro system throughout Santo Domingo, which would remake the face of the capital. Though as one Santo Domingo graffiti artist aptly noted in 2010, "Leonel=Balager+Internet." Misspelling and all, the sentiment—later circulated as an image on Facebook—reflects an ongoing critique of the way that the existing government perpetuates the same abuses of power as the dictatorship and of the limits of technological advancement to enact democracy.

The DR as a Site of Study

"It's so difficult to actually listen to all the voices and then pick the ones that build a solid concept about or opinion about the subject," observes twenty-four-year-old Jimena, after reading a piece that I had written about her peers.

"Yes," I agree. "It will end up being a snapshot of what's going on, you know, in 2010, and what's happening and what people were saying."

"I like that concept, a 'snapshot,'" she repeats. Indeed, I use the snapshot as a metaphor to refer to a containment and framing of the day-to-day occurrences in one location at one particular moment. In this case, Santo Domingo, from 2010 into the present. While Ingrid also understands my use of this metaphor, she nevertheless questions my terms of analysis—"Transnational? Why transnational?"—and I am reminded of the ways that this term, which has been so important to the framing of my project in the field of American Studies, has little resonance with her. "Because it really interests me how you can live in the Dominican Republic and speak English and identify with US culture," I tell her. Her reaction also reminds me that the "transnational" is so inherently a part of life for young people in Santo Domingo that it seems hardly to require remark. The Dominican women I have interviewed for this book do not know life any other way.

All of the women I interviewed had regular access to the internet and typically spent time daily consuming popular culture online via desktop computers, laptops, or handheld devices (in 2010 this was mainly the BlackBerry). By "consume," I mean take in—both intentionally and unintentionally—through images and other discourse the ideologies of race, gender, sexuality, Dominicanness, and much more.[58] True to ever-adapting Dominican vocabulary, the Dominican term and concept of *consumismo*, meaning "consumerism," is a telling play on words that names a noticeable shift from a collectivist culture to one that is more individualistic. It can also be understood as the Spanish phrase *con su mismo*, which translates as "with yourself" and as such conveys judgment about the selfishness of a product-oriented lifestyle, especially the desire for goods from abroad. In this way, the term marks the visible increased consumption within Dominican society today and is a critique made by some Dominicans about the acute impact of capitalism on the values of other Dominicans.

Like so many countries in Latin America, the Dominican Republic has relied on remittances—both cultural and economic—influencing social and political life back on the island. The number of Dominicans immigrating abroad steadily increased from the 1960s through the 1980s.[59] Massive migrations of Dominicans to New York in the 1980s brought US goods and cultural remittances to the island. Using a range of new technologies, Dominicans on the island today are able to maintain constant contact with family and friends in the diaspora, sharing goods, news, ideas, and culture across national borders. In 2004, the Dominican Republic–Central American Free Trade Agreement (DR-CAFTA) opened up Dominican borders to US industry in the name of development. Now billions of dollars flow from the United States into the Dominican Republic annually.[60] Neoliberal economic policies have the Dominican Republic developing in a fashion in which it lurches forward unevenly, leaving many of its citizens far behind. As in so many parts of the world, access to foreign goods has increased while incomes have remained stagnant. Even as new luxury malls continue to open, Dominican families in Santo Domingo subsist on locally produced staple foods, such as plantains, processed meats, white bread, rice, beans, and eggs. And they are significantly impacted each time the prices of these goods (and the gas with which to cook them) rise incrementally. Uneven development throughout Santo Domingo is emblematic of "structural disadvantages that have been shaped by the colonial process and by the uneven division of international labor."[61]

Participation in the global market entails producing something for consumption by other nations. On the island of Hispaniola, this has historically meant the addictive substance of sugar, which, among other things, produced a centuries-long dependence on the labor of enslaved Africans. Today, the extraction of goods and labor from the Dominican Republic for the benefit of more-developed nations continues—and often Dominican bodies are the goods being extracted. For example, boys and young men throughout the Dominican Republic have high hopes of becoming baseball players for North American leagues. To be sure, every one of the thirty US Major League baseball teams has contributed to the patchwork of training academies built throughout the Dominican countryside. At this very moment, the next big-league player is practicing for his "once in a lifetime" opportunity. One Dominican recruiter enthusiastically likened the town of San Pedro de Macoris (famous for producing outstanding *peloteros*) to a mine where he knew he would surely hit gold. ESPN also uses this language, stating frankly that these are "academies built to exploit what seems to be an inexhaustible gold mine of talent."[62] In the film *Sugar* (2008), a pivotal scene depicts the title character standing with a fellow young recruit in a US clothing store as we watch it finally dawn on him that he himself is the exported good. Having made the leap from a small Dominican town toward his aspiration of being a US Major League ballplayer, he glances at the tag of a shirt for sale that reads, "Made in the Dominican Republic."

Like elsewhere in the Caribbean, a vast informal economy of sex tourism impacts how outsiders view Dominican bodies as goods for consumption. Tourists travel to the island to find Dominican and Haitian men and women, boys and girls, cis and trans, who are willing to fulfill their sexual desires.[63] Sex tourism is so prevalent within Dominican society that low-brow popular Dominican films such as *Sanky Panky* (2007) and its sequels (2013, 2018) satirize the sexual economy that tourism creates, though in this case for Dominican men.[64] Yet Dominican women's most intimate relationships are informed by neoliberal policies under which their affective labor is commodified as part of a thriving tourism economy.[65] Dominican women's bodies are "made visible in the global context through particular articulations of gender and sexuality that are deployed by consumer culture and transported by mediated images."[66] Hypersexualized in popular media, they are marked and marketed as consumable goods on multiple levels under a neoliberal development plan that relies on tourism for economic growth. In her book *What's Love Got to Do with It?*, Denise Brennan reveals how Dominican women in the town of Sosúa on the northern coast navigate an economy of sexual tourism that renders their identities and livelihoods in terms of transnational opportunities. What Brennan terms a "sexscape" for the coastal region in fact pervades the entire country, where power dynamics in romantic relationships are visible in the ways that women are racially fetishized within the "transnational social field" of Santo Domingo as well.

Economic inequalities and the ever-present possibility of purchasing affective labor in the Dominican Republic is embedded in the social interactions between foreigners and locals. Kamala Kempadoo's research reflects how Caribbean economic reliance on sex tourism produces a form of cultural imperialism that relies on a desire for the exotic; today contemporary neoliberal processes of globalization sustain this legacy.[67] As Angelique Nixon states, "tourism reproduces the destructive psychology and race and gender dynamics of colonialism."[68] A version of this reality is visually confirmed throughout the Colonial Zone of Santo Domingo, and on beaches across the island as foreign men wrap their arms around Dominican and Haitian women and adolescent girls.[69]

La Mulata

How Dominican women's racially mixed bodies signify in the Americas today emerges out of a Latin American ideological framework of generations past and a global framework of the present that script the fair-skinned woman as muse, pure and positioned on a pedestal, in contrast to black women and *mulatas* as sexually available.[70] Dominican women have historically claimed an Indigenous identity rather than a mulata identity.[71] However, in this text I highlight the social currency of racial ambiguity and Dominican claims on blackness that are obscured by a long history of distancing from blackness. According to Daisy Cocco de Filippis, regarding the rejection of blackness (meaning Africanness) in Dominican poetry: "The mulatto woman as icon of Dominican womanhood does not enter the Dominican poetic landscape until well into the twentieth century; and even then she must be hidden under a protective cloak of euphemisms, such as *india* (light brown) or *trigueña* (olive-skinned, dark complexioned brunette)."[72] Moreover, as Dominican activist Sergia Galván has argued, as elsewhere in the Caribbean, the myths and prejudices perpetuated about black women sustain the trafficking of dark-skinned Dominican women in particular into sex work for the benefit of male European tourists.[73] Embedded in a historical legacy of Dominican anti-blackness, white and lighter-skinned Dominicans today experience preferential treatment and social benefits while brown and black Dominicans have internalized beliefs about their body as a commodity.[74]

Instituting practices of rape and bondage, French and Spanish colonizers early in the fourteenth century quickly decimated the majority of the Taíno, the Indigenous people inhabiting the island. Although Dominicans are predominantly a mix of European, African, and Indigenous heritages, it is routine for contemporary explanations of Dominican identity to omit African heritage, falling in line with the Latin American racial project of *mestizaje* in which being mixed race of Indigenous and European heritage is viewed as superior. As Licia Fiol-Mata points out, the racial project taken up by much of Latin America in the twentieth century invested in the notion that racial mixing would *disappear* less desirable lineages in a few short generations; the racial Other would be gone, opined Vasconcelos.[75]

Dominican national identity has long held the precarious stance that racially mixed bodies should represent a "civilized" Catholic, middle-class nation. Dominicans have relied on Haitian blackness as a fixed racial category against which Dominican racial identity could pivot.[76] Rules of Dominican national identity and with it racial identity are in no way uniform, but rather, as Milagros Ricourt has argued, are "a series of overlapping tendencies always in contradiction."[77] Just as the meaning of mixed-race bodies can adapt to context and social signifiers, structures of power contort themselves to put new values on racially ambiguous bodies—especially by mobilizing anti-blackness. Colorism further contributes to the ways that racism structures power by interpolating individuals within communities of color into social hierarchies that we maintain, even to our own detriment.[78] Historically, across the Americas "Mulattas and mestizas—in the feminine—have been targeted as the source, the cost, and the evidence of mixture."[79] Today, the "unique relationship between women and racial mixture" that Suzanne Bost recognizes is quite evident within a neoliberal global economy that relies so heavily on the labor of women.

Dominican anti-black prejudices are part of a centuries-long racial project; disparaging beliefs about black people and subsequently the black body emerge out of a cultural value system established under colonialism and systems of slavery that permeate all levels of Dominican society today.[80] The Dominican nation-state has long invested politically in distancing Dominican national identity from Haitianness, and its implied Africanness.[81] As García Peña states, "Through a discourse of pity, Haiti's misfortunes were racialized as results of the country's African religiosity and as signs of 'barbarism' and 'incivility.'"[82] Xenophobic violence and misogyny, perpetuated through conservative ideologies of race and gender among the

Dominican elite, were further institutionalized under Trujillo's regime.[83] In September of 2013, the Dominican Constitutional Tribunal ruled to revoked citizenship from all Dominicans unable to provide formal documentation of their citizenship as far back as 1929, thereby targeting Dominicans of Haitian descent. The late activist Sonia Pierre has asserted that Dominican elite have deployed "una óptica trujillista [a Trujillistic lens]" to erase the African heritage of Dominicans and construct a Dominican identity in contrast to Haitian identity, holding back the development of Dominican society in a globalizing world.[84]

Colonizers from Spain and France, and immigrants from Germany, Lebanon, Palestine, China, the United States, and elsewhere, have made the Dominican Republic a pluralistic society, yet the Dominican elite at different points in time have invested in a narrative of national identity constructed through xenophobia and anti-Haitianism. As geographer Marco Morales pointed out to me, you only have to look back a couple of generations in the Dominican Republic to see married couples of different racial backgrounds in almost every family. A couple of generations back interracial marriage was encouraged in an effort to lighten the population; choosing a lighter-skinned partner would allow for greater social advancement of one's offspring. Today, these values and language ("*mejorar la raza*" [better the race]) remain. Exhibiting features of European and Indigenous racial mixture has remained a superior position in the racial hierarchy since blackness and Dominican identity have been constructed in juxtaposition to one another, allowing Dominicans to embrace a narrative of national identity in the form of *Hispanidad* and thereby closer to whiteness. A Dominican identity that is nationalist, Spanish, Catholic, and white and rejects African culture represents the colonial racism of the state. Claudina Valdez argues that the anti-blackness of the Dominican state has been internalized among black people in the Dominican Republic through its state-sanctioned *hispanofilia*.[85] However, a recent trip to West Africa by Grammy award-winning Dominican American rapper Cardi B—and her stated desire to gain Nigerian citizenship—boldly defied a Dominican anti-blackness that is decidedly anti-African. Born to a Dominican father and a Trinidadian mother and raised in the South Bronx in part by her Dominican grandmother, Belcalis Marlenis Almánzar (Cardi B) has been outspoken about her visit to Ghana and Nigeria at the end of 2019's Year of Return.[86] In her solidarity with Nigerians and embrace of African heritage she publicly refused a Denial of blackness.

In stark contrast to the "one-drop rule" maintained by legal precedent in the United States that determines that anyone with any nonwhite lineage is not white, whiteness in the Dominican Republic functions as a social category that can be accessed by those with light enough skin. Within *Being La Dominicana* I reveal the ways that a consumable brownness or a narrative of blackness is utilized by fair-skinned Dominicans. Kimberly Simmons suggests that the racial mixedness of Dominicans serves to connect them to "a sense of shared history and pastness, Dominican ancestry, with a sense of *being* and *feeling* Dominican [emphasis in original]."[87] Perhaps for this reason, countless socially constructed and socially understood racial markers differentiate how Dominicans understand what they see on each other's bodies, in ways not readily discernable to people from outside of this racial system. Of course, a great many Dominicans are dark in color. They may be identified as "*cocolos*," or the descendants of non-Hispanic African peoples in the Caribbean; and there are many Dominicans and Dominicans of Haitian descent who are not mixed race of European descent.[88] Dominican historian Celsa Albert Batista argues that most Dominicans are a mixture of whites and blacks, resulting in a people that is "mulatos y mulatas por detrás, por delante, por fuera y por dentro," which is to say the Dominican past and future is one of racial mixture and Dominicans are this mixture inside and out.[89] The accompanying image she uses with this theorization is a simple silhouette of a white human head, with a darker silhouette inside of it; the illustration serves to reinforce the notion that all Dominicans have within them la mulata or el mulato. The Dominican expression "black behind the ears" refers to the practice of examining the crease behind the ear of even the fairest Dominican bodies for this visual trace of blackness—visualizable proof of African ancestry.[90]

While interviewing Dominican women in a Washington, DC, salon, Ginetta E. B. Candelario showed them headshots of women and men in hairstyling magazines in order to elicit a response about the meanings attributed to different hair types and their associated skin color. She concludes that among the diasporic Dominicans with whom she spoke, whiteness is not the ultimate goal, but rather a mixture of European (referred to as "*fino*" and suggesting "refined") features are preferred: "not Nordic or Aryan whiteness but mixedness that is more an approximation of Hispanic looks . . . straight haired, tan skinned, aquiline featured."[91] In short, argues Candelario, there is a Dominican preference to be "of color, but not black." Notably, the nuances of racial ideology and Dominican color hierarchy are not accessible to Candelario without her use of images as a barometer. Such hierarchies of color are enacted and maintained through daily interactions and an elaborate and detailed vocabulary of difference—both visual and verbal. Furthermore, Dominican women's investments in "self-beautification" are investments in the transformation of racial signifiers, as they exist within and rely upon beauty standards formed within a cultural value system embedded in centuries of anti-blackness.[92]

Alicia en el País de Maravillas

To be clear, I do not believe that there exists some authentic Dominican woman for me to document in my research. As E. Patrick Johnson states, the notion of authenticity easily becomes "yet another trope manipulated for cultural capital."[93] The narrowness of the construct certainly restricted the scope of my research in some directions, but it was relevant and responsive to the moment and social context. Within the Dominican social imaginary, "the Dominican woman" is a composite of different intersecting representations that reflect numerous social anxieties and expectations and new social and economic pressures within a rapidly changing neoliberal culture. La dominicana emerges in fragments over and over again in the zeitgeist, comprising a series of composite figures; at times she emerges as fully formed characters or caricatures on screen, in literature, and in stories told. This social construction remains fluid, in a process of becoming. Thus, viewing as surrealist the visual archive that I have compiled allows me to tell a better story about when and where resistances to hegemonic representation occur in Dominican contemporary culture.

Being La Dominicana accounts for the ways that an especially surreal visual culture is evident in the Dominican Republic today as not only an echo of the past but rather an organic response to contemporary disillusionment with neoliberalism. When I point to "surrealism" throughout this text, I am referring to the Surrealist aesthetics of André Breton's transnational avant-garde art movement—some of which was inspired by his visit to Haiti—and the various iterations that followed. Breton and his peers were interested in the subconscious, free association, and what they saw as pure thought without reason. In their cultural productions they used language experimentally and bounced meaning off found objects and objects out of context. As Dominican poet Frank Báez so aptly explains, "You see, for a Dominican it is normal for one to drink from different traditions. Maybe a writer from a European country could do his or her work without having to read literature from other countries. But for a Dominican, it is necessary to keep up with what is happening everywhere. So one develops these cosmopolitan interests."[94]

In the case of Dominican women in particular, surrealist art becomes a mode of art-making as well as a way of understanding contemporary reality in the process of producing subjectivities. Art historians Ilene Susan Fort and Tere Arcq note that "For surrealist artists of North America, surrealism became a means for gaining self-awareness, exploring their inner thoughts and feelings, dealing with their experiences, and locating their true identities."[95] What might this process of exploration mean for Afro-Dominican women artists locating their identities in a flow of global visual culture, a culture inherently drifting, or among identities perpetually see/sawing up and down hierarchies of power? The metaphor of the Dominican muñeca sin rostro that opens this book not only points us to the possibilities of racial ambiguity on Dominican women's bodies but is also a gesture toward that which is surrealist about Dominican women's cultural identities and experiences of race and gender in the present day. It is easily emblematic of the Afro-Surreal, a contemporary aesthetic that D. Scot Miller has argued is inherently fluid and ambiguous.[96]

Small Talk and the Big Picture

The more than forty interviews that I conducted with Dominican women in Santo Domingo inform my research and analysis of the diversity and specificities of Dominican women's identities.[97] The majority of my interviewees were in their early and mid-twenties.[98] The socioeconomic backgrounds of the women I chose to interview, and their access to education, had for the most part prepared them to critique their own subject positions. Interviewees generally wanted to help me accomplish my research goals; one said the reason she took time to meet with me was that she wanted her "fifteen minutes of fame." As savvy transnational consumers connected to people, products, and cultures abroad, they constantly negotiate raced and gendered expectations about their national identity and their mixed-race bodies, which are produced and reinforced by transnational media flows, a paternalistic state, and the misogyny of romantic partners. Opportunities for travel abroad, regular internet access, college and sometimes graduate-level education, as well as sustained contact with family and friends overseas, all inform their transnational perspectives.

By handing out business card-sized flyers that carried the Facebook logo, I was able to draw volunteers from several university campuses in Santo Domingo to participate in an online survey I constructed about existing stereotypes of the "authentic" Dominican woman. "La dominicana," I confirmed, was seen as a "fighter," who is strong (meaning solid or sturdy), a hard worker, a good cook, talkative, friendly, and extroverted. She is a "well-put-together" morena (brown-skinned woman), with her hair, makeup, and nails done. She is sexy, with "a lot of ass," and typically with "*pelo malo* [bad hair]," they told me, suggesting that "true" Dominican women have hair that requires straightening in order to be socially acceptable.[99] Then, through a Facebook group I created called "Un proyecto sobre la mujer dominicana (A project about the Dominican woman)," potential interviewees were able to self-identify and contact me there to learn about the topic of my research. Those who participated also referred their friends. In 2010–11, I sat down with thirty Dominican women in Santo Domingo, ages eighteen to thirty-eight during my initial research; and in 2016, I completed ten additional interviews to sharpen my analysis.

Stereotypes of Dominican womanhood perpetually overshadow the realities of complex contemporary identities informed by a constant engagement with global culture and networks online. Without a doubt, transgender Dominican women would have many insights into the lived experiences of race, gender, and sexuality that I explore in Santo Domingo; however, I did not pursue that possibility. In 2010, trans women were not especially visible in Santo Domingo, something that has shifted with the growth and investment in resources around LGBTQ+ activism in the capital. Young trans women did not self-select to participate in interviews with me nor were they to my knowledge a part of the relatively privileged networks of college students I connected with in Santo Domingo.[100] For some time, social networks for transgender women have remained distinct from that of queer and heterosexual cisgender Dominican women in the circles to which I had access; however, a decade later this is changing.

Interviews, participant observation, and detailed notes on ethnographic observations have allowed me to examine the influence that racial malleability and a culture of the visual has on Dominican women's processes of identity formation. As transnational subjects, Dominican women construct their identities—exterior and interior—from what are often disparate cultural influences. Rather than feeling torn across constructed boundaries, they articulate themselves as whole, yet made up of many cross-cultural signifiers and cultures, even as they exist in fragmented global formations that take the shape of a dynamic "constellation," or multi-sited collage (or pastiche).[101] Doing so through tools of visual culture in producing Dominican identity and as a form of resistance is no way a new phenomenon, but it does look different with the advent of social media.

Throughout this text, I include myself as an example in moments of cultural observation and unwitting exchanges around what the mixed-race body signifies in Santo Domingo. I engage with Dominican women's ongoing negotiations of the body throughout this text because "it is impossible to think about cultural memory and identity as disembodied. The bodies participating in the transmission of knowledge and memory are themselves a product of certain taxonomic, disciplinary mnemonic systems. Gender impacts how these bodies participate as does ethnicity."[102] Constant remarks about color are a part of daily life in Dominican society and continually produce racial meaning. As one interviewee assured me, after a third stranger on the street told me that my natural hairstyle was a mess: "Yes, here *el dominicano* feels at liberty to comment on these things . . . because it's part of the of our culture. El dominicano is very extraverted, likes to make commentary. You can get in a *guagua* [bus] next to a person that you don't know and they feel at liberty to comment on your clothes, your hair, *que crema* you should put on your face *porque el dominicano es así, porque la dominicana es . . . ,*" she then paused, thoughtfully. "Nosotros somos así," We are like that, she explained. In fact, the constant discourse around racial difference is one of the things that drew me to study identity in the Dominican Republic. It is a stark contrast to the dominant culture of the United States of the 1980s and 1990s in which a notion of "colorblindness" among those who saw themselves as the most liberal silenced comments about difference. To tell a story about Dominican women, I must tell it with and through ongoing negotiations of the body under global capitalism and my own reflexivity is a tool of knowledge production. I must also tell it in terms of blackness that is constructed in relationship to whiteness as much as it is constructed in relation to Haitian Otherness.

Early in my research, I identified four Dominican celebrities who were transnationally recognizable and whose images were available through popular media both online and off: Zoe Saldaña, Martha Heredia, Rita Indiana, and Michelle Rodriguez. All exist within the visual discourse and transnational imaginary of Dominicans on the island and each interviewee drew on existing narratives about these women's identities in order to make sense of what they saw in their photographs. It was not until I arrived in Santo Domingo that I got to know the work of Rita Indiana, though I had been told to keep an eye out for her locally. I also did not know anything at all about Martha Heredia, who had won the singing competition TV series *Latin American Idol* the year before. Rita Indiana appeared to be at the height of her popularity as a musician in 2010 while Heredia was already on the decline. Meanwhile, that year images of Hollywood actress Zoe Saldaña could be seen all around town and circulated in the press. Actress Michelle Rodriguez was the person I added last to my study at the urging of the sixteen-year-old daughter of the family hosting me. Though not particularly popular among the women I interviewed, she was recognizable because of her role in the *Fast and Furious* films, and in 2010 she would star as Minerva Mirabal in her only Dominican film. I gathered their photographs off the internet for the purpose of photo elicitation: everyday images of these four women speaking or singing in front of live audiences.

My use of these four images was critical to inciting a more nuanced discussion of differences in skin color, hair type, and class aesthetic. The photographs allowed interviewees to engage both their *visual* eye and their *narrative* eye in deciphering the women's embodied identities. Symbolic references within each celebrity's photographs were also critical to how interviewees read them in terms of class and color. The Dominican women I spoke with volunteered their thoughts and opinions on the many nuances of phenotype that North American researchers talk about broadly as racial difference. Consistently in conversation they would seek points of reference to explain color, saying something like, "She's darker than you but lighter than me." Images seemed to capture what we shared as common knowledge—to which we could jointly refer—and allowed me to get people to open up about race and color, leading to conversations about experiences of racial ambiguity in their daily lives.

Ay/I/Eye

As a black transnational feminist scholar, I aimed to produce a text through which the women I interviewed might have space to define themselves, thereby disrupting power dynamics between the researcher and interviewees as subjects. They are most certainly my interlocutors. I ask readers to privilege these women's words and cultural productions and the stories they tell. Interviews were conversational in style, with the dynamics of relationship-building. Each woman acted as a "cultural informant," educating me about details of Dominican culture that I could not have initially understood. The themes that I explore exist as part of the scopic regime of race and gender in the Dominican Republic and reflect the ways that communities are organized across an extensive diversity of hierarchies, undergirded by specific structures of power.[103]

"I thought she was going to be *morenita*," my friend's father says to her in front of me when they pick me up from the airport in Santo Domingo. Presumably, this is what she had told her parents about me, but after one long winter in Michigan I had grown many shades lighter. I had only just met her parents, but they sized me up in terms of my phenotype in the first fifteen minutes of our drive into the capital. They remarked on the color of my eyes and said that I had a pretty face; my eyes they said were the color of . . . I can't remember the word. It was something different than "ojos de miel [eyes like honey]" that I had heard time and again. As I expected, people I knew in the Dominican Republic were surprised to see me now so pale in color; they also remarked that I looked better than before. My friend from the neighborhood would soon ask me why it was that I identified as "negra," especially since now I look "casi rubia [almost fair-skinned]," she said. It was difficult for me to explain it to her, but I tried.[104]

My ability to offer self-reflexive insight about the experiences of women of African descent in the diaspora is essential to the praxis of my feminist ethnographic research, as many scholars have argued.[105] My own body offers me insights into what it means to shapeshift across the permeable boundaries of race, gender, sexuality, and culture, experiences that my interviewees describe. Since many Dominicans are racially mixed of West African and Eastern European descent, my own body is legible to them when we encounter one another on the island. In fact, the Dominican Republic is the only place I have ever lived in which I can visually blend in as part of the majority; in the United States, I am considered black like my Ghanaian father and in West Africa I am understood as white, like my Jewish-American mother. Interviewees tell me that because of my color, because of my mixed-race background, they are more willing to share. "Well, you understand," they say to me, punctuating their response to my inquiry. My brown skin, light brown eyes, and curly hair seem to place me there, allowing me to move in many spaces undetected, even as my status as a foreigner kept me feeling just out of place enough to provide an outsider's observation.

My precarious position as participant observer and researcher—building meaningful relationships with those about whom I write—actively disrupts a simpler binary of insider/outsider.[106] As a transnational Black feminist queer scholar, I do share a reality of diaspora experience with Afro-Dominican feminist lesbian activist interviewees and peers that involves having my body read as black and as queer. I also now share in common with the women I interviewed intimate ties to Dominican culture and the geographies of the island; beneath this emotional attachment lies a deep frustration with the racism, sexism, heteropatriarchy, corruption, and bureaucracy. I also empathize with their experiences of diaspora longing, as feelings that align with my experiences as part of a Ghanaian diaspora.[107]

"Why did you stay away so long?" a friend organizing for the Santo Domingo Pride Parade asked me. "You are part of us." In those moments, I shed my feelings of outsiderness. I take on the role of "insider," having worked my way into the lives and communities of these Dominican women not only in hopes of a better understanding of some kind of truth about their lives but also because for short time I made my life in their world as well. My own epistemic knowledge has informed each question I have asked, each space I have had access to, and the conclusions I have drawn. I have inserted myself into many different contexts in order to gain a firsthand experience of the worlds my interviewees inhabit. Although I am neither Dominican nor Latinx, time and again friends and acquaintances on the island have encouraged me to claim Dominicanness: "Ya estás bien aplatana'o [you are already Dominicanized]," they assure me, willing to include me despite my Otherness.

The methodologies of transnational feminism that I embrace center collaboration.[108] I have taken on the responsibility of engaging interviewees as collaborators with ownership over their own words. My task has been to draw out narratives and themes embedded in Dominican women's daily lives. In reality, I have failed frequently in my efforts to build feminist solidarities, and this project about Dominican women may not necessarily look the way my interviewees would want. Some suggested that my research should focus more on rural Dominican women, since they imagined them to be more "authentic." While I agree that they too would have valuable critiques of their own social conditions, in this project my interest lies in working-class and middle-class women with the privileges of education that allow them greater global media consumption, transnational movement, and transnational connectivities. At the same time, educational privilege (my own and that of my interlocutors) has significantly shaped my project. It has provided those whom I chose to interview with a greater understanding of my work and thus diffused a layer of unequal power dynamics between us, as did a shared understanding of the geography of Santo Domingo and the landscape of its artist and activist community.

There are a great many spaces into which as an outsider I remain uninvited: activist spaces, religious spaces, and sacred spaces. Those who chose to sit down with me, a "gringa researcher," expressed some faith in my intentions. Others were comfortable enough to convey their distrust, feeling that I would use their words for my benefit alone. I understand the possibilities of friendship between us as reflecting "our resistance to the divisive and fragmenting lies of structural power."[109] Cross-cultural and transnational friendship as a collaborative project always remain in a state of possibility. I learned repeat-edly that interview conversations with strangers could become in-depth and personal over one or two hours and turn into lasting friendships. Early on in Santo Domingo, I cast my net wide not solely to find interviewees, but in an effort to make community and to build a life. For several young women I interviewed, I would become as much a part of their world over the last decade as the many other non-Dominican friends they had met online.

1

Sites of Identity

Facebook, Murals, and Vernacular Images

> He watched me for a moment, then whispered, "Who are you?"
> I didn't say anything. I just stared at him in the dark for a
> moment, thinking of all the different answers to this question
> I had already given. You know how it goes. The disclosure,
> followed by the edifying speech. My body the lesson.
>
> Danzy Senna, *Symptomatic*

When a snapshot of two young Dominican women appears in my Facebook feed, I glance at it in passing. But something about it sticks with me and I return to look again at the image. Penélope's photograph is a deliberate critique of the medium.[1] It is an image squared by Instagram's stylistic format but she has posted it simultaneously onto her Facebook page: two young brown-skinned women in the Caribbean standing side by side outdoors in late afternoon light. Penélope, standing on the right, is dressed in shiny black Doc Martin–esque boots, a white T-shirt and hoodie, and torn jeans reminiscent of the 1980s. Her short hair—recently dyed green—is a shock. She points her left index finger at her friend standing close beside her while at the same time she curls her tongue (à la Miley Cyrus circa 2014) and strikes a pose for the camera. Her friend Álida Reyes purses her lips, chin tilted up at the photographer. You can almost hear the sound of disapproval that might accompany this expression. Álida is wearing a baseball cap, a Wu-Tang Clan T-shirt cut to a high midriff, and high-waisted shorts (the fashion of the moment) hitched up with a narrow belt. Her feet are clad in the type of thin faux-leather sandals in metallic colors that are common across the island.

As a visual artist, Penélope Collado has used social media to share many images from her daily life. Because of her self-conscious awareness of the ways that images signify, the photographs Penélope shares often act as what

Figure 1. Instagram photo of Penélope Collado and Álida Reyes. Photo composed by Penélope Collado.

Deborah Willis refers to as "frozen racial metaphors."² Penélope posted this photograph online with the text: "Con la Jíbara en #SantoDomingoParadise." Her comment makes cynical reference to things being not quite as one expects them to be in the Caribbean and sarcastically names her friend "Jíbara," which, in Dominican terms, would imply that she is rural, uncivilized, and perhaps uncouth.³ Penélope's hashtag in English serves as a sardonic reference to the ways that the reality of Santo Domingo does not conform to foreign viewers' imagined paradise of the Caribbean. Rather, if you take another look at the photograph, you see that the two young women are standing in front of four or five oil barrel trash cans overflowing with garbage—a far more common sight on the island than a pristine beach. Comments written in colloquial English and Dominican Spanish below the photo range from shocked to supportive, encouraging to teasing, capturing the ways that community response is a part of posting curated images online.⁴ Penélope, who has much experience modeling her thin, racially mixed Dominican body in professional photos, is well aware her short green hair and the garbage in the background disrupt the dominant narrative of an exotic and appealing Caribbean. The image she has produced documents an alternate reality of Santo Domingo and provides a critique by way of a counter-image that demonstrates to viewers her awareness of the popular Caribbean visual discourse in which she is embedded.

Photographic images produced for a burgeoning tourism industry in the nineteenth-century Anglo Caribbean, especially in Jamaica and the Bahamas, have been fundamental to shaping the significance of the Caribbean in the popular imagination today. Those who lived on the islands internalized a postcolonial narrative about the space and were invested in bringing tourism, and thus worked to present their island communities in ways that conformed to dominant conceptions of the Caribbean "picturesque."[5] In the Caribbean of the 1800s, Krista Thompson explains, "a genealogy of images . . . inform[ed] representations of the region."[6] Images that romanticize a particular notion of the Caribbean associated with escapism, the natural world, and the exotic remain a highly marketable currency. "Visual images and visuality (specifically sightseeing), were crowned the 'new sugar,' the means through which the islands were subsequently consumed."[7] Professional photographs remain part and parcel of constructing what the Caribbean signifies today: palm trees, unspoiled beaches, and "happy natives."[8] Moreover, Thompson notes, "the picturesque, in contradistinction to the aesthetic category of beauty (which encompassed objects and landscapes that appeared symmetrical and balanced), privileged wild landscapes that were 'free from the formality of lines.'"[9] Today, a new rapidly changing and erratically-fashioned genealogy of images contributes to how Dominican women see themselves. These images are produced out of youth culture, an established scopic regime.

Internet users now face a tidal wave of globalized visual discourse. Unlike ever before, our daily engagement with airbrushed and photoshopped bodies, fake food and staged interactions—and the repetition of particular visual discourses—reinforces and produces racialized logics in our real and virtually mediated worlds. The reality of the Caribbean exists intimately alongside the fiction and the two remain in constant dialogue; what we see is informed by what we have come to believe about the region. For example, when a young Dominican woman posts on her Facebook account a picture of herself lying in a bikini in front of a sunset at the beach, the self-crafted image responds to a ubiquitous online visual discourse: "You look like you're on a postcard," comments a viewer. Embracing a range of cultural expectations while representing themselves online often means Dominican women are echoing a visual discourse that accentuates their physical features or celebrates a sexualized pose. Photographs of people convey not only the hierarchies of color that exist in the Dominican Republic but also the dialogic construction of racial meaning. Just as people value images that confirm that which they want to believe about themselves and others, representations of Dominican women are deemed authentic only when they align with beliefs that viewers already hold.

In this chapter I look to a Santo Domingo landscape marked by Latin American *muralismo* in order to understand the cultural context in which Dominican women make use of visual culture to define themselves.[10] Facebook, as the most popular social media network among Dominican youth in 2010, extended beyond serving as a tool for narrativizing individual identity to facilitating a broader trajectory for Dominican visual culture. For those with access, Facebook has proven an effective tool with which to maintain diasporic relationships over the long term, promote community education, and organize movements of resistance. If it is the case that "we are now, each of us, a little media outlet unto ourselves," what narratives are Dominican women advancing online and off?[11] Most of the ethnographic research I conducted with Dominican women in Santo Domingo in 2010 and 2011 took place when increased access to Wi-Fi meant a significant portion of daily life involved circulating digital images, short videos, blogs, messages, and personalized pages via the internet. My connection to and observations about a changing Santo Domingo from 2006 to the present have been able to continue via social media, namely Facebook, in between return visits to the island.[12] Facebook has allowed me to remain part of a transnational viewing audience for Dominican friends and acquaintances, and my relationships are sustained via this transnational bridge.

While the omission of images of enormous malls, the Metro, or the Ikea in Santo Domingo often make the reality of the urban Caribbean unimaginable for tourists, these locations appear in innumerable selfies by locals who themselves participate as if they are tourists in these newly developed public spaces. Modernization is regularly excluded from the popular imaginary outside of the Dominican Republic because it does not confirm what is believed to be true about the Caribbean or the rest of the developing world, let alone the African diaspora. The image of the Caribbean-as-destination is so firmly entrenched that it will not disappear.[13] Dominican visual cultural producers create art that inherently negotiates this reality. In resisting the dominant visual narrative, their work reveals a contemporary surrealist aesthetic emerging from leftist roots and influences existing across the island.

According to Franklin Rosemont and Robin D. G. Kelley in their study of the often invisibilized black and brown surrealists, "Rejecting all forms of domination and the dichotomous ideologies that go with them—intolerance, exploitation, bigotry, exclusiveness, white supremacy, and all race prejudice— surrealists make the resolution of contradictions a high priority."[14] It happens that the roots of surrealism in the Dominican Republic run deep, revealing not only the ongoing impact of Spanish colonialism on Dominican culture and resistance to the rise of European fascism but also the sustained influence of Haitian cultural productions on the visual culture of the Dominican Republic.

Dominican women, whose bodies are interpreted through the Eurocentric gaze, as evidenced by ongoing discourse about hairstyles and other aspects of their self-presentation, have had to navigate with sophistication the transmission of the visual. They must decide whether or not they will adopt the visual language of the dominant culture and beauty standards that privilege whiteness. For, as Ella Shohat writes, "Colonial hierarchies have ramifications for the everyday negotiations of looks and identity."[15] And, argues Shohat, part of the work of resisting global hegemony is understanding the transmission of the visual—which needs to be combated with images and media representing us as we choose. According to Stuart Hall, popular culture "is where we discover and play with the identifications of ourselves, where we are imagined, where we are represented, not only to the audiences out there who don't get the message, but to ourselves for the first time."[16] Facebook in particular reflects the kind of popular culture that might easily be described as a "profoundly mythic" and a "theater of popular desires."[17] Many who are marginalized by society use social media to connect with one another and carve out a space for themselves in which they are recognized.[18] Women of color have newfound access to virtual spaces, while at the same time they themselves may be newly accessible to others in particular ways via the internet. Across the diverse and dynamic online archive that is Facebook today, I examine a series of what Françoise Lionnet and Shu-mei Shih describe as "creative interventions that networks of minoritized cultures produce within and across national boundaries."[19]

"Maldito Feisbu"

With more than 483 million daily users worldwide at the time of my initial research in 2010 and some 1.84 billion daily users more than a decade later, Facebook is the most popular social networking interface on the World Wide

Web. It far surpassed the once-popular sites HiFi and MySpace by quickly adapting its programming and applications to avoid losing young users; it has outlasted sites such as Friendster and acquired its greatest competitor, Instagram, in an effort to sustain its influence. Users worldwide have adapted themselves to life with social media, shifting culturally to meet the demands of this technological tool.

Early on, a great deal of Dominican cultural nostalgia circulated on Facebook, through quizzes and applications to test how Dominican you are, or give Dominican "gifts"—symbols of Dominicanness like plantains and Brugal rum—to friends online. Popular pages such as "Orgulloso de Ser Dominicano" (Proud to Be Dominican) and "Dominicanos Ausentes" (Dominicans Living Abroad) boasted tens of thousands of "likes." Users could upload digital snapshots to what Facebook once called a "wall" and then later a "timeline," so that they would show up in the "newsfeed" of their connected friends in real time.

Facetiously referred to as "Crackbook" due to its addictive qualities, Facebook provides users with a personalizable online location in which to share words, images, websites, games, videos, and more. Over time, the newsfeed has become a space curated by algorithms, shaped by each click, post, and preference. Travel photos mix with informal images in an online album that can be called up at any moment for sharing. Moreover, the digital image in proliferation becomes a way in which we document the same moment from a million different angles, offering a range of witnesses to the same event. With cellphone cameras, the photographer now exists within every community, and a new value is added to the visuals of everyday life.[20] Selfies, family photos shared for #tbt (Throwback Thursdays), and vernacular images gathered together both archive and produce personal narratives of identity.[21] For some time now, Facebook has served as a way for diasporic communities to stay connected and hold onto something left behind. Dominican Facebook users produce a rapidly corporatized transnational space of cultural transmission with its own unique rules, meanings, and expectations, and typically remains highly prescriptive of gender, class, race, and nation. As elsewhere in the world, Dominican women readily employ visual culture and online networks to connect, seek information, sympathize, assert ideologies, mobilize one another around personal and political issues, and so much more. They do so from anywhere they are at any moment of the day—and often right from the palm of their hand—via BlackBerry, smartphone, or other internet-ready electronic device.

In her hypnotic ode to "Maldito feisbu," a decade ago Rita Indiana named the ways that our whole lives were already being swallowed up into a virtual world online, in which it is possible to literally lose ourselves in an alternate reality. Nuanced lyrics in her ominous song carry a *doble sentido* (double meaning) that showcases her creative brilliance, wit, and awareness of the impact of technology in the social moment: "Tenia de to' / no tengo na' / todo por una computadora / 'toy enganchá' igual que tú / por esa maldita vaina / maldito feisbu / miro tu foto / mira la mia / a toda hora de noche y de día / me puse a taggear sin compasión / mientras en mi casa se metia un ladrón. / [I had everything / I have nothing / all for a computer / I am hooked just like you / By this damn thing / Damn Facebook / I look at your photo / You look at mine / Every hour of the night and day / I tag you without compassion / while in my house is a thief.]" Rita Indiana suggests that the character she represents in her song, like you the listener, has been robbed while sitting at the computer. The *ladrón* is Facebook itself—or anyone *on* Facebook— grabbing your pictures, your personal information, and your identity off the popular social networking site. While this is now a well-known risk of using social media (with the additional awareness that the US government is tracking all our online interactions), the allure of such a dynamic social space is hard to give up. Yet, as she acknowledges in her song, interactions online today tend to be no more than a superficial gazing at one another's curated images or a "you show me yours, I'll show you mine" visual currency.

A Dominican friend in my social network, Yosaira, began displaying a series of snapshots taken on her BlackBerry phone that she shared to her Facebook page under the heading "parte de me vida en pocas imágenes [part of my life in a few images]." In her real-time archiving of these vernacular photographs she gathered together blurry snapshots of her parents, a picture of a bike, a favorite gelato shop, and several selfies taken outside on the street at night in Santo Domingo. I am able to witness love, rebellion, community, family, and identity conveyed within the frame of each of these vernacular images. As Coco Fusco writes, "We are increasingly reliant on photographs for information about histories and realities that we do not experience directly. But we also create and use photography to see ourselves."[22] For black people in particular, argues Tina Campt, we must consider self-making photographs as sites off both "*articulation* and *aspiration* [emphasis in original]."[23] Yosaira's choice of images from those she had taken with her BlackBerry camera required her active curation and a self-conscious awareness that what she shared would be scrutinized or at least witnessed by others. By way of audience confirmation, she crafted a way of seeing herself and produced a public identity while coalescing community around her narrative. Fifty-five people "liked" Yosaira's post.

Yosaira's reality became viewable through the window of a series of cell-phone snapshots that served to critique the romanticized nature of online representations. When she posted the series online, she understood it as part of a larger visual project. In her textual response she criticized the relatively recent constant use of social media and its misrepresentation of reality: "When I see my memories on Facebook, it seems like I have never felt bad in my life. That I have always been smiling or enjoying time with friends or acting and receiving applause. Sometimes one is confused, it turns out that this is not real, this parallel world that we have created is false. The trick is to know this and avoid confusion."[24] Some of her Facebook followers commented in response, one stating, "I started posting things that are ugly too and they asked me if I was going crazy."[25] Images posted online are inherently surveilled and users are thus encouraged to share only beautiful and polished representations of themselves. The same commentator goes on to decry the superficial nature of Dominican society, a frequent complaint. She writes, "I think that people are afraid of the authentic, that which is real. It is better to pretend, you'll do better in this comfortable state. But neither you nor I want to be comfortable," she laughs, in an online gesture of "Jeje."[26] Another friend of Yosaira who felt the same way suggests she had read her mind, "*Bruja*, this morning I was thinking the same thing . . . luckily I'm just dipping into this parallel world but I am very selfish and I am not going to share so many good things that happen to me. But when I'm not very happy, I go on [Facebook] and I see so many people who think they're so special and blessed for so little, that I immediately realize how lucky I am."[27] As a "parallel world," Facebook is a place to share in someone else's joy. And it is a space of comparison, measuring one's self against virtual reality of someone else's life. Suggests another in Yosaira's network, "It's as if we live in a bubble of eternal happiness, but as you say, the trick is to know it and not get confused."[28] In this "bubble," photographs manage to bind together a group of people, in dialogue around what the visual images signify for each of them.

Raisa and Ingrid: Social Networks as Sites of Identity

"What I love about the internet," twenty-four-year-old Ingrid tells me, "is that you feel completely crazy and then you find people who grew up in completely different cultures with the same fears and desires as you."[29] Her remark captures the ways that so many of the Dominican women I have spoken with live within Dominican culture yet feel far outside of it. Her sentiments remind me of those of James Baldwin, who once articulated something similar: "You think your pain and your heartbreak are unprecedented in the history of the world, but then you read. It was Dostoevsky and Dickens who taught me that the things that tormented me most were the very things that connected me with all the people who were alive, or who had ever been alive."[30] Like several other women I spoke with who regularly surf the net, post on Facebook, and connect with friends online, for Ingrid, the line between her online identity and her actual identity is blurred. She actively cultivates an audience, reinforcing a particular identity that she has shaped and selected in her act of *doing* identity. Facebook offers her a chance to see herself—and having others see her—in ways in which she is highly invested.

"Everyone can testify to my love for my BlackBerry," Ingrid tells me when I interview her with her best friend Raisa.[31] Ingrid's social media tool of choice, the BlackBerry phone, or "BB," as it is fondly referred to, has long been a popular mode of communication because it allowed for free text chatting to other BB users anywhere in the world, at no additional cost, and it is durable and economical compared to personal computers and smartphones. Throughout Santo Domingo in 2010, you could walk into shops, corporate offices, beauty salons, art galleries—even the police department—and go unnoticed because one or more young people at work there were leaning over their BlackBerries, messaging friends or reading Facebook status updates. Omnipresent digital technology means that at concerts, lectures, and birthday parties, Dominicans are recording the details of their lives to share on the internet; there is even greater incentive to record for those who have family and friends living abroad with whom they desire to share an affective moment.

"It's a love-hate relationship because it stresses me out too much," Ingrid explains about the technology and its influence. "For example, I maintain contact . . . with all of my friends, those of us who started university together, now that they are finished some of them finished and are doing their master's in different parts of the world. Therefore, it makes it very cheap and very easy to communicate, we keep up, talking a lot, they send me music, and we keep up as if they were still here." She says her friends might send news about what is going on where they are, in Europe or in the United States, and she can include that information in her blog. Her friends studying in faraway places (Germany, Spain, Switzerland, and the United States) open her world up even though she has not yet had the opportunity to live abroad.

Raisa describes herself as not being "*muy* [very] Facebook" or "muy Messenger," and says she just uses her BlackBerry to send messages and make calls. As for Facebook, she says, "I am always connected at work. I connect to Facebook and right there I can talk to *todo el mundo* [everyone—or literally, the whole world]. Normally at work, not at home. But yes, I share a lot of information, my new passions . . . information about cinema, new movies." She says she has family in Spain, the United States, Canada, and Mexico. "We connect in different ways, through Messenger. Now we all look different, we can see each other and see who has had gotten fat," she says; Messenger had recently added a video component.

"There are others who close their Facebook accounts," I say, playing devil's advocate.

"Yes, I'm against Facebook," Ingrid contributes. "It seems very . . . maybe, impersonal. The people are divided. . . . Before Facebook, there were social relationships." Ingrid's additional complaint is that people get their information about you via Facebook rather than going directly to you to learn what is going on your life. Furthermore, she says, "People construct false lives on Facebook." They also construct false Facebook accounts in order to get information about others. It becomes increasingly difficult to trust what we see, and we learn not to trust who people say they are online.

"How many hours are you connected to the internet?" I ask Ingrid and Raisa.

"24/7," says Ingrid, "I am always connected."

"Ay," gasps Raisa at her friend's response. "When I leave work I don't want to know about Facebook, that nobody said nothing. Not Messenger, nothing. I go to school and then I go home. This is my life."

But internet access also means access to films and books that are otherwise unavailable to Dominicans on the island. Ingrid elaborates: "I spend a lot of time on the internet reading, when I don't have other work. I love the blogs about feminism. . . . My friends that are in Holland, in Germany, send me messages: 'Look, read this!' And maybe that page has a link to something else that leads to something else. I like to read the news from BBC, the edition for Latin America." She goes on, "The books, I try to download them in PDF wherever. It is really difficult to get them in the country because they are very expensive."

"Yes," says Raisa, immediately.

"In English here, they cost a lot of money," says Ingrid, who reads American pop culture websites like *Jezebel* and *Gawker*. If her friends do not send her books from abroad she gets PDFs and prints them out. Via email, and across feminist networks throughout Latin America they circulate essays by Angela Davis and bell hooks alongside Dominican scholars such as Ochy Curiel and Denise Paewonsky. For many, the practice of reading in English—even if they do not speak it—still tremendously broadens their access to information and resources, though. The internet now provides tools for translation and desired texts are increasingly available in Spanish.

Sites of Resistance

On a day in late February 2010, I headed to La Universidad Autónoma de Santo Domingo, Santo Domingo's large public university. La UASD (pronounced "la wha-s") has long been dynamic public space in the capital and a site of political fomentation; and it is where the vast majority of my interviewees, friends, and acquaintances in Santo Domingo have studied. Founded in 1528 as La Universidad Santo Tomás de Aquino, it is the oldest public university in the Americas and the main university in Santo Domingo. It was, as Tirso Mejía-Ricart notes, constructed for the purpose of educating "administrators both spiritual and material" of the new world.[32] In the first decade of the twenty-first century, nearly half of all university students in the Dominican Republic were students at la UASD. The school has educated numerous generations of Dominican professionals, artists, and intellectuals.[33] Credentials from la UASD are recognized worldwide, a factor of great importance to those who aspire to travel abroad for further education. Professionals throughout the country sport the UASD class ring— the school's emblem engraved on a square black background—as a marker of educational attainment. Doctors and politicians in the news can be seen wearing it, as well as actors on local TV.

On this day, the campus is flooded with students streaming across broken sidewalks and sitting out on cement benches and low walls, beside weather-worn concrete buildings that hold blocks of classrooms. Cars line the narrow streets within the campus walls, while almond trees and other vegetation provide much-coveted shade across the campus. In some areas, the grounds are kept green with sprinklers, while in others there are bare patches exposing dry cracked earth between clumps of determined crabgrass. Just by watching the flow of student traffic on campus, it is obvious that the majority undergraduates at la UASD today are women.[34] Equal access to education is "how the playing field gets evened out," my neighbor Porfirio informs me, as we walk to campus together one day. The campus of la UASD does not compare to the facilities at numerous private universities that emerged throughout the Dominican Republic after 1961. These institutions (each known by their acronym), including UNPHU (Universidad Nacional de Pedro Henríque Ureña), INTEC (Instituto Technológico de Santo Domingo), and APEC (Universidad Acción Pro-Educación y Cultura), are better maintained and seem to draw a different student body. In 2010, the newer business school and the engineering building at la UASD starkly contrast with the sparse and decaying classrooms of the humanities block, where there are not enough chairs in each classroom. Students from different socioeconomic backgrounds can all afford the cost of tuition at la UASD, which at that time was a remarkable 100 Dominican pesos per class, about 15 dollars per semester for a full courseload; transportation to and from campus throughout the semester costs students far more.

La UASD has long been considered a site of political struggle because of leftist student organizing and it remains a bellwether for political activism in the Dominican Republic. Throughout the 1960s and into the 1970s Dominican President Joaquin Balaguer used the university to co-opt leftist activists who could otherwise prove a threat to his regime. According to historian Frank Moya Pons, "Intellectuals and professionals were mollified by their appointment as professors to the state university with total disregard for their professional qualifications. More than a thousand members of the minor leftist parties became professors or employees of the Universidad Autónoma de Santo Domingo."[35] Though they may not have come across as revolutionary in their political discourse, writes Moya Pons, these new administrators did bring a leftist approach to the university after the Trujillo era.

"Balaguer used the university as a ghetto for the left," one interviewee would later explain to me. "The police could not enter. It was if it were a little free zone . . . as an exercise. For the prosecution, it created a concentration of all of his enemies," she said. By allowing revolutionary organizations to feel ownership of the campus community, Balaguer could keep any and all organized acts of resistance contained; Dominican intelligence agencies kept university groups under close surveillance. Activist protest and violence on the university campus is a constant occurrence as students at la UASD attempt to maintain a left-wing public sphere within Santo Domingo, where they might sustain an ongoing critique of the state.

In 1993, when moves toward privatization of the public university were in full force, there were 45,000 students at la UASD. A couple decades later, there are over 170,000 students who, beginning in 2012, could enroll in classes online. Such rapid growth reflects the dramatic population increase in the Dominican Republic, as well as steady migration toward cities and a desire on the part of all Dominicans to have access to education as a means of social advancement. The difference in class background between students at la UASD and those attending private schools is discernible not only in how students dress but also in in the color of their skin.

In the popular Dominican comedy *Ladrones a domicilio* (2008), this reality of color and class being tied together within the university system is a visual gag. When the film's protagonist, Bruno (Manolo Ozuna), quits his job as a professor at a Catholic university, it is out of sheer frustration with his own exploitation. The private school has pulled out of an agreement for free tuition for his daughter who, like him, is dark-skinned. Bruno tells his boss that he knows he is being discriminated against because wealthy parents at the school do not want his working-class daughter mixing with their privileged children. In a pivotal scene, one of Bruno's wealthy students shows up late to class again and he can do little but threaten the youth and run him out of the classroom. When the camera pans across the room, it is full of light-skinned Dominican youth, several of them with straight blond hair, in designer clothes and polo shirts, sitting in front of open Apple laptops. The visual commentary on the racialization of class is one that Dominican viewers recognize, and it underscores fact that upper-class Dominicans are in fact a world away.[36]

At la UASD, inside the Pedro Mir library, there are banks of black Dell computers on every floor for students to access the card catalogue—though only a few of these computers actually work. Other computers with limited internet connection are scattered along the walls of several of the study rooms, and spotty access to Wi-Fi is available in different parts of the building including at the entryway. The students I spoke to agreed overwhelming that it was far easier to get answers to questions they have about the world online at home, on a handheld device, or at an internet café, than to seek out a few well-worn books from the library's sparse collection. In the library's open foyer, however, is a large painting on canvas that seems to encourage Dominican students to strive for an education. It is superimposed above an oft-recited narrative of Dominican history and identity.

Rewriting Master Narratives

Like numerous other works of art on the walls and facades of buildings throughout the campus, the painting in the library foyer is part of a culture of the visual that has long shaped Dominican thought and leads us to a highly visual present. Executed by Jose Altagracia García Espino and collaborators, the commissioned piece was installed at the time of the building's opening in 2005. It hangs high on the western wall, to the left of the main entrance, and one can view it in its entirety from any of the three landings on the down staircase. Stretched across a wooden frame that is several floors high, the canvas has already begun to sag under its own weight and the light and heat of the library's unairconditioned building. García Espino's mural narrates Dominican history from conquest, through colonization, to the social and technological advancements that are the backdrop of Dominican identity today. While Dominican history and national identity are firmly grounded in a patriarchal narrative representing the forefathers of the nation, a new story about the vital role of internet technology in how Dominicans understand themselves in the twenty-first century emerges from this work: at the bottom left-hand corner of the painting, García Espino has included an IBM desktop computer, circa 1995, suggesting that the entire history being portrayed here materializes out of it.

The story starts in the lower right-hand corner, where Spanish conquistadores arrive on the island of Hispaniola and stand waving their flag. In this first encounter, the Taíno people have their arrows drawn on the far left. Immediately behind the triumphant image of the Spanish is an illustration of the period of *encomiendas* that would follow, in which enslaved Taíno were rapidly killed off through brutal labor conditions, violence and abuse long-sanctioned by the Catholic Church. García Espino depicts these Indigenous people wearing loincloths and headdresses, as they are forced to pan for gold and carry heavy goods under the watch of Spanish overseers on horseback. Although positioned at the center of the mural, enslaved Africans in this history seem to fade into the background; they appear as mostly nude, monochromatic, and anonymous figures and the depiction of them pouring sugar is so faint it is easy to overlook.

Tracing upward along the painting, one sees the figure of Gregorio Luperón, famous for winning a second independence for the Dominican Republic, ending the country's annexation to Spain in 1865. García Espino portrays Dominican history anachronistically in this work, since above Luperón at the top and center is Juan Pablo Duarte, standing in trinity with Matías Ramón Mella and Francisco del Rosario Sanchez; the three led the country's war of independence from Haiti in 1844, well before its reannexation to Spain. Duarte, Mella, and Sanchez are known as "*la trinitaria*," the country's founding fathers, and drive the narrative presented. To the right of these three men is an image of the Aula Magna, la UASD's iconic edifice with its round red roof and distinct pinnacle. To its left is a co-ed group of students in class and just behind them a satellite drifts in orbit. A satellite dish nearby points out into space and beyond the nation, a suitable reminder of the desire of the Dominican Republic to extend itself past its borders.

Eddy De los Santos Nuñez, assistant to the director of the Pedro Mir, who worked at the library at the time the painting was installed, tells me that García Espino had intended to convey that all of this Dominican history could now be accessed through the World Wide Web: "*I* would have put un *aroba* [@] on there to indicate that the computer was connected to the internet," he tells me. Indeed, at the time the aroba had become a highly recognized symbol, used on internet café signboards throughout urban and rural Dominican Republic. Instead, the artist opted to paint rays of light bursting from the computer screen and winding their way up the wall, to tell this tale in which the past intersects the technological present. The painting sends a clear message regarding access to knowledge for Dominican students in the twenty-first century: that the whole history of the republic is accessible via a computer screen. It also suggests that the Dominican nation and a narrative of national identity are influenced by new technology. New technology changes the narrative: Dominican identity in Santo Domingo may now be about looking forward through the internet toward a new type of *progreso*, one that can align with global progress.[37] In contrast to this vision of a future that clings to the past, an older artwork I encountered on campus tells a different story through symbols familiar to Dominican students.

Everybody's Protest Mural

In 2010 I came across an extensive, noncommissioned mural fading on the outside of a block of humanities classrooms at la UASD. Comprised of a nuanced Dominican visual discourse, I was eager to know more about it and began asking around. Eventually, I learned that it had been painted in the late 1990s by the student group known as ERA (Espacio de Reflexión y Acción [Space of Reflection and Action]). The mural critiques the cultural changes occurring in the Dominican Republic under neoliberalism, not only the privatization of the university but also the foreign cultural values fed to students by government aligned with the United States and its capitalist agenda. Across the top it reads: "¡PAREMOS LA PRIVATIZACION! [WE WILL STOP PRIVATIZATION!]" and "¡CONSTRUYAMOS EL PODER ESTUDANTIL! [WE WILL BUILD STUDENT POWER!]." It reflects Dominican student opposition to a free-market development plan for the nation enacted by the Dominican Republic–Central American Free Trade Agreement (DR-CAFTA) in 1995. Nestor García Canclini describes the rise of neoliberal dogma in Latin America that has so much shaped the Dominican Republic in the following way: "All of the tendencies we observed a decade ago, toward abdicating the public in favor of the private, the national in favor of the transnational, have been accentuated."[38] He notes that digitization has changed "rural processes of production, circulation, and consumption, which transfers the initiative and economic and cultural control to transnational corporations."[39] Of course, all the while informal markets continue to expand as well, greatly influencing the national economy and its politics.

The United States is represented in the ERA mural as a cartoonish figure, a bearded Neanderthal with a bulbous nose leaning back confidently on the spiked club in his right hand and wearing a tall top hat striped in the red, white, and blue of the American flag. Behind him are a bulldog, a wolf, a pig, and a vulture—symbols of greed—along with figures including the pope and the president of the university at the time, who supported its privatization. To the right, two Dominican students stand in front of the Neanderthal. Directly above the students' heads are funnels overflowing with different symbols of capitalism and corruption. They are wide-eyed and dizzied by the effects: the centers of their eyes contain dark spirals so they appear as if drugged; the mural suggests that their heads are being filled with vices from the West, such as pot, alcohol, guns, money, and other symbols of degenerate materialism. Foreign emblems of the BMW, the Nike swoosh, and the Toyota logo are being funneled into them.

ERA students have painted the female college student as lighter in color than her male counterpart, making legible her femininity within a Dominican visual lexicon I had become familiar with; her straight hair is cut

Figure 2. Espacio de Reflexión y Acción (ERA) student mural on La UASD campus. Photo by the author.

Figure 3. Mercedes García pointing to different symbolism in the ERA mural. Photo by the author.

Figure 4. Closeup of the ERA mural. Photo by the author.

into bangs. The preference for fair-skinned women with straight hair is also reinforced in the funnel above the young man's head where there is a figure of a white woman along with the bottle of alcohol and the US dollar sign. In contrast, the female student has a marijuana leaf above her and a copy of *Jasmín*, a popular romance novel (like a Harlequin paperback) once viewed by Dominicans as immoral and damaging to society. In fact, the young woman has also let go of the book she held in her arms, figuratively letting her education slip away, although the male student clutches his firmly under one arm. In his right hand he grasps a picket sign that reads "Made in Gringolandia," a critique of the damage done by North American values.[40] Behind the two students on the lower right side of the mural is the Aula Magna again with its recognizable round red roof, representative of la UASD. But hanging from the pinnacle is a bar code, or effectively a price tag. To the right of the building, streaming out at an angle from its roof like the stripes of a flag, are the colors red, green, and yellow, which, I am later told, do not represent claims to an African heritage but rather stand for the ERA's themes of passion, hopefulness of youth, and the glow of light under which they are to educate themselves. The ERA's logo is a drawing of a hand grasping a pencil, symbolic of students' fight for "public and cost-free education." In the mural, this same fist is held high by an unclothed male figure running forward, almost leaping from the wall.

Questions that came up for me about the mural could not be answered at the university library nor the National Archive but eventually led me to Rocío y Rafael, two self-identified activists who attended la UASD in the 1990s. When I met Rocío and told her about my research she assured me her husband would know more about the mural and in fact, he was part of producing it. Rafael was a member of a group of students who founded the Espacio de Reflexión y Acción at la UASD back in 1993. It was, he says, a response to "the menace of privatization of the university." He was a student there from 1993 to 2000.

While Rafael could provide further insight into the significance of the mural, Rocío shared ephemera from student activism of the 1990s that she had carefully preserved in a personal archive. The three of us meet for an interview in their living room one rainy afternoon. We are in a ground floor apartment, looking out at a tree-lined street just after a torrential rain. The windows are open along the street, with no screens, only the iron security bars common to most households in Santo Domingo. Framed artwork lines the walls from top to bottom, including some made by the couple's young child, which are tacked up on doors and in extra spaces.

"We are a bit unconventional," Rocío explains almost apologetically, when she invites me to stay for *pan y chocolate* and Rafael heads to the kitchen to prepare it. Since Rocío has a fulltime desk job, her husband is responsible for the cooking in the household, in what is an uncommon dynamic in Dominican society. Rocío is a tall and lanky Dominican woman with light brown hair and blue-green eyes. When we meet at her house, she is wearing a pale blue blouse with denim shorts and a dark blue glass evil eye hangs around her neck, the type from Eastern Europe that they sell at the tourist craft tables in Samaná. She sits with Rafael on a long low sofa, its narrow wooden spindled arms framing the dark upholstery. Rafael is also tall and thin but with a darker coloring and dark eyes. He graciously responds to my questions about the mural with many details and speaks passionately about student activism during his time there and the issues students rally around presently. At moments, he lowers his voice to talk about particular political figures, embodying his familiarity with a culture of political repression and hyper-aware of the digital audio recorder I am shuffling around. I see him occasionally self-edit before allowing his words to go on record and recognize that these tensions convey the level of state repression to which student activists have been subjected when they seek to express themselves through organized acts of resistance.

"[La UASD] was in the process of being privatized," Rafael explains, "with greater policing and control of the students." The ERA was the only student group addressing the issue of privatization at the university beginning in the 1990s. "It started with two or three projects of privatization at the university that the students became aware of." One of the ways that the university privatized in the past, and the way the government continues to privatize the university today, is that different individuals appropriate valuable campus property and sell the prime real estate off for private projects under the guise of construction for the university. Rafael informs me that administrators, under Roberto Sandoval (from 1993 to 1996) began building with money from la UASD on land owned by the UASD and yet no one knew for what. They closed access to the university on different sides, narrowing the flow of foot traffic through a small number of guarded gateways. "Barbed wire was put up. . . around the campus to keep people from crossing in different areas." These actions began to shift the relatively open culture of the university and narrow the public space. La UASD denied the accusation of privatization, but the administration was aligned with Balaguer: "They had a rather fascist mentality," Rafael says flatly.

After Trujillo, Balaguer ran the country with an authoritarian regime supported by the United States, stealing elections and maintaining his hold on the presidency well into his eighties, at which point he had become completely blind. He would continue to run for president into his nineties. Some of his success appeared to be based not only on election fraud but also anti-Haitian propaganda, and a patriarchal culture in which Dominican voters felt reassured by the fatherly figure in leadership, a political approach regularly deployed by contemporary candidates.[41] During the three decades after Trujillo's death, some forty private schools opened up, yet as Rafael tells me, la UASD was the only state institution. "There were *institutos* that opened and closed, but they didn't have credentials or rigor . . . they were businesses . . . and they couldn't find students. To privatize la UASD as well meant that there would be nowhere for poor people to study. . . . We realized if they privatized it we would not be able to study there."

Rocío chimes in throughout, pointing out that the government offers very little for the people and now they wanted to take away public education. Rafael tells me that the language of privatization was not used; it was the "capitalization" of state businesses that was being pitched to the people, and capitalism was supposed to save the country. "I tell you so that you can see how we are living here," Rafael confides. "The government does not attend to the public services. The social programs do not serve the people. Institutionalization, but not to serve the people, rather 'institutionality' in the sense to control the people . . . that is what they want." During the 1990s, the students of ERA were reading Francis Fukuyama's *The End of History and the Last Man* as they critiqued the changes occurring in the country. Fukuyama's insights into liberal democracy resonated with Dominican youth, as did his declarations about privatization and technology's impact on society—decades before the existence of the BlackBerry and the iPhone. Fukuyama warned of technology as advancing neoliberalism in ways that would lead to "an increasing homogenisation of all human societies, regardless of their historical origins or cultural inheritances."[42] Fears of homogenization reflected in the ERA mural were well-founded. Furthermore, writes Fukuyama, "Such societies have become increasingly linked with one another through global markets and the spread of a universal consumer culture."[43]

Rocío describes being a student at la UASD in the 1990s under the administration of Miguel Rosada as "insane," due to his brutal, aggressive, and oppressive regime. "Students were being terrorized. They had to sleep away from their homes for fear that he would go after them." Her anger contrasts Rafael's calm, matter-of-fact descriptions of the period. Rafael recalls the actions students took, and how the mural looked when it was brand new. The paint, he says, had been donated and the students camped out overnight, "with a lantern [and] pan y chocolate, working to complete it before graduation. "Surely many people have pictures of themselves in front of that mural with the colors bright and fresh," he says looking over the photographs I had brought. He deciphers some of the mural's images for me: "It was a figure to say that if he was naked, he had nothing to hide, healthy, using a pencil like a spear," says Rafael, of the naked man depicted. A student I spoke to on campus said she interpreted the figure with his brown skin, simple sandals, and bare chest to be a cimarrón [maroon], a symbol of resistance and liberty.

"Tío [Uncle] Sam," is there, symbolizing the intervention by the United States in 1964. "This represents the Independence," Rafael says, pointing to the wolf, "but it is a caricature, because independence from what?"

"From the Haitians!" Rocío pipes in sarcastically; all of us laugh at the grossness of her humor, and its truth.

"Yes, from the poor Haitians," Rafael responds with a knowing grin. It is laughable because of the painful truth of it. The Dominican Republic celebrates its independence on February 27 each year, not from Spanish colonialism but in honor of the day in 1844 that the Dominican people overthrew a twenty-two-year Haitian occupation. It was this same Haitian occupation that brought the abolition of slavery and freed an estimated eight thousand people enslaved in Santo Domingo at that time. Dominicans attribute their independence from Haitian rule to Juan Pablo Duarte and celebrate him with parks, statues, and roads in his name, but notably the country later sought re-annexation to Spain in 1861, only to fight for independence again 1865.

"This is a vulture here." Rafael points to the figure behind "Tío Sam" with its head poking out and its body a large gray mass with other heads emerging from its back; each head is a caricature of a greedy politician or global figure, including George H. W. Bush, Pope John Paul II, and Muammar Gaddafi. When I ask why this type of political action against privatization had fomented at this moment, Rafael offers me a nuanced and relatable explanation: "A form of degeneration . . . [the Dominican elite] depoliticize and become indifferent to others because all that they have is imaginary: 'it's good to study in order to be rich and imitate the model North American lifestyle.' You know? . . . to live imitating the things of the empire. For example, you see poor people that can't come up with 300 pesos to buy a book and understand reality but to buy a BlackBerry, yes. It's a mess, right? And the poor boys in the barrio rob, do it all, to have this type of thing."

Off the Wall

Neoliberal privatization in Santo Domingo is visible in the ways that protest murals fade and walls of abandoned buildings around the city today are "tagged" by corporate advertising made to look like graffiti or rebellious street art. Artists are commissioned to produce murals along major thoroughfares that draw tourists to encourage photographic moments (standing in front of the murals) and make a city more visually appealing. Long gone from the visual landscape of the university are *las vallas* that students at la UASD once employed to send a clear political message to the university administration. Las vallas were enormous metal billboards on which students painted political messages and then placed them, for up to a week, at central locations on campus or in the breezeways of particular departments where students and faculty would pass by, see, and discuss the topics presented.[44] This manner of inciting dialogue in the campus community through visual culture preceded social media campaigns. It was also effective, I was told, for challenging a sexist university culture in which faculty were harassing female students.

"It was the size of this wall," Rafael gestures with his hands, "but wide and low with images and brochures. . . . We covered it with paper or painted right on the metal doing art, we would make art on it." In explaining the culture of las vallas, he makes what he suggests is obvious link for me between students' artistic renditions of their political concerns and the lively culture of performance that exists in Santo Domingo. "We also did a lot of theater. The theater also carried a lot of symbolism, you know?" Rafael explains, "Like the *caja de muerto* [casket], which symbolized privatization." For a few years before attending university, he had participated in activism in through a theater troupe.[45]

Las vallas were different from how today's youth use the internet for organizing, yet there are some surprising connections. Rafael agrees, it is "otro medio de publicidad abierta [another means of open advertising]." Like posts shared via Facebook, las vallas could draw the attention of 300 or 400 people walking by. Images, symbols, and written discourse could incite face-to-face debates and discussions on the university campus.

"I don't know if there are images of this," says Rafael, seeking to better explain the moment. We eventually discover a newspaper clipping in Rocío's files that includes a picture of one of the vallas. It is a photograph in color from *Listín Diario*, in which two female students stand gazing at the enormous billboard; the photographer snapped the picture over the left shoulder of one of the students facing the valla. We can see it from her vantage point. She has raised her left hand to her cheek as she views the message from the ERA: "RETROCESO EN LA UASD [SETBACK IN LA UASD)]."[46] The valla

Figure 5. Newspaper clipping from the personal archive of an interviewee. Original image by Miguel Gómez for *Listín Diario*.

responds to ongoing organizational troubles at the university throughout the 1990s.[47] Along the left side of the valla, the ERA has painted a life-size cartoon of a Neanderthal, club in hand, and a red swastika on his pale bare shoulder. In the newspaper's caption, student onlookers are described as indifferent but this commentary seems far more to reflect the politics of the newspaper than the women's intense gazes upon the information being presented.

"Once a woman made una valla when several women were being harassed by a professor in the Economics Department. There were several women, sometimes crying, because this professor would have them come to his office to take their final exam, then ask them what grade they wanted to get," explains Rafael.

"[A female student] brought us this issue and first we went and investigated it, because you can't just go accusing professors or you could get yourself into trouble. But understanding our 'super *machismo*' and other things, we said yes, we could take action. . . . We made una valla and left it there in the Economics Department for a week. . . . Then we had an assembly with the students and they gathered in front of the valla to testify about all the things that this guy had done." The reaction that the valla received around the issue of sexual harassment by professors was so threatening that the administration destroyed the valla late one night, says Rafael. In response, students painted another, this time in front of their peers. With such support, they felt confident enough to further the confrontation: "We went to [the professor's] class with a mass of students, and the woman he harassed, and he pushed us out of his classroom."

"This was a truly interesting process," he says, "because maybe we never could have imagined that it would awaken such discussion and debate in the street." This occasion of student organizing not only captures some of the obstacles that Dominican women face in their struggles to access education but also provides a concrete example of the type of action by youth mobilizing visual culture. "It was another type of pressure on the administration, with el muralismo, las vallas, la caracatura," Rafael says with pride.

Photographic Resistance

"¡AHORA NOSOTROS DAMOS LAS NOTICIAS! [Now *we* make the news]" reads a sign held over the head of an anonymous protester who could be located anywhere in the Spanish-speaking world. The logos for Facebook, Twitter, and YouTube are hand-drawn across the bottom of the poster board, while the top is embellished with the logos for Color Vision, TeleAntilles, TeleMicro, and TeleSistema. A photographic image of the hand-drawn sign with only the forehead and eyes of the protester revealed below it circulates on social media.

In 2010, a YouTube video shared on Facebook encouraged all Dominicans to "párate y protesta [stand up and protest]" around issues such as environmental degradation, protection of water, conservation, and pride in the country.[48] The video urges Dominicans to speak up so that the government will represent their interests and encourages viewers to make sure that their friends and family watch the video. A series of speakers tell viewers to share the video: "Mandalo por Facebook [Send it by Facebook]," "Por Facebook," chimes in the next, then the next, "Mandalo por BB [Send it by BlackBerry]," "Tweetealo," "Twitter . . ." echoes one voice and closeup headshot after another. "Mandalo por HiFi, si todavía está allí [Send it by HiFi, if it's still there]," jokes another talking head. "Messenger," "Por Second Life," list the voices. "De cualquier manera tú que puedas [In whatever way you can]." Videos like this one circulate "virally" through Dominican social networks that are not bound by national borders.

Although a visual approach to political engagement is a longstanding tradition in the Dominican Republic, posting your photos or thoughts from the comfort of your own home or typing a comment from your cellphone is quite different from standing up and speaking your mind on campus and can contribute to a sort of passive political allegiance. Nevertheless, acts of resistance through visual culture have been effective with the expansion of LGBTQ+ Pride festivities in Santo Domingo and their documentation on-line.[49] Photographs have long been used as a tool to combat dehumanizing propaganda through the inundation of positive images.[50] Dominican Pride photos circulating en masse online have effectively countered a dominant narrative that homosexuality is a Western construction and gay, lesbian, and transgender people do not exist in Dominican society. Both professional and amateur photographers capture Santo Domingo's annual Pride festivities. The flow of images from tens of thousands of revelers who happily celebrate the *caravana gay* each year has become a critical intervention for the insertion of marginalized identities into a mainstream Dominican transnational imaginary as part of a project of queer visibility.[51] These efforts by minority groups are rewarded through the distribution of NGO resources; incentive to do visibility work online.[52]

Organizing and messaging that was happening via email networks and on blogs shifted over to Facebook in the later part of the first decade of the twenty-first century. One important example of this type of mobilization in Santo Domingo is El Besatón, which first took place in Santo Domingo in 2010 and occurred again three more times while expanding its reach as a social movement via Facebook and Twitter. The word *besatón* translates as "kiss-a-thon" but the event was a procession that looked a lot like a protest march and culminated with a collective performance of public kissing. It was organized in response to Dominican media's shaming of a heterosexual couple of Haitian descent living in Santo Domingo, who were working as cellphone card venders, and were photographed kissing in the street. A cellphone image of their kiss had circulated via social media. The conservative media called for the couple to be thrown out of the country and conservative politicians sought to investigate their legal status.[53] El Besatón was a "*lúdico-político* [playfully political]" act of mobilization, the organizers state in the email that they circulated. They were inspired by similar actions by LGBTQ+ groups from Costa Rica, Colombia, Peru, Spain, Brazil, Mexico, and France. El Besatón also aligned with a tradition of street theater in the Dominican Republic as a "performance-based political practice" that provides what Raj Chetty describes as "a Brechtian blurring of the distinctions between performers and spectators."[54] The circulation of the initial image incited racist public outcry, and led to much public dialogue via radio, TV news, and social media. A call to take to the streets was mobilized via an email circulated by artist and activist Yaneris

González Gómez, and it intersected with the movement for social justice that Dominican women have been working to build online and off.[55]

"To show affection is a human condition, not a delinquency," argued the organizers. "It is a democratic act that allows one to construct social, political, and economic relationships that challenge the system of torture, dictatorship, and violence," they contended.[56] The protest was framed by organizers as an intersectional movement response to overpolicing, calling for the defense of human rights. They saw it as an issue of democracy and tied it to a larger crackdown taking place in Parque Duarte, the public plaza popular among artists and queer Dominicans located in an area of the Colonial Zone that was being gentrified. "Hay que estar alertas [One has to be alert]," suggested Sergía Galván, who was at the time executive director of the NGO Colectivo Mujer y Salud, because tides of conservativism can quickly turn to increasing restrictions and violence.[57]

Paloma: *La Calle Será la Calle*

I meet with Paloma in a corner of the library at la UASD, on the third floor. She finds time to talk to me in between classes in journalism and social communications. She has been to the United States, she tells me. Like many students in Santo Domingo, she has studied English, and when she was eighteen years old, she went abroad through a summer work program to improve on her language skills. She paid a US company to travel to a small town in rural Georgia for four months, where she earned minimum wage while working at McDonald's. After that, Paloma spent three months in New York City visiting relatives on a tourist visa, and then traveled to Puerto Rico and Colombia. She carries to our interview at the library a beat-up laptop that does not pick up Wi-Fi or have a working battery. When I ask her what she uses the internet for, she says mostly for reading the news, for Facebook, and to communicate with family abroad.

Paloma is brown in color, morena, and growing out her own tight curls into a natural hairstyle. At the time of our meeting, I do not read her as particularly femme in her gender presentation, dress, or mannerisms. In contrast to the many other women on campus, she is taller and heavier, not dressed to conform to a particular aesthetic. Over time, our friendship deepens and I see her in old pictures on Facebook in which her hair is in fact straight, or out at parties where she is wearing bright red lipstick, with which she claims a particular type of femininity. When I ask her about existing stereotypes about Dominican women, Paloma has little difficulty naming numerous characteristics with which she is familiar, ones I had by then heard many times: "I have always thought, kind of, that the stereotype of the Dominican woman is that she is very sensual, that she is very extroverted, that she is very . . . um . . . affectionate, that she works hard . . . but that she is also conservative in many things." Paloma continues her list, "That she has to have a big butt. That she has to know how to dance, that she has to like to party . . . That all dominicanas know how to dance, that all dominicanas know how to cook; that all dominicanas have an ass, that all of us are hot, that . . . we are very *comparona* [we like to show off]."

"Where do you get this?" I ask, impressed by her specificity. "You hear people talking about this? Or you see images?"

"You see it in the street. For example, the manner in which they refer to a woman. . . . Also you see the same in foreigners because when you talk with foreigners, they have in mind the image that they have of us. . . . Talk with a Puerto Rican and their image of a Dominican woman is submissive, hard worker, good body, very sensual, knows how to dance, knows how to cook. Things like that," she says, seemingly detached from these constructions though highly aware of them. What Paloma describes, however, are the ways that these dominant constructions of Dominican womanhood today, unlike fifty years ago, are also informed by not only Dominican standards but also by transnational desires. Outsiders come with a social construction in mind and look for a particular type of Dominican woman, wanting a color, a body shape, a cultural aesthetic, and behaviors that they already have imagined. These ideas circulate broadly, as Paloma says, on the street, in public spaces. Traditional discourses around acceptable ways of representing Dominican-ness are so pervasive that, for the women I interviewed, the social identity exists as a kind of "common sense": a reservoir of knowledge that young women readily draw from as they envisage the "Dominican woman" trope and her associated stereotypes. Their experiences of race and gender soon became a part of my own "common sense," as I hear variations on the same theme from many different interviewees.

Like most Dominicans, the majority of the young women I spoke to were Catholic by culture, but they and their families were less and less observant. Nevertheless, the Catholic Church is hypervisible in daily life, often to det-rimental effect, with its promotion of homophobia on daily talk shows and lobbying against women's rights.[58] Dominicans are "officially Catholic," says Paloma, but now embrace all kinds of different religions. "This is a very con-servative country, very conservative," she wants me to know. "People don't go to church every Sunday but they identify as Catholic." She herself has been a

Hare Krishna for two years. She says a friend brought her to a meeting and she liked the philosophy and stayed; they meet and talk about vegetarianism and do workshops to educate others. I later witness her involvement in educating others about her religion, observing her work with the community of Hare Krishnas both in real life and by way of her postings on Facebook. Religion did not come up often among the women I interviewed, though one interviewee, when asked how she identified, declared herself to be "first and foremost a child of God."

The perennial tension between the Church and Dominican culture is conveyed in a photograph widely circulated on Facebook. In it, only the robust cleavage of a young Dominican woman is shown as it bursts purposefully out of her shirt, while a gold cross on a chain dangles between her breasts. The photograph is emblematic of a performed contradiction between the moral demands of the Church and the hypersexualization of brown-skinned Dominican women and their lived realities. As Paloma explains to me, it is this culture of the *doble moral* that allows so many extreme contradictions to coexist in the Dominican Republic.[59] She gives as an example the contradictions around homosexuality in Dominican society, which she says is accepted on some level while at the same time it is violently rejected. During this conversation, I share with her my own discomfort around performing femininity in Santo Domingo. When Dominicans see me they often think that I am Dominican, I say. Because of this, when they see me wear my hair the way I do (medium-length curls in their natural state), some have asked me to my face why I haven't combed my hair.[60]

"They ask you why you haven't combed your hair? People ask you that?" Paloma sounds surprised at first, but she clearly understands. "Because . . . yes, here el dominicano feels at liberty to comment on these things . . . because it's part of our culture. El dominicano is very extroverted, likes to make commentary. You can get in a guagua next to a person that you don't know and they feel at liberty to comment on your clothes, your hair, what cream you should put on your face because el dominicano is like that . . . we are like that. Sometimes we don't try to do it, but we can't help it . . . *zafa*." This constant policing of personal aesthetics in Dominican culture, and more accurately people's bodies, profoundly shapes individual identity. People live in close quarters and travel via public transportation in even closer quarters. Strangers will readily make it clear to you if they feel you are stepping out of line, especially in terms of how you look. Adults and children making comments in the street was a regular occurrence for me and the many Dominican women I knew who were growing out their permed hair and opting for a natural hairstyle. Walking out the door each day involved facing scrutiny, while coming home to family could be equally onerous.

One evening, stepping out of a packed *carro público* after a day trip to the beach, I thanked the driver. Glancing in his rearview mirror he responded, "Goodbye, *joven* [youth]." Then he swiftly followed with an explanation of his word choice, "I say 'youth' because I can't tell if you are male or female." In that moment, as in so many others, a Dominican man felt entitled to publicly chastise a (presumably Dominican) woman for not performing gender to *his* standards. One shrugs off these incidents, but when they are constant and never-ending, it becomes obvious to me why women and girls might elect to conform, or leave. Dominican women have educated me on how Dominican culture is highly conformist with the general population striving to fit in to a homogenous dominant culture.[61] Many suggest it is a holdover from living under a dictatorship in which social behavior is policed and failure to meet social expectation is punished. Incessant commentary about people who look different is just one example. See/sawing between "you are one of us" and "you aren't one of us" in response to each minor remark is something that Dominican women experience within the scopic regime and transnational context of Santo Domingo—as well as when they travel beyond it.

2

Me Quedo con la Greña
Dominican Women's Identities and Ambiguities

> My grandmother was a mulatto woman, daughter of
> a mulatto mother whose grandfather was jet black.
> So black in fact, that she tells me that as a child when
> she saw him in the street she would hide—so as
> not to have to say he was her grandfather. I mention
> this because the subject of Caribbean racism will
> surely come up throughout this conversation.
>
> Magaly Pineda, interview with Margaret Randall,
> *Our Voices/Our Lives*

Over the years that I have conducted research in the Dominican Republic, natural hairstyles have come into fashion and a "natural hair movement" has gotten under way. It has heavily relied on the proliferation of images of black women who have decided to "go natural" and shared photographs of their process on Facebook pages, Instagram, websites, and blogs. For Carolina Contreras with her hair care business Miss Rizos and Patricia Grassal's Go Natural Caribe, it was sharing these personal experiences online with other Dominican women that helped them launch successful businesses. Contreras's social media project in particular, built first around her own natural hair transition and later her growth as a young entrepreneur, recast how Dominican women could imagine themselves. Her social media project has been to decolonize Dominicans' relationship to their natural hair, reaching beyond the island to include Dominicans in cities in the United States and Europe.

A plethora of images shared online work to counter the Dominican dominant visual discourse about black female beauty and what was previously acceptable. Dominican women have long been committed to presenting themselves with pin-straight hair that might elide any African heritage. Dominican salons on the island and throughout the diaspora have a reputation for their expertise in transforming black hair in this way. Hair is an important site of transformation of the body through which to conform to social pressures or confirm racial expectations—it is a key signifier used by Dominicans to distance themselves from blackness.

"There are people who are enslaved by the salon and spend tons of money on it," twenty-one-year-old Dulcina Abreu informs me.

"The whole world here is enslaved by the salon!" shouts her friend Michelle Ricardo in agreement. Indeed, beauty salons are everywhere in the Dominican Republic and some 70 percent of women in Santo Domingo go to the salon every week.[1]

"The salon, and the nail shop," Dulcina goes on, "and I think many of the people could use the money to buy themselves a book that would help them with their careers." The two young women express opinions I have heard numerous times among educated working-class and middle-class Dominicans in Santo Domingo in everyday conversation.[2] They respond with frustration to a dominant culture that fetishizes a particular type of female beauty within patriarchal Dominican society. In addition, these young women complain that the culture that surrounds them is highly superficial. Dominicans invest in symbols of status: the brand of clothing they wear, the handbags they carry, and the straightening of their hair.[3] Transforming one's appearance is frequently more feasible and more socially acceptable than transforming one's social position through educational attainment.

There is a mutually constitutive relationship between the elaborate microeconomic structure around which Dominican beauty salons are built and cultural standards about how Dominican women should look.[4] In the Dominican Republic, beauty salons are almost exclusively owned by women.[5] Salons have been so embedded in Dominican culture that for many little girls their first hair straightening is a veritable rite of passage. Often the beauty salon is little more than a tiny storefront, a sole swivel chair in front of a mirror at the back of an internet café, or a woman's back patio (where the smoke from blow-dryers does not linger). The salon is such a ubiquitous space within Dominican culture that even if a woman does not invest in mainstream beauty practices, she is still likely to spend time in this important community space. Women and girls may sit and wait for hours for their turn to have their hair straightened in rollers, under "*el blower.*" By devoting time and money to physical appearance and racial transformation (producing a feminine Latina identity that conforms to social expectations), Dominican women increase their value within Dominican society. They are making astute choices in pursuit of social access and economic stability, but some-times that looks like playing the lottery at the popular *bancas* throughout the country, or investing a great deal of money into their appearance for a chance of securing a better job opportunity or attracting a wealthy partner. In a neoliberal *machista* culture, can Dominican women empower themselves by investing more in education and less in their appearance, or does one's physical appearance have greater social currency?

Fluctuations in Racial Meaning

"Do you know who Martha Heredia is?" I ask each interviewee as I share images with them. I myself had not heard of Heredia until I moved to the Dominican Republic in 2010, right on the heels of her rise to stardom.

"The one who won that thing, *American Idol*?" is twenty-six-year-old Sobeida's response.

"Did you watch when it happened?" I want to know.

"No, it didn't interest me. The saddest part was that the final day coincided with the date of the death of Luis Días," Sobeida tells me, "and it irritated me so much that the newspaper came out with a column on the death of Luis Días and another one that announced that it was the final day of *Latin American Idol*. I was so irritated because I thought: she's a stupid new star, who's going to disappear in a short time and to give space to her cuts into the space of one of the most important artists that this country has ever had, a composer, *un tipo completo*, a revolutionary, a guy to whom we owe much musical credit." Sobeida is correct about Heredia's social significance by 2010: "Now hardly anyone mentions [her], like, she has disappeared, the fever has already disappeared." Nevertheless, Heredia proved a fruitful site of analysis in how she represented Dominicanness to broad audiences that tuned in to the fourth and final season of *Latin American Idol* in 2009. What I heard from friends and interviewees was that Dominicans on the island and in the diaspora had gone wild in their support of the young singer from Santiago de los Caballeros and spent money texting in votes to ensure that she would win the competition, thereby securing a moment of national visibility in Latin America.

"Yes, everyone had this pride because she's Dominican." Sobeida con-firms. "Even my dad said it was good to support Martha, so he sent in a text of support, to give his vote for Martha Heredia."[6] Perhaps Dominicans also looked to Heredia to represent Dominican national pride because she looked like them with her brown skin and straightened hair. By placing her image alongside those of Zoe Saldaña, Rita Indiana, and Michelle Rodriguez, I drew out many conversations about class and color that would not have otherwise emerged. Although in my mind (and to my eyes) Heredia was quite similar to Saldaña in color, how she was read by interviewees in terms of color was quite different. She was born in Santiago, yet to Dominican audiences she represented the working class and *Dominicanyork* (Dominican immigrant to New York) in her aesthetic in ways that Saldaña, as an established Hollywood movie star, did not.

With the images laid on the table in front of Sobeida, I suggest, "We could say, academically, about the phenotype of the women here . . . that you have to decide what color Zoe is, in comparison to Martha. And I know it's a bit difficult because these are photographs printed on paper, but there are some things you can say about her phenotype that are revealed."

Sobeida responds, "Zoe Saldaña, I think she's more mixed, because of her hair . . . because of her hair and her nose. The other [Heredia] looks more like an average Dominican, I dunno, like one of those that you see out there on the street, with her straightened hair so ugly—with her afro treated . . . and her little nose. I think the two of them seem to me to be the most dominicana. . . . Zoe is a little more fair. . . . Here the women who look a little like Zoe are in the Cibao, in the central region of the country, where there was the most racial mixture in comparison with other regions. There are more whites in the Cibao or quote unquote 'whites' than in other areas of the country." Specificities of region are also revealed through my use of images. When I say to Sobeida that it seems like in her description of these women and the differences among them that there was some attention to class, she responds, "A difference in class? You think so?"

"Yes, because *she*," I say, pointing to a picture of Heredia, "is a woman that you might see in the street every day, and *she*," I say as I point to Saldaña, "is not."

"No, I didn't say that you wouldn't see Zoe in the street," Sobeida says, pushing back at my misinterpretation of her words. "I said that her origin could locate her in the Cibao, but you can also encounter women like Zoe in the street. . . . She [Heredia] looks *mas pinta como de pobre* . . . making her more Dominican, because most Dominicans are poor."

"'Más pinta como de pobre?'" I ask, "What do you mean by that?"

"That is to say, well, I'll explain . . . Zoe appears to dress with better taste, she looks different; and she [Heredia] looks like one of those girls that has taken on a popular aesthetic, who looks like everybody else, like all [Dominican] women . . . like any woman you see on the street has that same aesthetic, the same hair, the same extra-long nails. Look, for example, Zoe does not have long nails. *Esta tipa*," she says, pointing to Heredia "has those extra-long nails." Sobeida offers a critique of the type of clothes that women like Heredia wear as provocative and revealing, even though I had only presented her with a headshot because there was always much more to the story than the image. And the image was just the tip of the iceberg.

When I presented a sheet of paper that included an image of Rita Indiana alongside pictures of actresses Michelle Rodriguez, Zoe Saldaña, and singer Martha Heredia, I heard the same thing from many young women as they pointed to Rita's image—"Culturally, I think *she's* the most Dominican of the four." Sobeida explained to me that this is much more of an ideological determination of Rita Indiana's significance, since she is not in fact Afro-Dominican, or "verdaderamente dominicana [truly Dominican]." We are sitting at my dining room table in the stuffy, ground-floor apartment that I have rented in Los Jardines de Norte.[7] Sobeida responds to my line of questioning about Rita as follows:

"There was a lot of curiosity, and a kind of mythology around her has been created. There were many people, young boys especially, who wanted to see more, to know who Rita Indiana was, even though there were many fans who already know her . . . and in general terms, for whom, I felt, like a lot of closeness from the public, a lot of warmth; the public wanted to see [her work] and identified 'con esa loca [with this weirdo]' and it's incredible, that this girl Rita comes to break through many taboos and so much bullshit. With that height with that skin color, it's something else. And no, I don't know to what extent they like her or are drawn to her physically for those uncommon traits, the people maybe see 'something white in her' if, like you say, Xiomara Fortuna could be as alternative as her, or represent as much rupture. I don't know why but the people do not identify with [Xiomara]. Of course, Rita's music is more commercial and uncomplicated, for youth. Xiomara being Afro-Dominican invites reflections and romance and young people don't always respond positively to that. Xiomara had many problems because they said that she was black, that she was *una bruja* [a witch], I dunno. And this girl [Rita] doesn't have that. She doesn't have this 'problem' of negritude."

Sobeida's comments emphasize Rita Indiana's Otherness in terms of her height and color, an observation that was regularly remarked upon in other interviews, and something that stands out visually as much as her queerness or marker of ambiguously representing "una loca." Although she breaks taboos to a degree, Rita's whiteness is not stigmatizing in the ways that Sobeida—who was responding to my own juxtaposition of the two popular artists—suggests Fortuna's Afro-Dominican rhythms, practices, and representation have been.

Rita's sophisticated deployment of Dominican sound and language that is racialized as black seems to allow her to shift her firmly established Dominican identity toward queerness, with less of a social cost. Dominican audiences dismissive of Afro-Dominican culture produced by black bodies are willing to embrace black culture packaged in this way. Says Sobeida: "And they know she is a lesbian and they applaud. Yes, for me that was motivating. I think that the constructions of homophobia and of heteronormativity cannot . . . can't always be imposed and many myths can be deconstructed and we can open up spaces collectively, as a community, through figures like her. Hate is not everything. The people may simply repeat all the *porqueria* [crap] and all these constructions but when they encounter something too good, these other things don't hold so much weight, those things they perceived as negative, what they were taught was negative, which in this case is homosexuality, now it doesn't hold sway." She notes, "Acceptance is an interesting phenomenon . . . in which the people, at the same time they that they hate us, they can applaud us and arrive at the 'collective hysteria' of enjoying a type of music." She draws this observation from living with the contradiction. As long as queerness is kept in its territory, typically that of the artist, it is acceptable by viewers and cultural consumers.

I ask Sobeida directly about her reading of Rita in the photo in front of us because I want to determine a scale through which to talk about difference and whether we are seeing the same thing or have disparate understandings of Rita's racial meaning.

"So, is she white or not?" I ask.

"Yes, I think she's white. She is from families that are rich and white." Sobeida's response demonstrates how the appearance of whiteness in the Dominican Republic may need to be confirmed by lineage even as it is assessed through the visual image. Class becomes the qualifier for Dominican whiteness. I push to understand the color hierarchy that she sees in my set of images because initially when I showed her my four photos she also told me that the two women that were most Dominican were the morenas (Zoe Saldaña and Martha Heredia) and that in the fourth image Michelle Rodriguez "looked very white." Sobeida explains, "Yes, in this photo she appears very white and maybe because of that I said she seems less Dominican for that reason and because, the truth is, I don't know much about Michelle Rodriguez. But I think since I did not know much about her coming here or her having some important contact with this country, that's why I think she's not very Dominican." Narrative, or lack thereof, is determining how Sobeida sees Rodriguez's identity—and how she interprets her image. Her comments also reflect the ways that knowing someone is Dominican serves to racialize them as nonwhite.

When asked why she thinks Rodriguez is beautiful, Sobeida responds—candidly and without self-consciousness—based on the racialized measurements of the actress's mixed-race body: "I think her smile is really pretty. Her eyes are very pretty. . . . She has a well-proportioned face. She does not have a very large nose, I dunno . . . her nose and eyes, she looks really good." Sobeida's comments are commonplace. Like others I interviewed, she suggests that Rodriguez's features are European enough to appeal to the eye; a wide nose might signify too much Otherness or too much blackness. This response seems to echo a long history of active documentation of racial difference and racial assessment in the Americas, where part of the process of colonization involved cataloguing that which was new and different and making scientific conclusions about species and peoples, including demarcating racial mixture.[8] At the moment of cataloguing, racial identity appears as if it is fixed, yet those of us who live in bodies that are of mixed racial heritage experience firsthand how highly dynamic a construct race can be.

To Be Black or Latina?

"My first experience was a dilemma filling out a form at the YMCA in the US," Yaneris tells me, describing her own challenges as an Afro-Latina in identifying herself within the social boundaries that invariably defined her as Other. She and I are sitting in her living room in Santo Domingo one evening.

"To be Black or Latina? It's like, 'okay,' I am not fucking Latina," she laughs, "but I am not Black either, eh? What am I? I put Latina because geographically . . . it's a geographic identity." Yaneris is a dark-skinned Dominican woman in her early thirties. She has long dreadlocks that fall down her back—an exceptional aesthetic in the Dominican Republic. She agreed to participate in my research project only about six months into our friendship. She took her time deciding to trust yet another gringa researcher like myself who had come to Santo Domingo to write about race and the lives of others. My own privilege initially distanced us, and yet I soon discovered that we shared a black feminist politics that would bring us together on many issues. At the time, I did not recognize that we also shared in common an experience of straddling multiple categories of identity informed by the color of our skin. The moment of being forced to choose between two presumably disparate racial categories and racial identities that Yaneris described was familiar to me. During our conversation, I shared with her how my own experiences with this type of racial "dilemma," as she called it, inspired my scholarly pursuits. The "what are you?" question inevitably lays a foundation for each story told about mixed-race experience in the United States. Accordingly, in the multiracial movement initiated in the US in the 1990s, mixed-race experience has been perceived as an anomaly probably because it emerges in the context of middle-class whiteness.[9] How does a mixed-race narrative of identity emerge—and play out—in the predominantly mixed-race society of the Dominican Republic? Dominican racial logic frequently contradicts what US scholars think they know about how race works.[10]

"I have a book of Dominican races," Yaneris tells me. "There are like, twenty-eight, and a census of slaves, from *zambo* to I don't know what. . . . *E' loco*," she says, "It's crazy." Yaneris has reevaluated her racial identity in numerous situations throughout her life, negotiating the line between blackness and Latinidad that Dominicans embody. "I can make a list of the things that people say are ugly and that which they say are pretty," Yaneris says, explaining that blackness is always on the former list, never the latter. "It's like many people say we are a mix, we are pretty, we are Taínos [native people of Hispaniola] . . . but it is mostly to say that we are not black, you know?" For generations now, Dominicans have been taught that they are "indio" in color, romanticizing their Indigenous past while rejecting their African heritage, regardless of the fact that the vast majority of Taínos were killed by Spaniards in the early years of conquest. While Indigenous identity is viewed as noble, blackness—signifying Haitianness—is highly denigrated and ever suspect.

"Negra Latina . . . this is something new," Yaneris says. The terminology is foreign in that the two racial identities might seem to cancel each other out in Dominican racial logic: a black Latina? It is "new" at a social moment in which the considerable number of people of African descent in Latin America has just begun gaining greater recognition.[11] As an Afro-Dominican woman, Yaneris has often felt invisibilized in Dominican society. She says her racial identity has led her to self-censure. She keeps her observations about the daily racism she experiences to herself because her objections and concerns, along with those of other dark-skinned women in the Dominican Republic, are generally dismissed. In our interview she explains, "I can identify as Latin American but it is much easier [to identify as] as black." Every day on the street people shout at her to get her attention, calling her by color: "Negra, how are you?" Dominicans are aware of her difference and do not hesitate to comment on it. Sometimes they use the term "morena" instead, which suggests blackness, too, though more politely. "It's ambiguous," Yaneris says about the term. Yet black bodies are perpetually associated with an African origin because of how we think about and recognize skin color as defining racial narratives.

Black visual artists (and the white collectors of their work) have made an effort to contextualize Black art as part of a broader African diaspora, changing the meaning and value of the work and its style. African diaspora work, argues Kobena Mercer, is about representing the race, and working against a narrative of absence for black people.[12] It is fascinating to consider Mercer's gesture to the repeated use of the image of the African mask—a removeable face, if you will—as tying together works of "Afro-diaspora modernism," while the Dominican muñeca sin rostro, symbolic of racial ambiguity in the African diaspora, requires the erasure of a face. It is not that Africannes can be taken on and off but rather it requires signifiers in order to be legible.

For Yaneris, a dark-skinned Dominican woman, those who view her often make decisions for her about her racial identity. She faces discrimination at the intersections of blackness and queerness. As Dulce Reyes Bonilla reminds us regarding the experiences of dark-skinned queer dominicanas, "Day by day there is a struggle to fit in to places in which one belongs, which creates a feeling of not belonging anywhere. Every day decisions have to be made about what aspect of one's identity would dominate at which moment."[13] The language of ambiguity reflects the unspoken contradictions around race and identity and challenges of belonging that Dominicans negotiate daily. We cannot avoid seeing the racial meaning of black and brown bodies even if the meaning of what we see can see/saw from one moment to the next as we articulate what we are seeing; these are the very moments in which we produce "mixed race."

Marked on the Body

This time, when he looks me over, I wonder what it is he is looking for. Where does his gaze rest? What was it he thought he recognized in me? Is it true that I am not Dominican, he asks, not at all Latina? He sizes me up. After I assure him, I wonder if he still sees a marker of ethnicity there. Being able to shape change and shift meaning front of the eyes of others makes me feel guilty of something, as if I'm trying to pass myself off as something I'm not. Why aren't I recognizable as "American," after hundreds of years of slavery in the United States? What erasure makes unrecognizable my existence as such? From moment to moment, the color of my skin allows me to either fit in or be read as out of place—as researcher, as scholar, as mixed-race brown body in Santo Domingo. Another black woman indistinguishable, all too often expendable; I am the subject of my own study.

The Dominican Republic is the only place I have ever lived where I didn't stand out because of the color of my skin; I blend in. Outside the United States, I am rarely identified as "American." I am, by someone else's gaze, dissociated from my national identity, my vantage point on the world, my privilege. Interactions like the one above lessened as my body assimilated to place and culture and I began to move more like the people around me, imitating and then assimilating the way Dominicans move in the street. I stopped lingering under the blazing sun unnecessarily and developed the habit of always crossing to the shady side of the street. A hardening of my mannerisms and facial expressions in public places occurred, along with a softening of my way of being in gatherings in groups of friends, out late at the park, *chismeando*, refilling each other's plastic cups of beer.

I walk all over Santo Domingo and blend in, sometimes. Some days I receive no comment at all. One day I head to the Colonial Zone to go to the Payless Shoe Source along El Conde. I am in need of serious walking shoes to traverse the city in the heat, between torrential downpours, across wide puddles and open sewers, from beaches to parking lots with mountains of trash.

"Were you just in here a few weeks ago?" the woman at Payless register asks me. Once Santo Domingo's most bustling commercial street, El Conde is a long pedestrian street that is lined with an array of shops, hotels, restaurants, and a few chain stores. It is now exhausted. Enormous, decades-old Spanish buildings look down on the corridor and slowly weep rainwater after each tropical downpour. With so much going on at the street level, one often forgets to look up at architectural details that hint a different historical moment.

Shiny new malls in the further reaches of the city have sprung up, drawing the populace away from the old city center. But here, in shop after shop they sell amber, larimar, rum, cigars, and Dominican paintings rendered by Haitian artists—and Haitian paintings rendered by Dominican artists. Across the plaza from the first cathedral in the Americas (Haitian history says otherwise), there is a Hard Rock Cafe.

"About a month ago," I tell her.

"I thought so," she says, "I remember your eyes."

I didn't find any shoes I would consider wearing, not then or now. But I was reminded by her comment about how often Dominicans make note of difference, especially eye color, though all physical features receive comment at some point. I think of the big billboards of Dominican politicians' faces that line the roadsides—driving along it seems one can pass hundreds of them in a matter of minutes. "The coloring has been photoshopped," people remark under their breath; politicians portrayed with pale skin and icy blue eyes are the most striking. When my Dominican host sister and I look into a crowd of teenagers as we drive through a town intersection during a festival, we are both struck by the same thing: a boy with golden eyes. As if we have observed an anomaly, even though there are lots of brown-skinned Dominicans with light-colored eyes, I had learned to see it and comment on it too. Just the slightest lightness in eye color becomes a social asset. I listen as my other host sister tells her Dominicanyork cousin who is visiting about how when I first got to the island I was "*clarito, bien clarito, limpiecito*—and now look how dark she is!" she says, pointing at me. Whether or not that was the case, it was how she remembered me.

A Swiss woman who has lived in the Dominican Republic for over a decade asks me and a friend where we are from. I look over at my friend who explains she's American but also Dominican—her parents are Dominican, so she is Dominican. My response, however, leads to further questioning:

"You're American? You aren't Latina at all?" she asks, looking me over, trying to see something. My story doesn't satisfy her.

"No," I say.

"Well where does your *colorcito* come from?"

"My father is African," I tell her, "my mother Jewish."

"And the part of you that's American?" she questions further.

Like the young Dominican women in Santo Domingo I have interviewed, observed, and written about, I'm forced to reconcile my own cross-cultural movements with my mixed-race identity. So many Dominicans are not of Spanish descent. There are the Jews, the Lebanese, the Japanese, the Chinese Dominicans that run *pica pollo* cafeterias on every corner, for generations. There are the Dominicans of French and Belgian descent, living along the coast. Raising kids in Dominican schools. Preserving their French with home tutoring. Producing fine French pastries in small beach towns along the Caribbean coast. But narratives of Dominican national identity doggedly obscure these heritages.

One day I walk past a young white woman on the shoulder of a busy road and she stops to ask me to ask me whether I speak English. She is a Norwegian Jehovah's Witness, contentedly doing missionary work in the Dominican Republic.

"What gave me away?" I ask, wanting to know how she was learning to see others in the scopic regime of Santo Domingo. My common skin tone allowed me to blend in so surely there were other tell-tale symbols. "It was the shoes," she said, "and the sunglasses." True, my Dominican friends might on occasion wear Nike knock-off athletic sandals but not the Keens that I had on. It was much more likely to see Dominican women in strappy gold lamé sandals with thin faux leather soles, a popular and available style at the moment.

Michelle and Dulcina: Ambiguity and Alienation

"Mángame una visa!" the taxi driver shouts at Michelle, reciting lyrics from a popular reggaetón song of the moment that incessantly repeats the lyrics "I want *una americana* to snag me a visa!"[14] I am standing with Michelle and Dulcina on the grounds of the Plaza de Cultura. As we exit the gate and walk along the street toward El Museo del Hombre Dominicano, taxi drivers talk to us from their parked cars. They speak to Michelle as if she were an *extranjera*, not from the Dominican Republic. At the time of our interview, Michelle had recently returned from studying in Mexico, going back and forth from the Dominican Republic over the course of several years. As she is just beginning to settle back into life in Santo Domingo, something observable about her demeanor makes her a target for verbal abuse because she now appears foreign to these Dominican men.[15] Michelle tells me that street harassment in Mexico was far worse for her than in the Dominican Republic because the men actually grabbed at her and even followed her off public transportation. In contrast, women in the Dominican Republic "merely" face the constant barrage of sexually suggestive verbal commentary from men, referred to as "*piropos*" or "compliments."[16]

As we walk away, Dulcina tells Michelle that she looks like a gringa and that is why the taxi driver harassed her. Michelle tells Dulcina directly that this comment irritates her. It isn't a compliment. Michelle does not want to be seen as an outsider or to be misinterpreted in this way. Yet just as Trinh Minh-ha has suggested, the problem with identity is that it *requires* a process of essentializing the individual in order to make meaning and come into one's self, distancing one's self from what she suggests is a singular "core." "The further one moves from the core the less likely one is thought to be capable of fulfilling one's role as the real self, the real Black, Indian, or Asian, the real woman."[17] Dominican women in Santo Domingo, who are broadly exposed to cultures from outside of the Dominican Republic, move away from a presumed core identity and subsequently struggle to be recognized as truly "Dominican" or see themselves as such. It is a struggle that diasporic Dominicans regularly wrestle with in the production of art, literature, and scholarship. A constant quest to be seen as authentically Dominican for the purposes of legibility and in selling their work simultaneously perpetuates the act of essentializing, even if their identities disrupt the dominant discourse in representation.

Michelle is fair-skinned, and the color of those considered white in the Dominican Republic. However, as is a common story in the Dominican Republic, her thick black curly hair, associated with African heritage, has made her the black one in her family. On this day, Michelle has pulled her hair back with a headband. It is true that her hair worn in its natural state, along with other details about her "look," might lead other Dominicans to perceive her as foreign, since the majority of Dominican women at the time still straightened their hair. The necklace she wears is one that she no doubt picked up in Mexico: a black cord, with three black hand-formed clay figures on it, one of them shaped like a chunky cross. It gives her a bohemian look, which she balances out with long dangly earrings that have orange clear plastic beads at the ends and match her plastic narrow-framed eyeglasses. Dulcina says later that Dominicans typically wear gold jewelry, as symbols of class status; because Michelle is not wearing these things she is not recognizable as Dominican. Her demeanor as a woman, also conveys a unique sense of independence.

Sitting along a concrete wall under a tree just behind El Museo del Hombre, I first explain my research project on gender and race in the Dominican Republic to Dulcina and Michelle. They are interested, and enthusiastic about the opportunity to express their own opinions on these topics. Each of them has studied at the renowned Dominican art school Altos de Chavón, which greatly informs their trajectories as artists.[18] Our afternoon conversation is lively, as the two friends have known each other for nearly a decade now and the rhythm of the interview is, in and of itself, entertaining. Both are fluent in English and so the interview takes place mostly in English with Spanish mixed in. Michelle is a performer; she has a big personality and much to say. Dulcina frequently interjects thoughtful comments with a youthful hesitance. Both young women are intelligent and well-informed and the subject at hand matters to them.

"I feel exaggeratedly dominicana in every context because the stereotype is an alienating stereotype, that is, it doesn't fit," says Michelle.

"How does that work?" I ask about the stereotype, "and why does it continue?"

"Aha," she said, "but it isn't authentic in reality. Like, the stereotype of the Dominican woman is an alienating stereotype, not a stereotype you can say is real. The people have to change their hair, have to change their eyes, have to change practically everything to achieve the stereotype and to be dominicana." Michelle's distance from the social construction allows her to zealously critique the ways that it is controlling, while she refuses to conform.[19]

Dulcina responds to Michelle's comment, turning first to her friend to argue, "Like you say, neither you nor I nor Rachel fit this stereotype, but there's another Dominican stereotype that is taking over the arts [scene]." She is referring to an aesthetic among privileged Dominican youth, who, like those in the United States, are known as "hipsters" in their efforts to be cool and alternative.

"Most of them go for 'cool' and for fashion. Right now, to be gay is fucking cool. Everybody's gay or if you aren't gay, you're bi. Because it's cool. Because Rita Indiana is gay. Because suddenly, these countries in Latin American are interested in legalizing *matrimonio* between homosexual couples."

"Look what happened in California with this revolution and what happened with Harvey Milk. It's a little bit of this," she says, and I assume she is referring to the 2008 film about the gay politician in 1970s San Francisco whose assassination ignited a movement. "But in a version *aplatonaa . . . aplatonada.*" She corrects her own pronunciation of this slang term that refers to making something dominicanized, of the people.

"That is other bullshit too, excuse me. I am the first one to criticize because I am a woman of the stereotype 'so cool' I am an artist," says Michelle. Dulcina and I laugh at and with her about her claims on this particular stereotype of the artist. She reveals the same loathing I have heard from many other Dominicans about a widespread hipster culture in the Dominican Republic. These are youth whose parents have provided them with the money to buy whatever they want in the way of cars, expensive clothes, and the newest electronics.[20] They are often art students and they manufacture a bohemian style, dressing down, assembling a look that becomes uniform among them, for all of its effort to be edgy and different—and they spend a whole lot of money to look this way. The critique that I have heard repeatedly is that, like the style they embrace, their thoughts on culture and the state of the Dominican Republic are completely superficial. Yet these youth, the ones with buying power, are the ones to whom the Dominican government caters, as they spend and consume at the same level as youth outside of the Dominican Republic.

It's "an aesthetic vision," that you project, Dulcina assures her friend, "that you are beautiful as you are, that you can have curly hair."

"No, no, this is still being the stereotype of 'cool,' according to the people 'so cool.' I'm an artist, I'm alternative, I like indie music, I am *super* Rita Indiana. I can listen to Omega, I don't like Los Jevitos, 'so so fucking cool,'" she underscores with her hands making quotation marks. Her taste in music, from Rita Indiana to Omega, is almost expected of her. "I can be included exceedingly well in these categories: *una mujer alternativa*, writes poetry . . . I dunno. Without a doubt, I didn't notice the transformation. I do not wear my hair curly because it is so fucking cool . . . I wear my hair curly because my hair is curly, but there are people who do it because it is 'cool, so fucking cool.'" She draws out the o's for further emphasis. Michelle points to the ways that she inadvertently takes on the culture around her, even in her efforts to be different from the mainstream. She remains a product of the culture of which she is a part.

Michelle searches around for the right word to describe Dominican culture and then tells me frankly, "It's a pigmentocracy." She understands this privileging of whiteness as most educated Dominicans do: "Trujillo set and advanced this ideology." Yet my curiosity about identity pushes me to ask, But how is it changing? Who perpetuates new values around race, color, and identity today? In what ways do individuals continue to participate in this prejudicial color hierarchy? Does every Dominican family still talk of a distant European relative? As another interviewee had explained to me matter-of-factly, "Yes of course, everyone talks about a very, very far away grandfather or ancestor that is from Spain or Italy, like mine. I don't know where the black part of my . . . myself comes from, but I do know that some part of myself comes from Italy. Thank you. Pretty fucked up. But I'm blacker than whiter. So, really, what's the important part?"

"Mi Negra"

Race and gendered expectations take their toll on young women, particularly those unable to conform or who have no interest in conforming. As a poet and visual artist, Michelle demonstrates how the identity-based cultural productions of Dominican women can circulate transnationally, garnering response online. Michelle's poetry is also emblematic of a theme in my research—those women who are considered the "darkest" in their family, or who are otherized by the phenotypic features of blackness, bring particular insights into how race functions in Dominican society. Their own observations about life in a racially mixed family as well as experiences outside of the Dominican Republic shape their insights into how race functions transnationally.

Michelle explains well her tenuous relationship to her own culture and her own country in ways similar to some of the other young women I got to know: "I had a war with the country, *era una Guerra* . . . I, with myself, with my appearance. In Mexico, I made peace." The war with herself began in adolescence, as quests for identity typically do. Not until she left the country to study art in Mexico was she able to come to terms with her own identity as a Dominican woman. Her return four years later was one more step in the process. Her racial identity as she understands it, tied to her hair texture and coloring within an otherwise white Dominican family, was a negotiation with blackness, not indigeneity.

"All of my life, I have struggled with this issue of my hair and it has pushed me to think about who I am," she confides. I later see Michelle on a panel with women talking about their experiences in the Dominican Republic while wearing their hair natural. There she tells a story of her high school teacher not allowing her to enter his class with her hair out in a natural afro. She had to bring her case to the head of the school and fight for the right to take his required class in order to graduate.[21] Michelle conveyed the story as a moment of triumph: the teacher was ultimately forced to publicly apologize for his discrimination and she ended up being his best student.

During our hour-and-a-half interview, Dulcina takes out her camera several times. With her digital SLR, she takes candid snapshots of our conversation and at some point begins recording us on video. One of the photos she takes end up as Michelle's Facebook profile picture the next day; the visual archive is in constant production via social media and the power dynamic in this visual and cultural exchange moves back and forth between us.

"You will never find a photo of me with straight hair," says Michelle, "Because I don't have straight hair and I wear my hair like this; I like my *greña*."[22] Rather than her childhood friend's testimony at that moment being enough substantiation, Michelle immediately gives this example of the photographic record as proof that she has never straightened her hair. Photographic representations actively construct Michelle's identity as cool. In professional photos with the hip-hop artists of Quilombo, her image circulates on Facebook. She is wearing her hair in a huge round afro and artsy attire. Her hair becomes a signature part of the image for the group, representing both blackness and what was at the time a Dominican counterculture.[23]

Dulcina speaks up to say she does not change her own hair, which is long, thick, and dark brown. It easily flows past her shoulders or she piles it up on her head with a hair elastic in very organic ways, much like the other art students at her school.

Michelle responds, "Listen, it's different, your hair . . . your hair isn't curly, your hair is wavy, accept that. My cousin, my aunts, are straight-haired women . . . my grandmother. They wear their hair straight. But I don't have straight hair; I don't wear my hair straight," says Michelle.

"Do they want you to change your hair?" I ask her.

"No . . . not all," she says laughing. "Not anymore . . ."

"My grandmother is 'muy open-mind,'" she explains in Spanglish, "a person, a woman, with a very open viewpoint and I have to say that I have never had problems. This is my hair. She taught me to be proud of who I am and how I am.

"My mother is a white woman, you understand?" Michelle asks me. "When they see me she tells people 'this is my child.'" As it happens, I do understand.

"Yes," I say, "my mother is a white woman too." We exchange a knowing laugh. I am aware of how this particular difference—this Otherness marked by the texture of her hair—has shaped Michelle's identity, her relationship to Dominicanness and blackness.

"I have a little sister who was born rubia [fair and blonde] with ojos claritos [eyes light in color]," Michelle explains. "I know that I was born looking more like my mother, but with the only exception of my color and my hair. And my little sister doesn't look anything like my mother. Yet when they see her, people say [to my mother], 'this child is identical to you.'" This example is one that is common of narratives of mixed-race people in North America and underscores the way that Dominican experiences of racial identity can at moments parallel a more general "mixed-race experience."[24] Michelle and I connect around this experience for, I, too, look like my white mother but strangers were unable to see this at first glance because of my color.

Michelle is clear, "We are a culture, unfortunately, we are a country that lives for appearances." Indeed, what Dominicans see transmits a lot of information about social hierarchy.

"You can see it," says Dulcina, "you can see it because really in all of the neighborhoods you don't see, you don't see books . . . here there are four bookstores, four bookstores!" She pointed to a major frustration for intellectuals and writers in Santo Domingo, that the population does not read books with much voracity, and they rarely can afford to buy books. Michelle says to her friend, "But you just have to look at the politics of this government, which is . . . ?"

"*El progreso*," Dulcina responds so quickly that I can see that as a Dominican the language of "progress" has been drilled into her.[25]

"Exactly! And what do they base this progress on? . . . the *macroconstruciones*, in making parks, *coño*, that are very badly constructed but that look 'super bonito' [very beautiful]," clarifying that she is putting the term in quotation marks. Architect Melisa Vargas writes harshly about the changing landscape in Santo Domingo, "The Dominican Republic reflects a long history of the United States impositions and influence on Latin America. Today the country builds its image on a clumsy idea of progress, in a collective dream that its society synthesizes in the image of one city: New York." Vargas concludes, "Maybe if making parks, creating programs for education and organizing the population were more profitable for the engineers and entrepreneurs that donate to political campaigns, probably the little New York would be less about expensive roads, tunnels, and metros and more about its organization and the qualities of its public spaces."[26]

"I mean, this is an embellishment," says Michelle, in reference to how Santo Domingo has been made to look through numerous recent development projects including luxury condo towers, malls, and Metro stations. "We are a culture and a people of appearances . . . and this is what you are, up until what your personal image is, so as to what foolishness this is . . . *carajo*." She emphasizes her disdain with a few choice swear words. Extensive construction is taking place in the Dominican Republic but on a superficial level, Michelle explains. She sees it as typical of Dominican culture.

For most Dominicans, life remains a struggle and skepticism about government continues. This skepticism is often captured in graffiti around the city—images of which may be encountered online—communicating sentiments of anti-establishmentarianism to the many Dominicans stuck in traffic: "Ese no es mi constitución [This is not my constitution]" and the classic "Fuera Yanki [Get out Yankee]!"

I ask Dulcina and Michelle about the recent popularity of natural hair in the Dominican Republic in just the last year, "Do you think it is changing or is this just a fad?" I increasingly saw images of women with natural hair in advertising campaigns and on billboards in Santo Domingo beginning from 2010 onward.

"I see it changing," says Michelle, "but it also has to do with fashion. Now an afro is in style . . . men were able to do it, and now bit by bit women are able to." Images of young people with natural hair, both men and women, would later show up in Danilo Medina's presidential campaign materials plastering the capital in 2012.

"We are in a *machista* culture," Michelle says for emphasis as she repeats a fact of which Dulcina and I are all well aware. "For men, kinky hair was seen badly, it reflected badly on their character. They might be viewed as *mariconas* [faggots], or as drug addicted . . . but now it is in fashion for men." Long hair on young men in the Dominican Republic had previously represented activism, resistance, and an unwillingness to conform. There are consequences for resisting an aesthetic imperative, something experienced by the young man outside of the capital who in 2012 was kidnapped by police who then took it upon themselves to shave his head.[27]

Like so many other Dominican women who have lived abroad and then returned, Michelle wrestles with the question of whether to try to leave again or to make a life as a liberal-minded, educated woman within the constrictions of Dominican culture. Her perceptions of Dominican culture remain framed by her understanding of culture beyond the bounds of her home country, and like so many other Dominican women I have spoken with, she embraces a truly transnational identity. Michelle's epistemic knowledge and insights about the transnational world she navigates have been shaped in part by her own racial ambiguity, as someone who is read in different ways depending on context.

Navigating a Transnational World

One story Michelle narrates for me is about an experience while living with family in Texas.[28] She boarded the wrong bus one day and ended up in a part of town that she described as "*muy* creepy." She found herself out of her element in a poor African American neighborhood when a Black man at the bus stop asked her, "Where are you from?" When she responded with "I'm Dominican," he told her, "I thought you were from here [the United States] . . . I thought you were from Florida." Michelle tells me that this brief interaction revealed a lot to her about US preoccupations with race and difference. In that moment, she understood that she was being read within a different racial framework from her own. "I said 'no,' I was not from Florida," she explains. "It was at this moment I realized that everyone thought I was a Black woman. Now I wasn't Latina. I wasn't Latina because I wasn't *Mexican*. I was Black." The man who spoke to her was aware of her foreignness, and asked the standard questions that racially mixed and racially ambiguous people are asked: "What are you?" and "Where are you from?" In this case, the man tried to contextualize Michelle, to make racial meaning, within the bounds of the United States. What Michelle realized in that moment of interaction was that it was possible to move across racial categories depending on one's social location—even just relocating your body across town and into a Black neighborhood. The moment was memorable because it changed how she understood herself in the world; she came into consciousness about her own racial ambiguity.

Michelle jokes with Dulcina and me about how illogical racial constructs are: "Whatever part of the world I go to, I am going to say no, I have a white ancestor so I am white. . . . because people here say this." We all laugh together at the thought of this truth.

"You are white because you have a great-grandfather, or great-great-grandfather who is white. Spanish or German . . . they say that here," adds Dulcina. "Imagine me going to Finland and saying, 'I'm white!'" she says. We have a good laugh about what we know to be true about the how race does and does not work, each of us understanding its instability because of our experiences of racial ambiguity while crossing national borders.

Michelle also recognizes the influence of African American culture in the Dominican Republic—namely through New York City and hip-hop music in which Dominicans in the barrios have seen themselves since the 1980s. Now they identify with the marginalization of African Americans, she explains. "This you can see with the boys in the barrios, they began to assimilate themselves as Black. . . . Of course, not the same black as the Haitian, but they, too, in the barrio, began to assimilate like a group of people that aren't white." As she describes it, the poverty of the barrios of Santo Domingo "blackens" Dominicans.

"Ultimately, we are never going to assimilate as black people," Michelle concedes. "Maybe not white, but not black. . . . Like in my poem, 'Como indios, no indigena' . . . here there are so many indios because there are no blacks," says Michelle, frustrated. She is openly critical of Dominican desires to distance themselves from blackness. While she enjoys privilege because of her color and her class, she is also familiar with outsider status.

"It is strange that we haven't revolutionized this," Dulcina offers, suggesting that these concepts of race in the Dominican Republic have not moved forward, as if there is a clear, linear direction for ideological change that looks like other development projects in the country. She has her own stories and experiences of being racially misinterpreted. She is a Dominican of Iranian descent, with light skin and long, thick, brown hair that falls nearly straight down her back. "Before people thought I was Spanish. Now people think I am from the Orient, my father is from the Orient. Before, it was Spanish or Arab . . . Spanish or Turkish. Never placed . . . but now the people are assimilating more things, more culture." She says someone finally identified her as being of Iranian descent because they actually knew of Iran and therefore they could conceive of her identity. Dulcina, who is quite similar in coloring to Michelle, is not simply viewed as "black," rather she carries with her a Dominican national identity and a narrative of Dominican immigration that intersects her racial and gender identity, informing how she is perceived abroad. Unlike the experience of non-ambiguously racialized immigrants, however, she is well aware that variables based on context could allow her to "assimilate" into different countries differently. Because immigration is so much about the movement of labor, racially ambiguous bodies have more options for such movement; they change shape and meaning within a global capitalist culture.

The two friends also share a laugh about the culture of primary school in the Dominican Republic in which it is always the fairest students who are selected by teachers to play the lead roles in school performances. "And that was me," Dulcina tells us. She was the one always chosen, the one always preferred over her darker-skinned peers.

"You are white," Michelle says to Dulcina in an accusatory tone, teasing her. Yet Dulcina, too, has traveled abroad and had experiences in which she definitely was not white. Like other middle-class Dominican youth, she has been to Europe. In countries such as Holland, Belgium, and Germany, she quickly learned that she was no longer white. She says that it was in Spain that she experienced the most discrimination. According to Dulcina, there are many women who travel there for work, who become domestic laborers. Employers want them to be attractive because they are "expected to use their sex appeal to advance themselves," she says.

According to Michelle, these challenges of daily life in the Dominican Republic, including the sexism and colorism, are integral to who the people are. It is such a hierarchical culture that people are submissive, unwilling to talk back to a boss. Obviously, doing so has real, negative consequences, so complaining happens behind people's backs. For Michelle this is particularly frustrating because, as she says, "I am not a person that can keep silent." She describes herself in school and in work as arriving on time and getting her work done, serious about the tasks at hand. Michelle earned her art degree from Altos de Chavón before leaving the Dominican Republic to study at Universidad Nacional Autónoma de México.

"Everyone knows that *no soy facil* [I am not an easy person]," she says. "I am a person who is very direct." This has certainly been my experience with her.

"Is this very Dominican?" I ask.

"—No, it's very my grandmother," she responds with quick wit. "I don't like to talk crap . . . Dominicans like to talk just to talk."

Digging into the broad generalizations, I ask Dulcina and Michelle about "this thing about the strength of the *mujer dominicana*, it's a way of being in the world? Of getting what you want?"

Dulcina says, "Yes, this is very powerful."

"Honestly, I think that yes," said Michelle, "*la mujer dominicana* has an [advantage] and I don't know if it's just la dominicana, that's all I know. She is a person. . . . very strong. I consider . . . all the dominicanas that I have known to be *luchadoras* [fighters] and they are very strong. I think it's a question of survival. We are in a society *machista*. But here, *las mujeres se comen en cualquier tíguere* [the women take up with whatever guy off the street]."[29] Women's options are limited.

To be clear, this is about nothing less than survival, these two young women explain. Dulcina educates me about the reality of trying to get work in an art gallery in the Dominican Republic: "You have to know people . . . and you have to be pretty." As a woman, to get your work in a gallery, you have to sleep with the owner of the gallery, she tells me. At nineteen, she is well aware of the obstacles she faces to advancing herself in Dominican society. Like Michelle, she comes from a matriarchal household in which the women do not rely on men for support.

Dulcina lays out the predicament that poor Dominican women are in: "I am young, I want a career, I have to marry *con capo* [a drug dealer]. . . . Women now look for men who have a *yipeta* [an SUV], not just men who can afford to buy them a stove and a washing machine the way it was in the past." As Dulcina explains it, they are happy to have a man who can pay for everything for them. Because, what they quickly learn is that no matter how much a woman studies, when she is no longer pretty the boss will no longer want her. Just as unskilled labor is expendable, it seems that attractive young black and brown women as wives and girlfriends are too—particularly because so many are desperately trying to gain social access or just survive.

"I have friends who say, 'I am *fulano's* [so and so's] woman," Dulcina says, horrified by the way that the women describe themselves as little more than men's accessories. They have learned, "I'm intelligent, but I'm a woman," and so they focus on getting married in order to have economic security. "I don't know if you have noticed," Dulcina says for emphasis, "they start going to the salon . . ." I have noticed.

"They reach an age of twenty to twenty-five at which they say 'okay, I'm not going to make myself beautiful. I'm going to study. Now I have to marry, and I have to have two boys to keep a man tied to me so that he knows that if he divorces me he still has to support his kids.'" The familiar scenario was well-scripted in Dulcina's head; Michelle corroborates it: "They have kids so that they have the money secured," says Michelle, matter-of-factly.

The two women talk about other women they know—and those they imagine—in ways that distance themselves from these same cultural values and experiences. Because of their racialized, classed, gendered realities and their perceptions of the world, which have been influenced by their education, class privilege, and travel abroad—but also because of the matriarchal families in which each of them grew up—Dulcina and Michelle struggle to imagine sharing these same cultural values around gender. They do understand what it is like to live within Dominican society and why other women make the choices that they do. No woman is exempt from the patriarchal structures that limit how men perceive her because of her gender, race, and class. Dominican women are encouraged by their families to have children no later than the age of twenty-five, which very often slows down or completely diverts any educational plans they may have had. Dulcina has said something in our interview that I had heard elsewhere in the Dominican Republic, about how Dominican women are already thought of as old and less attractive by the time they reach the age of twenty. It is of course women over this age who are better educated or have obtained greater life experience who are more likely to recognize and critique their own precarious social positions under patriarchy.

Michelle: "Negra Caribeña Soy"

The first time I met Michelle, she was standing out on the street in front of a local bohemian bar where she had just finished a performance of her poem "Negra Caribeña." She was wearing a T-shirt showing a map of the Dominican Republic, with the collar cut to fall over her shoulder, emblematic of the ways that 1980s fashion had come creeping back in 2010. Earlier that evening, readying for her performance, I had seen her bent over the bar with this same shirt and a thick black Sharpie, drawing in the missing half of the island of Hispaniola; Haiti had not been included on the map. Later, we ran into each other in different circles until I finally requested an interview with her. Eventually, we connected on Facebook where the site quickly confirmed for us the many friends and acquaintances we already held in common in Santo Domingo. Online, I could see another way that Michelle represented herself as an artist. I would see her publicly perform "Negra Caribeña" once more before she recorded it with Quilomboarte as an audio track set to the hippest of jazz tones, and shared it on YouTube.

In her live performances, Michelle speaks in fast, syncopated bursts, putting an emphasis on every third or fourth word, emphasizing the sounds of Dominican Spanish and animating her slam poetry by using her hands, posturing, and taking up space. On YouTube, you see a still image—like album cover art—of Michelle's name in large white stenciled letters, slanting above the Plaza de Colón toward a blue sky, and the name of the song in smaller black letters below.[30] The image includes the full statue of Christopher Columbus in front of the Cathedral of Santa Maria. Columbus stands proudly immortalized in bronze, his left hand outstretched, like so many statues throughout Santo Domingo. At his feet, climbing up the concrete base of the monument, is another bronze, the scantily clad Taíno woman Anacaona. Michelle is seated on the steps at the left of the monument, in an uncharacteristically empty plaza. While the sound of her voice emerges from the track vibrant and certain, in the corner of the image she is a small, almost indiscernible figure, in a moment of contemplation. I include the poem here translated into English, leaving untranslated a few terms that stand on their own.

On the island they practice
a culture of colonized idiosyncrasy.
Long hair, straight hair, white hair.
They get in the hair through . . . Fear.

Fear of assuming that we have too much blackness.
—Black? You? And who told you that? If you are
a little *india caribeña*.
What blackness? Nothing more than the mop of hair. And just in case.
Because in truth your hair ain't that bad.

Therefore, they put an "I" for me under type of skin on
the identity card.
Because in this country *indigenismo* is limited to
a letter, for this sacred color
that atoned for the damn African.

¿Ofrécome and what rudeness is that!?
India ¿Me?
Not me.
And do not get me wrong.
Even if I was the granddaughter of Enriquillo, niece of
Caonabo or the daughter of Guacanagarix. I would be the first
that would be saying so VERY PROUD.
But here, to be *indio* right now
is synonymous with many other things.

To the *indios* of the present what they like most is to assume
the position of slaves.
Of the telephone, of the radio, of the TV, of money, of cars,
of the pimps, of the girls, of the tennis shoes, of drugs and
saying they had an ancestor who was
white.

It's because of this that nothing more than my *greña* is black.
I'll keep my *greña*.
Because it is me . . .
ME.

Negra caribeña soy.
Negra caribeña soy.[31]

The phrase "Negra Caribeña" becomes a chorus on the audio track, as an interlude at the middle of the piece. With this poem, Michelle indignantly responds to what she identifies as a racial ideology specific to the peculiarities of Dominican culture. Generally her cultural productions, from slam poetry to sculpture to performance art, critique the racial hierarchy in Santo Domingo, which is alive and well, even as the roots of it continue to be buried by new narrations of Dominicanness emerging from elite circles.[32] Like so many other women I know in Santo Domingo, Michelle is angered by the daily injustices of life in the Dominican Republic, including a disregard for human life and a lack of care or respect for the natural environment, which has increased under the economic calculations of neoliberalism. However, she is unique in her choice to always talk back.

Directing her energy into art and poetry, Michelle tells me, has been about coming to terms with some of these internal conflicts about identity and her place in the world. In her poem above, she captures the nuances of negotiating the politics of identity as a transnational subject. The national project of distancing Dominican citizens from Africanness as a racial identity is exasperating for so many Dominicans who claim their African roots and their connection to the other side of the island. With the stylings of a slam poet, Michelle affectively narrates the hispanophilia of Dominican society, in referring to the *I* marked on her national ID card that categorizes her as "indio." It was a story I had been told many times by friends, colleagues, and acquaintances while living in the Dominican Republic. All of them were indignant about the ongoing state-sanctioned racial categorization and some even pulled out their ID to show me how they had been misidentified in terms of race, their blackness omitted or obscured by the use of the term "indio." Michelle defiantly rejects this label put on her by others who tell her that her skin is "not too dark," and her hair "isn't so bad." She clarifies for her audience that this rejection is not about a shame in having Indigenous roots, but a recognition that this is not in fact what being "indio" means. To Michelle, claiming "indio" means being invested in the superficial, and becoming a "slave to a consumer lifestyle" (not unlike the one represented in the ERA mural in figure 2). With her slam poetry, she conjures up an image of indios as peoples reenslaved by present technologies—perhaps through the instant gratification of drugs, money, and television. She does not include the BlackBerry phone or Facebook on this list of vices that keep Dominicans trapped, though; at the time they seemed like liberating tools.

While Michelle's point goes to the many ways in which Dominicans elide their affiliations with blackness, her articulation of the experience of being black, as defined by hair texture and accompanied by a critique of how the nation deploys indigeneity, differs from that of the self-identified Afro-Dominicans I have interviewed who are dark-skinned, whose bodies are viewed quite differently. Michelle's experiences of Otherness appear rooted in her hair type and tied to her refusal to conform to gendered expectations. Yet she enjoys the social privilege, I argue, of not having her gender questioned. She does not have a formative experience to draw on of being denied entrance, access, or opportunity because of an accent or the color of her skin. At the close of her poem she states, "Me quedo con la greña [I'll keep my mop of hair]," using the common term *greña* and knowing firsthand the ways that hair is a political issue. At the end of the second stanza, she captures effectively the ways that Dominicans can make backhanded remarks about difference: "in truth, your hair is not so bad" they might say, making an exception to the rule to include those they want to include. According to Michelle, Dominicans invest in hair out of a fear of blackness.

Michelle's poem circulated on YouTube garnered some response, including one user who comments in Spanish: "*Muy chulo* [Very cool], but I think that '*la isla*' still isn't totally ready for the profundity of this writing. I think that's why Rita Indiana left. But keep at it if it is not there it will be here :)) [*sic*]."³³ The comment echoes the challenges of living within Dominican society and implies the usual assumptions by those on the outside—that Dominicans on the island are stuck in the past. In fact, they are stuck in an extremely patriarchal present. The commentator reassures Michelle directly that she should keep expressing her convictions through her art and should rest assured that if she is not successful there on the island, "it" (her success) can and will be "here," meaning where the commentator is located in the diaspora; in this case, Spain. The commentator also invokes Rita Indiana as a contemporary of Michelle (though Indiana is about eight years older) to provide an example of someone for whom it was necessary to leave the Dominican Republic in order to escape the heteropatriarchal conservative culture. Life beyond the boundaries of the island has been imagined as more liberal-minded about gender roles and sex and race. The diaspora is perceived as a safe place from which to be critical of the Dominican Republic—even as those in the diaspora no longer know what life back "home" is actually like. Many of my interviewees have expressed that they intend to stay and do what they can to make the Dominican Republic better. Others leave, but then make their way back again, bringing with them a shift in perspective based on new experiences of race and gender, culture and society. Upon returning to the island, if they stay a while, they unpack a metaphorical suitcase of ideas and cultural influences.

Dominican women navigate a world in which color and hair are constantly remarked upon while imbedded in experiences of racial mixed-ness and racial ambiguity. Because of this, individual Dominican women very often can move in and out of positions of power and influence and develop unique views of these structures and of race and gender. This sharply contrasts the experience of North American whiteness. A key component of racial privilege lies in the fact that most white youth are unaware of the power that they hold within structural racism. Experiences with the blurred lines of race and the pressure of Dominican gender roles come across in the majority of my interviews. In turn, my research demonstrates the intricate ways that race and color matter in the lives of women in contemporary Santo Domingo. The ability to transform one's identity may mean acting more "feminine" in order to move closer to a hispanidad that values whiteness, in which straightened hair and lightened skin are rewarded by patriarchal attention.³⁴

Access to privileged spaces or permission to advance in order to earn a degree may also be a "reward" for altering one's appearance to conform.

Michelle has the option of straightening her hair in order to access the privileges of Dominican whiteness, but she has never done so. While I may find myself at times misinterpreted as Dominican because of my skin color (and my efforts to assimilate into my host country), light-skinned Dominican women like Michelle, though Dominican-born and raised, may find themselves interpreted as foreign to the nation if they refuse to conform to expected gender roles. For the women with whom I spoke, physical transformation—the ability to move in and out of racial and gender categories—is a constant negotiation with power and the possibility of social acceptance.

3

Whiteness, Transformative Bodies, and the Queer Dominicanidad of Rita Indiana

It is the combined thoughts, conscious and unconscious,
of all of us that hold the machinery of racism in place.

Toi Derricotte, *The Black Notebooks*

Many a late night in Santo Domingo, I went to bed with the sound of bachata in my ears; it drifted down the street where I lived. When I sat down to write on many afternoons, I could feel the beats of reggaetón pulsing in my chest cavity, as cars decked out with elaborate sound systems rolled through my neighborhood or parked in front of the center of activity on the block—a *colmado* selling cold beers. The layers of sound that shape the urban space of Santo Domingo are as remarkable as in any urban space and yet uniquely Dominican: honking horns and loud public conversations, neighbors shouting up to balconies and open windows, the sing-song of Dominican Spanish, the sound of telenovelas drifting out from doorways. One can also hear the squawking of caged birds—roosters raised for fighting—and the loud engines of motorbikes zipping around the neighborhood as young men make colmado deliveries. Eventually, these sounds fall into the background alongside the swish of early morning sweeping and palm leaves scraping against one another in a strong breeze. As boys in athletic gear shout across the baseball diamond, even the sound of their cleats hitting the dirt is audible.

Rita Indiana's electronic sounds mixed with the Afro-Dominican rhythms of merengue drifted through this Santo Domingo soundscape. Her project of self-making as an artist riffed on and responded to the fluidity of the Dominican transnational cultural context and moment. As Maja Horn has argued, the "psychological infrastructure" of the Dominican Republic post-Trujillo era—including the period under Balaguer—was ripe at that moment for a

new and different type of identity construction.[1] "Rita" became a Dominican phenomenon both within the country and throughout its diaspora at a
moment that coincided with my February 2010 return to Santo Domingo.
That year, she could be seen on the front of the "Alegria!" section of *Hoy*,
the *USA Today*–like Dominican paper circulated in Santo Domingo in print
and online. There, Rita looked like a teenage boy: thin and pale with her hair
cut short, and wearing dark glasses—as if somehow she might be hiding
something, or signaling the "open secret" of her queerness. Inside the pages
of the newspaper, however, she is wearing the full makeup of a supermodel,
harkening back to her past career trajectory.

Across these two contrasting images and juxtaposed in one publication, we
are able to see one of the many ways that Rita Indiana is able to transform:
her bodily performance challenges dominant notions of gender, sexuality,
and race in the Dominican Republic. Her gender is fluid. Her ability to exist
as what is often referred to in Dominican society as a *transformista* (a trans-
former) is emblematic of Dominican culture and identity in the twenty-first
century. I use the term *transformista* here with all of its queer significance to
point to the ways that Rita adapts her dress and physical appearance. In turn,
our understanding of her identity shifts and expands with her gender performance. Like the muñeca sin rostro that has no definitive facial features, Rita
manages to be a race and gender transformista—able to transfigure herself
based on narrative and desire.

In this chapter, I read several of Rita Indiana's visual culture productions
to consider the ways that she mobilizes and capitalizes on the ambiguities of
race and gender in her work. Her race and gender consistently transform in
her public performances, including appearances in Santo Domingo advertising, and in her representation in music videos for the album *El juidero*.
Because of the ways her cultural production of identity is emblematic of
what I seek to explain regarding mixed race, gender, and visual culture in the
Dominican Republic, I consider Rita Indiana's multimodal work to be critical to how we understand Dominican women's identities in contemporary
transnational Dominican popular culture. As I have suggested elsewhere in
this text, I argue here that bodily representation and visual culture productions serve as a necessary surrealist response to the contemporary moment.
Rita Indiana's performance of masculinity in the "El juidero" video, and her
performance in blackface for the video "Da pa' lo' do'" as well as the surrealist
aesthetic that she mobilizes in "La hora de volvé" are all notable. Yet, I add
to the existing scholarship on her work by questioning how Rita Indiana's

class privilege, fair skin, and transnational mobility—along with her identity as an artist—intersect with her queer identity, thus informing the ways that Dominicans perceive her to be "authentically" Dominican.

While living in Santo Domingo, I regularly overheard people discussing Rita Indiana and more than once in passing someone called me by her name—for my height, perhaps my hair that was not long, my way of moving through the world. Yet, as one of my interviewees noted, Rita is understood by the Dominican public as *rubia*, roughly meaning "blonde." It is a color category that does not necessarily refer to her actual hair color but rather lightness in skin color in the Dominican racial hierarchy.

"She resembles her," a guy on the street tells his friends after shouting "Rita Indiana" in my direction as I pass. I do not look anything like Rita. I am, I have been told, india in color. I am quite tall with long arms and legs, but not as tall and thin as Rita is—she has five inches on me—nor do I have any of the aesthetic of cool that makes her so popular. What then is this man on the street pointing to? Is it my queerness, my inadequate performance of femininity, or my somewhat gender-nonconforming way of inhabiting my body? His labeling of me as Rita was not an anomaly. What is it that people are seeing when they look at our mixed-race bodies and read for gender and not color? Here again, I am led to question what we see or believe we see when we look at the intersection of gender ambiguity and racial ambiguity. And what does it mean that Dominican women that I interviewed consistently identified Rita Indiana and her white queer body as representative of that which is authentically Dominican, or "domin*icana*-dominicana"?

When I attended Rita Indiana's concert at the Hard Rock Cafe Santo Domingo in early 2010, it was only her second concert in that venue and it was the first time I had seen her perform. At the time, the venue was located on Christopher Columbus Plaza, across from the Catedral Isabela Católica, the oldest cathedral in what had been deemed "the New World." Hard Rock Cafe is a popular chain that caters to tourists with a decidedly American ambience, and Rita performed there for an audience of middle- and upper-class Dominican youth. Ticket prices were high to keep the event exclusive, despite the fact that such concerts are heavily sponsored by large corporations: the cell phone company Claro was that night's sponsor, though many other advertisements bombarded us via television screens during the hours we waited for the show to begin. Ads intermixed with images of Rita Indiana and past and upcoming Hard Rock Cafe concerts. As an audience member, I was surrounded by an economic class of Dominican youth that I was not usually around, all recognizable by their fair skin, straight hair, and brand-name clothes. To my right, a group of teenage girls from the Bronx, New York, demonstrated that they were dedicated fans with a great deal of screaming. "She's like the Lady Gaga of the DR," I overheard one of the youth nearby tell her friend in English. She is claimed so fiercely by Dominican youth that they just call her "Rita" because there is no other.

At the height of her career, Rita was also often referred to as "La Montra" because of her drive and skill as musician, though this nickname probably also makes reference to her stature and her queerness; it is a dominicanization of *la monstra* (the monster).[2] I refer to her throughout this chapter by both "Rita" and "Rita Indiana" because this is how I heard her most often referred to on a daily basis in Santo Domingo. However, I will include her second surname, Hernández, when I reference her literary publications because it is how she is also cited. The popularity of Rita Indiana Hernández's writing is a testament to the ways a new generation of transnational Dominican youth are piecing together identities from a sea of global media with a level of sophistication many underestimate.

While her poetry and prose circulated in the networks of my interviewees, the buzz about Hernández's award-winning literary contributions made the rounds among my academic peers. As an author, she has gained a great deal of recognition and esteem within and beyond the Dominican Republic; her books have earned her numerous literary awards and her writing has brought visibility to the nation even though she has chosen not to reside there. In her depictions of life in Santo Domingo in the 1980s in her early novels *Estrategia de Chochueca* and *Papi*, young protagonists capture a transnational cultural fluidity familiar to the generation of Dominicans I write about. Hernández explains in an early interview that her novels are about making people who are so often invisibilized in mainstream Dominican society feel recognized, and understood.[3] She is inspired by the Surrealists, she says, who also blurred the lines between reality and alternate reality. As Horn writes, regarding the power of a transnational youth culture that Hernández captures in *Chochueca*, it is indeed the case that "shared globalized references and cultural repertoire help bring this group [of teenagers] together and it is with the help of these new symbols and vocabularies that they mark their difference from mainstream Dominican society."[4] There is a new subjectivity and popular imaginary among this generation, one that resists what Dominican identity had previously signified.[5]

Fernanda Bustamante Escalona edited *Rita Indiana: Archivos*, an important collection of literary criticism about Hernández's published work, giving her impressive body of writing its due in Dominican studies. Yet scholars have been hesitant to critique her for what E. Patrick Johnson generously calls "usurpations" of black culture in her work.[6] The fluidity of blackness in the Dominican Republic makes flexible who claims it, thus making it difficult to pinpoint when black cultural signifiers are being exploited by nonblack people. I read Rita Indiana's performances of "Dominican whiteness," masculinity, and queerness across several of her cultural productions in order to explore her racial malleability and gender fluidity at work. Throughout, I demonstrate how she strategically deploys ambiguous race and gender identity along with blackness in order to produce a consumable Dominican cultural aesthetic. Her ability to see/saw in meaning in terms of race and gender based on context, with whom she is interacting, and how she is read in relation to other bodies, demonstrates her power as a transformista. My focus on the queer, raced possibilities of Rita Indiana allows me to further explore what it is that we project onto the bodies of Dominican women. I argue that Rita's Dominican whiteness is precisely what makes it possible for her to produce such a safe, salient, and fluid identity through visual culture and popular media, in ways that resonate as authentically Dominican. In the process of self-making she has regularly aligned herself with Otherness yet still asserts many of the privileges of whiteness that she is able to enjoy in Dominican society.

I also examine Rita Indiana's aesthetic choices and surrealist tendencies in her music videos. In the 1930s, when high art began to influence culture, "Surrealism was able to function as an adaptable style rather than as a static quotation," writes Sandra Zalman. "It was Surrealism's adaptability that made it so appealing to designers."[7] Likewise, the adaptability or malleability of Rita Indiana's work today, particularly the sensation that her "Dominicanness as ambiguity" provokes, draws our attention to her work. Her emergence and popularity ushers in an exciting new era of Dominican cultural production, albeit an aesthetic born of disillusion and experimentation that echoes past Surrealist moments.

Cecilia Rabinovich's explanation of a Surrealist understanding of the extraordinary object is useful in thinking about the visual work of Rita Indiana and her juxtapositions of transnational objects. Rabinovich notes that the act of looking and the value of both context and perception are required to understand the meaning of the object at hand.

> Consider a group of objects on a table. If you pick up just one and concentrate on it alone, the surrounding objects fade into your peripheral vision. As you focus your attention, the object becomes larger and more compelling. Its

expressive character becomes psychologically more important. Disregarding the surrounding space alters our visual impression, for no context defines the object's relative size or function. Isolating the object removes the conventional frame of reference and introduces new perceptions of the ordinary, making it extraordinary.[8]

As an arts movement of the early twentieth century, Surrealism encouraged a transnational discourse among artists and philosophers from different parts of the world in order to pull from a range of cultural signifiers to create something new. Rita Indiana has described her penchant for the surreal in her creative work as coming out of the literary world. She states, "There's something about William Burroughs in particular . . . there's something about him being queer and part of a movement but you can't really put him in a box, in any of those boxes . . . he's so big, *tan genial, tan enfermo.*"[9] Indeed, Burroughs's writing and practice was shaped by Surrealist visual artists and the form of the collage. Rita Indiana's surrealist approach is evident in the stream of consciousness and ekphrastic style of writing she frequently utilizes in her novels.[10] In her visual work, it is her own body that becomes the point of juxtaposition for the viewer; it is unmistakable in the aesthetics of her music videos in which unrelated objects are isolated and then placed in juxtaposition with one another.

"La Hora de Volvé"

The music video for Rita Indiana's "La hora de volvé" offers an undeniably surreal experience. It echoes the work of well-known Surrealist artists Salvador Dalí and René Magritte: with hypnotizing rhythms, bright colors, and flying objects, the band Rita Indiana y Los Misterios can be seen levitating through a neon-colored outer space. Animated planets and crumpled colored paper serve as the terra firma on which they stand. At other moments, they are dancing atop a record or a hurtling planet. As her backup singers repeat a dance move, images of their bodies multiply as if in a chorus, but Rita remains singular throughout. Rita dances dressed in black, wearing dark red lipstick and blue eye shadow. She is at one moment looking like a backup singer for Robert Palmer, and the next, as the background changes and the camera zooms out, she is left standing on a yellow orb, reminiscent of the Little Prince.

The music video's collage-like aesthetic is reminiscent of Afro-Surrealism's celebrated artists, including Kenyan-born Wangechi Mutu. For Mutu's 2013 video installation, "The End of Eating Everything," musician Santigold swallows abstract shapes floating in the air as a disembodied figurehead of a ship. In "La hora de volvé," Rita's disembodied head with wide-open mouth spews animated shapes: record albums, pink birds, orange octopi, and seaweed made of origami paper. The floating objects in this video, acting as floating signifiers, function in ways that Surrealists of the twentieth century might have understood. While Western instruments are conspicuously absent as Rita's bandmates play air guitar, our attention is drawn to the *tambora* (a Dominican drum) we can hear and see being played throughout the video.

The appeal of Rita Indiana's visual, musical, and written work, not unlike that of Burroughs's writing, is in the shock of recognition it gives us in supplying new ways of seeing something familiar.[11] Fredric Jameson's theorization of Burroughs's value resonates with reactions to Rita's creative work. Jameson asserts that under late capitalism, writers must contend with the commercial by using language that surprises and "by restructuring the overfamiliar or by appealing to those deeper layers of the physiological which alone retain a kind of fitful unnamed intensity."[12] Some of the shock that Rita offers may emerge from the disjuncture of her gender identity and its performance, which does not look like traditional Dominican women's performances of gender. As she floats along like other objects in the video, Rita is herself decontextualized and able to take on new meaning. This is very much the way that race can operate in a society in which everyone is mixed race of African descent and signifiers beyond skin color are required in order to make meaning around what that person might signify.

Silent but ever-present in this music video are retro suitcases; colorful luggage without wheels serve as props or signifying objects. Rita sits on a lavender-colored suitcase as she sings, while resting her heeled boot on a black one. Each out-of-context piece of luggage, floating with her in the universe, is symbolic of a transnational Dominican life—a effective metaphor for the potential for movement, the space of transit, migration, and waiting for a chance to travel that is so much a part of the Dominican experience. Its color emblematic of queer resistance, the lavender suitcase next becomes a screen onto which a black-and-white film clip of a plane taking off from an airport runway is projected. Rita Indiana holds it out in front of her.

Just as Salvador Dalí's avant-garde work would go on to influence a consumerist cultural revolution of sorts, Rita Indiana's work pushing boundaries within Dominican culture in the early twenty-first century reflects a similar moment of disaffection. As Zalman argues, dynamism of Surrealist art is what makes it appealing to the eye: "Surrealism proved difficult to categorize: as a style, it was both abstract and figurative, automatic and academic, visual and literary; as culture, it shifted between high and low, transcendent and absurd, avantgarde and kitsch."[13] Rita Indiana's creative work, her identity performance, could also be described in this way. "But," as Zalman makes plain, "it was this very versatility that made Surrealism effective as a marketing tool," making the department store and art industry dependent on one another.[14] Rita Indiana's popularity teaches us about the allure of race and gender ambiguity and its marketability as something visibly consumable. Her bodily performance is surrealist not because she names her influences as such but because it seems to evade the rational; our attraction is an impulse.

Ritaindianístico Pastiche

"Rita Indiana is making fun of your Facebook obsession with her new song 'Maldito feisbu,'" writes *Remezcla.com* reviewer Rmessina. "The best thing to come out of the Dominican Republic since the concept of a bodega, the lateral-thinking songstress has penned a sardonic hate letter to Mark Zuckerberg's Little House of Online Horrors." The social media critic goes on, "what's a Rita Indiana song without some sort of genre-bending Latin music? The requisite ritaindianístico pastiche is alive and well in the lyrics. Just when your ear got used to the Dominican accents, 'Te tengo en la mira, carnal. Te vi, güey. Tengo tu passwoooord' comes and blows you a-güey. I love this woman."[15] Rmessina points to a reality of cultural production on the island by giving a name to the type of cultural mixing so prevalent in Dominican society at the turn of the twentieth century. This transnational cultural production is precisely the type of "ritaindianístico pastiche" that excites cultural consumers.

With the support of a creative team of her peers, Rita Indiana has been able to construct for herself a unique Dominican identity that seems to stay "on brand" and live up to our expectations. It is possible to see this very ritaindianístico pastiche throughout the visual culture that she has mobilized and produced around her persona. However, as another insightful interviewee once explained to me about the significance of Rita's work: "Para mi, no e' nada nuevo, nada novedor . . . para mi ella e' una sintesis de todo lo que hay [For me, it is nothing new, nothing special . . . for me, she is a synthesis of everything there is]."[16] Indeed, what is so captivating about Rita—the mixing that she does that has resonated so deeply with transnational diasporic Dominican subjects—is perhaps a quintessentially Dominican approach to cultural production. The *música raíces* of Luis Días and Xiomara Fortuna that came decades before is likewise quintessentially Dominican in its mixing of rock and pop and Afro-Dominican rhythms.[17] The pastiche that Rita Indiana presents is equally emblematic of Dominican culture and the manner in which Dominicans have always blended new cultures into Dominican society; an adaptation, one could argue, or one more synchronicity within African diasporic culture.

Through new media technology, and with the polish of good marketing strategies, Rita Indiana's music videos excite viewers with their juxtapositions of the familiar and *lo de afuera* (that which is from abroad). She draws us into her sounds and playful language with a complimentary visual culture through which she deftly mobilizes difference. Her own carefully curated image as an artist—a musician, writer, and intellectual—in and outside of her music videos is essential to her self-produced transnationally popular identity. Moreover, the type of Surrealism that Rita Indiana deploys has roots on the island of Quisqueya. Dominican experience of the transnational as an unexpected interaction of goods, ideas, and cultural values is one that scholars like me have rushed to write about, trying to articulate it in linear form, and interrogate it for its disruptive significance and resonance within a globalized culture.

The internet archive offers up an interview with Rita Indiana Hernández from 2006, conducted by Marisel Moreno-Anderson and Rubén Ríos Avila for the Oral History Program at the Institute for Latino Studies at Notre Dame.[18] There, a young Rita provides a thoughtful analysis of the Dominican context in the first decade of the twenty-first century. She states, "I think we are still living in a Trujillato, so that's what it's all about . . . it's not even *un trauma* yet. It's actually the present." It may have to do with Balaguer's death, Rita suggests, or perhaps the internet, that influenced a vibrant period of writing, painting, and performance art in Santo Domingo in the 2000s: "There's definitely something that's being—algo está exorcisando." Switching language mid-sentence, Rita points to a purging or exorcizing of the repression that Dominicans had been living under, growing up under. And the resistance that is taking place, she argues, comes out of this. It is "a rebellion that is concrete and focused," she says in Spanish. "This isn't happening in academia but among youth in the streets. And they are writing and producing works." Many of them are queer—in Rita's estimate 50 percent—and they are "doing really sophisticated work in terms of *respondiendo a esa cultura Trujillista en la literatura.*"

Drawing on aspects of popular culture and design, not only literature but also music and visual culture that resists the status quo, images that document and challenge Dominican culture and the socially conservative anti-blackness of the Trujillo era, all of this shapes her work.[19] She says, "If you read my first novel, it's like, a little bit of a grunge manifesto. . . . Kurt Cobain had just died. Maybe you think, 'this girl is in the Dominican Republic, what the hell does that have to do with Kurt Cobain dying? There was something that linked us in a way, I dunno. Maybe just that I wanted to wear flannels and it was too hot to do that. But I wore those flannel shirts anyway to go to the mall. I dunno. People think of a writer, they think that your *maestros* are always gonna come from literature." In fact, like a true Dominican, it is singer-songwriter Luis Días whom she holds in highest esteem, and recognizes for his poetry and prose as well.[20] Días's mixing of genre, music, and poetry, the roots of Dominican contemporary popular music, is precisely what Rita Indiana provides in her versatile writing and musical performances.

In 2010, she was on the program for the national Feria del Libro not once but twice: for her writing and with a musical performance that closed out the annual event. She performed merengue for an audience of students from la UASD who, like me, had probably come only to see Rita. A fusion of European and African culture, perhaps merengue itself is emblematic of a cultural mixing that unites blackness—seen throughout Dominican history as decidedly not modern—and modernity.

"Can you dance merengue?" one of the students seated in front me queried, reading me as a foreigner. Although it turned out that Rita was a very small part of the show that night, she did come on stage at some point to pour libations of red wine to the ancestors for whom she said the event was a tribute.[21] The African tradition of pouring libations is regularly practiced in the Dominican Republic. Performing merengue and this Afro-Dominican ritual for the theater audience, Rita positioned herself as undeniably Dominican—not to be dismissed for being queer. The red wine splattered against her long white flared pants and then she quickly disappeared behind the curtain on stage.

The Privilege of Being a Transformista

Along with her status of whiteness in Dominican society, Rita's status as an artist allows her certain permissions to position herself radically outside of social norms.[22] Her queerness is criticized and otherwise challenged publicly in the Dominican Republic, yet there remains a space for it in popular culture and among those who consume it, perhaps because of her transnational positioning, her ability to move across borders, her class privilege, and her identity as an artist. Certainly, her visibility challenges homophobic patriarchal systems in Dominican society and, as Gayatri Gopinath argues, "It is precisely by making intelligible those queer, feminist cultural practices that are rendered inaudible and invisible within dominant paradigms of nation, diaspora, and globalization . . . that we most powerfully intervene into these paradigms, and thereby suggest other ways of being in the world."[23] Nevertheless, making this intervention does not exempt Rita Indiana from the pitfalls of exploitative racial representation or reinforcing other aspects of a hegemonic structure in the process. Rather, her multifaceted performance of identity offers a rich example of how Dominican whiteness intersects with gender identity and performance differently than it does for black and brown Dominicans.

Rita Indiana's persona is made possible through her constant and deliberate manipulation of powerful symbols of dominicanidad.[24] Like the characters she creates, she draws on both mass culture and high culture in order to navigate social hierarchy.[25] Her creative palette, an assemblage of symbols, meanings, and resonances with which she is working, is Dominican in its mixture as well as influenced by globalized hip-hop culture. Says Hernández of her first book *Papi*, "La he escrito como un gran rap, tiene una cadencia de hip hop o de merengue [I have written it like a long rap, with the cadence of hip hop or merengue]." In sound and in structure, she combines symbolic language and forms of music that have African roots. For the Barcelona publication *La Vanguardia*, Rita says of her creative work: "I wanted to put into a kind of voodoo doll all the things that fucked with me and all the things I feel fascinated about."[26] Her mention of *vudú* references New World religions of Haiti and the Dominican Republic that are tied to African cosmologies. Her idea of acquiring difference and combining it into the object of the voodoo doll mirrors an outlook shared by Surrealism's forefathers. Along with the psychoanalytic, an internal stream of consciousness, and dreams, Surrealism past and present has focused the fantastic, including many influences from the African diaspora and in particular Haiti. The movement has long celebrated the curio cabinet of collected objects of inspiration. Rita takes up this same possibility of Afro-diasporic culture as an acquisition, a move we have regularly seen in popular culture among white working-class American and British artists. She is successful at mobilizing black culture—from the Dominican Republic and abroad—but without being marginalized for being a black artist.

To better understand at how Dominican women's racial ambiguity is impacted by the pigmentocracy of the Dominican Republic and to get a glimpse at how whiteness works in such a racially mixed place, it is useful to read Rita Indiana's racialized and gendered image in the ways that my interviewees have: in juxtaposition to other Dominican women celebrities, in particular Dominican American actress Zoe Saldaña. Saldaña has often played African American characters in Hollywood films. Her thin brown body and hyper-femininity contrast the queered whiteness of Rita Indiana and can offer us further insight into the ways Dominican racialized bodies are visually in-terpreted and consumed. Regular appearances by Saldaña on the island and her constant mention in Dominican newspapers throughout 2010 were, as with Rita, frequent enough to place her as a local celebrity at that moment. Saldaña's image could be found in Dominican advertisements for Avon de-livering donations for victims of the devastating earthquake that occurred in Haiti early that year. Her philanthropy would distance her by class and by culture from a blackness overdetermined by images and realities of Haitian poverty and loss.

Saldaña's performance of race, class, and gender fed into a Dominican politics of respectability that seemed to change her color before your eyes. Although she may proclaim on the internet that she is a black woman, Saldaña was referred to by the Dominican press as "trigueña" in an effort to lighten her in the racial imaginary. This color category, interpreted as "wheaten" or even "olive-skinned," often factors in hair texture as well. She had previously been understood by US audiences as African American because of the roles she played in mainstream films. Appearing in print and online in provocative photos discussing her sexual appetite, she simultaneously occupies the space of the mulata figure of Latin America and the Jezebel of US lore—a stereotype of hypersexualized black womanhood. Saldaña's visual proximity to black-ness informs viewers' imaginations about who she is, where she falls within a colonial legacy of racial hierarchy, and her use within a neoliberal society. As Dixa Ramírez has argued about the mulata, "global demands aided by neoliberal free trade policies accommodate centuries-old colonial fantasies."[27] In truth, no amount of respectability politics can position Saldaña at the top of the Dominican color hierarchy, but class privilege has lightened her color in the Dominican imagination. Saldaña's popularity challenges representa-tions of dominicanidad in terms of color in ways that Rita Indiana challenges mainstream media with her queerness. While Saldaña's value as a sex object is constructed in the media by simultaneously humanizing and exoticizing her brown (decidedly not black) body, Rita's Dominican whiteness prevents her from having to negotiate anti-black perceptions about her body and its value in these terms.

Queerness and Whiteness in the Dominican Imaginary

Yessica recognizes Rita Indiana immediately in the set of photos printed on a sheet of paper that I present to her during our interview. She says, "When I [first] saw Rita I didn't think she was from here. My impression was that she wasn't from here. She seemed more Puerto Rican."

"Probably because of her color and her height?" I blurt out my assumptions about her evaluation of the image, while making an effort to coax her into the conversation. Despite the many "white" Dominicans of the elite class and working-class Dominican known as "*blancos de la tierra*" (whites of the land), Yessica's quick evaluation of the singer reflected the ways that people, including Dominicans, read racially mixed brown bodies as Dominican and white bodies as foreign. Our interview takes place at Yessica's house, in her living room, in the neighborhood of los Jardines del Norte.

"Yes, she's very tall," Yessica agrees about Rita Indiana. Yessica and her neighborhood friend Ambar, at eighteen and nineteen years old, respectively, are the youngest Dominican women that I interview. Ambar is fair in color; Yessica a medium brown with dark hair and dark eyes. The two young women explain to me that Rita Indiana is especially Dominican in her way of *being*, if not in her physical appearance. Her style is provocative and sometimes outrageous, capitalizing on her otherworldliness in her performances. In white pantsuits with bellbottoms, hair shaped into a mohawk, thick chains worn like jewelry on her tall skinny frame, she is a riff on one of her inspirations, David Bowie.

Ambar says she sees "Rita" as more dominicana than the other women whose photos I have presented her with, because she draws on Dominican folklore in her music, performances, and visual representations. Rita "speaks Spanish in a way that is more local and of the people," Ambar tells me.

"I think she seems more Dominican because of her accent," says Yessica. When I ask the pair whether it matters that Rita is not heterosexual, whether this impacts her Dominicanness, Ambar tells me "No, because the role of Rita is that she expresses what she feels in her music."

"It's her personal life," says Ambar, with Yessica nodding in agreement. Ambar brings up Ricky Martin as another example of why it no longer matters, because perceptions of homosexuality have begun to shift. At the same time, however, Ambar makes clear that what is permissible for performers is not permissible for *her*. When she talks about a greater acceptance of gay and lesbian artists at this moment, she refers to a global public. These artists are able to find their place in transnational communities that Ambar and

Yessica, who are not yet transnationally mobile, simply cannot: "She is an artist and she is gay, right? But I am not an artist, and I live here in Los Jardines, right? And if I were gay, it isn't the same. They could reject me but not her. Because I'm not, you know, I'm here . . . dominicana. This is something here that they see as bad . . . although in other countries this might be something common." Furthermore, "artist" exists as its own loaded identity in the Dominican Republic, one that has associations with sexual promiscuity, I would come to learn later. But what Ambar also points to is the class privilege of Rita Indiana, and I would argue, the related privilege of her whiteness. Rita is not confined to the communities in which her queerness is not accepted; she leaves the Dominican Republic for New York, and eventually goes to reside in Puerto Rico.

Discussing what is and is not socially permissible, the two young women laugh in discomfort at the thought of seeing Dominican men kiss one another on the cheek in greeting, the way that Dominican women always do, or Dominican men do to women. On some of the telenovelas they watch they have seen men greeting one another this way. It happens in other parts of Latin America, they tell me, but it's something you would never see in the Dominican Republic. Homophobia and hypermasculinity are deeply embedded in the culture.

"All of this has to do with the culture . . . and the development we have in the country," says Ambar. In the way that she uses the term "development," she suggests it is both structural and sociocultural. Thus, it would mean progressive politics around gay and lesbian identity as well as an importation of ideas from abroad.

"Do you think it's changing?" I ask them both. Yessica is quick to say yes. Says Ambar, "It's changing . . . people are accepting more the reality, and discriminating less against homosexuality." The reality is that gay and lesbian people are present and highly visible in Santo Domingo. Publicly, though, they face unrelenting stares and abusive comments. In dance clubs and after dark they are part of the attraction in a local nightlife and tourism-based Caribbean economy in which some of what is being sold is sex and Otherness. Yet, simultaneously, the presence of queer bodies causes a great deal of anxiety within Dominican patriarchal culture and non-heterosexual individuals are often met with belittling comments and violence. Like women and black people on Dominican television, gays and lesbians are made a spectacle and are often the butt of all jokes.[28]

While overt and state-sanctioned discrimination of LGBTQ+ people was commonplace in the Dominican Republic in 2010, global popular culture had

Ellen DeGeneres advertising Clairol makeup and Lady Gaga and Beyoncé in the music video "Telephone" performing characters in a romantic relationship. It was the same year that Ricky Martin came out as gay on Twitter, and queerness seemed to be gaining new traction in the mainstream overall. Such media representations celebrated in popular culture counter generalizing narratives of social conservativism and homophobia that Americans reserve for other parts of the world like Latin America and Africa. At that same moment, the pope was forced to speak out against the ongoing pedophilia within the Church, as Catholic priests continued to abuse children all over the world; the Dominican Republic was no exception. In terms of the presence of the Church in Dominican politics and community life, all of the women I interviewed wrestled as Catholics with significant contradictions. Not all Dominicans are equally impacted by the pressures of the Church, and the patriarchal system "has its favorite victims," those who are most vulnerable because of gender, age, class, color, and health.[29]

Paloma, the student I interviewed at la UASD, explained, "It's a double standard, because here in this country there's what's official—we are Catholics, moralistic—but when you go out to the night life, when you go to *la zona* (the Colonial Zone) and the areas that are criticized, you see the same people who criticize them. They use the double standard a lot, speaking against what others do . . . therefore, religion influences a lot." Dominicans have learned to live with contradiction.[30]

Reyes Bonilla explains that the views of racial identity of her and her fellow Dominicans hold contradictions, asserting that "In popular culture, our intolerance with difference manifests itself in what I call a 'culture of *complejos.*' It is as if diversity were synonymous to *diversion.*"[31] This is part of the of the fabric of Dominican culture, she suggests, where one does not even recognize one's own internalized prejudices. Even as a dark-skinned Dominican, she, too, was raised to fear Haitians as the Other. Likewise, several of my friends have told me that growing up, they were chastised by their parents to "behave or a Haitian will come and eat you!"[32] According to Reyes Bonilla, she must daily choose her most salient identities because others do not see it as possible for her to be all of her many identities at once: "dominicana, lesbiana, negra, activista, inmigrante."[33] Moreover, she suggests, "lesbian" does not equate with Latina (the category of identity she uses in the United States) and comes across as a betrayal of this other aspect of her identity.

The transnational popular imaginary of which the Dominican Republic is a part dictates that "the homosexual other is white, the racial other is straight."[34] Such a notion of sexuality may explain why Rita Indiana can publicly represent queerness—as the most open of secrets—in ways that an Afro-Dominican artist may not. When we learn these rules about whiteness and sexuality, they make it more difficult for us to view Rita's queerness as a true disruption of the hegemonic structure.

For quite some time, Dominicans did not publicly acknowledge Rita Indiana's queerness, though they knew her to be queer. It is a taboo, "un hipocracía muy sofisticada,"[35] Rita Indiana once explained. The public was collectively committed to keeping her "open secret." She ruptured that reality in March of 2010 with a televised kiss between her and her partner Noelia Quintero. By visually performing her queerness she was able to break through the hypocrisy. She showed up with her girlfriend on the red carpet of the Casandra Awards in a sleek white suit and her girlfriend on her arm in a dark purple dress. In some ways, the two challenged the heteronormativity of the event by appearing as a couple, and in other ways their performances of gender still bent toward homonormativity. Despite the fact that, for many, her gender performance had always made her legible as queer, this act of resistance in the form of a kiss on live television determined Rita's sexual orientation beyond what had existed as rumor.[36] Not unlike the much contested and circulated image of a heterosexual Haitian couple's kiss in the street that led to the Besatón discussed in chapter 1, the image of the kiss between Rita and Quintero drew dramatic public response. Video and stills circulated online became spectacle and evidence of the transgression. Yet her act of resistance to Dominican homophobia, rather than disruptive, made Rita Indiana even more appealing to her viewers and listeners, herself a surreal object of curiosity.

In 2006, Rita had suggested that there was more space for her in Puerto Rico, more freedom, more safety as a queer person; eventually she went to live there. In that same interview at Notre Dame, she hints at her own rejection of Dominican patriotism, subscribing to a notion of the "global citizen"— an identity she later seems to exploit: "I would much rather be part of that [queer global] community," a young Rita Indiana explains, "than to say I'm a Dominican. Definitely. And be part of that struggle which is more imminent to me . . . than to be part of something called *patria*."[37] Self-imposed exile, one could argue, not only helps her to see her homeland from outside but allows her to identify with so many Dominicans who are part of the vibrant diaspora. Her outsiderness allows her to be gender-queer and foreign to the nation while also authentically representative of it. For Rita Indiana to claim her own erotic autonomy would in fact be a threat to the nation and its construction of citizenship in which good citizens are all imagined as heterosexual.[38]

"El juidero" as Masculinity Deployed

The highly anticipated music video for Rita Indiana song "El juidero" (The hustler) appeared on YouTube in October 15, 2010, months after her album had dropped. The music video was primed to become a sensation.[39] Fans were already familiar with the album by the same name, released by record label Sony Music Latin. As a whole, it was well received by the Latin American music community and described by music critic Carlos Reyes at Club Fonogram as "Música Dominicana with a universal eye."[40] Rita explains the video for "El juidero" in the following way: "It was imagined as a short film of the era, a drama in which a clandestine organization traffics in arms and executes operations during a difficult political moment for the nation. . . . It was delicious to see how these historical, artistic, and social planes converged in ways that up until now have not been represented audiovisually in the Dominican Republic."[41] Rita's partner, writer-filmmaker Noelia Quintero Herencia, envisioned and produced the music video for "El juidero"; she also produced the music video "La hora de volvé."[42]

Rita Indiana's lyrics are revealing, but her visual representations, including the central role she plays in the narrative of "El juidero" as a masculine figure, are even more striking.[43] Her queered body makes her performance particularly provocative and popular among Dominican youth, making visible a distinctly Dominican queer imaginary. We are able to see Rita Indiana from many vantage points across her videos but she seems particularly at home in the aesthetic performance of a queer masculinity in "El juidero" that is visible both on the cover of the album and in the video for the title track. Her masculine gender performance allows her to visually access power. Photographer Lorna Simpson once stated about her experience of dressing up in men's clothing to perform for the camera (in her photo series "1957–2009 Interior") that "the slippage of gender brought to life a whole 'nother side of who I am."[44] According to ethnomusicologist Sydney Hutchinson, queerness can also be *heard* in "El juidero" through the inclusion of a Santería prayer to Oyá, of whom Rita is a devotee; Oyá is a Black Madonna who is reputedly the patron of transgender women and lesbians, gays and bisexual men.

As the music video for "El juidero" opens, we hear a radio announce that leftist journalist Orlando Martínez has been murdered near la UASD, an event that took place on March 17, 1975. Through the visual, we are thrown into the period of Joaquin Balaguer's first presidency (1966–1978), known as *los dos años*, an era in the Dominican Republic that was experienced as an extension of the Trujillo dictatorship.[45] Rita Indiana is cast as leader of a clandestine anti-Balaguer organization, hidden away in a cinderblock apartment. Dressed in a burgundy pantsuit and matching burgundy-and-black jacket, she tucks a gun in her pocket and marches to her long black car. Writes Hutchinson, "As she drives away in a black 1972 Lincoln Continental, Rita sings, 'Exodo,' voy pa' Puerto Rico [Exodus, I'm going to Puerto Rico]" in a homage to Bob Marley. The Continental she drives off in had in fact belonged to Balaguer.[46] A pay phone on the corner further marks the time period, while a Volkswagen Bug passes her on the street. Yet when backup dancer Vincent Santos appears on the corner stepping to the rhythm of the music, we are reminded that we are in an alternate reality, not a period film. Rita's character drives to pick up a suitcase full of weapons while dressed in a tuxedo shirt and pants; down to her pinky ring, she blends in among the men around her, also dressed 1970s attire. The goods are swiftly handed over to her by celebrated Afro-Dominican musician Johnny Ventura in a cameo appearance. Hutchinson attributes the aesthetic vision for "El juidero" to Quintero, while noting that Rita Indiana's performance of and investments in performing Black culture and dominicanidad are evident all throughout her audiovisual work. The popular photograph by Maximo del Castillo of Rita Indiana holding *la güira*, an instrument used in Dominican merengue and bachata music, captures this contradiction when Hutchinson captions it, "Rita Indiana with güira. While she doesn't actually play the instrument, it seems here to symbolize the 'power of cultural origins' she discovered while making *El Juidero*."[47] The object is symbolic of Dominican musical tradition and held in her hands it imbues her with this cultural heritage.

The cover art of the *El juidero* album is designed like a movie poster. It reads, "Rita Indiana y Los Misterios" and is seemingly subtitled with the "El juidero" lyrics "Mándale la horma a to tu tío en el e'tranjero pa que manden tenni, que se armo," as a call to youth (who presumably have family in the diaspora) to "Be ready!" Scrawled in text that looks like paint strokes is the title of the album and then the cast of the "film" is listed with the actors and their roles or nicknames. Four men in different frames surround Rita on the cover, as she sits at the center behind the wheel of a Cadillac driving off into the sunset. In the frame at the bottom, shotguns and pistols of black metal and wood lay beside a case of bullets. Being surrounded on the cover by these images of cars and weapons, and in the company of men, masculinizes the images of Rita. By the same turn, familiar visual tropes from 1970s Blaxploitation films racialize her. In fact, her image evokes the movie poster for the Blaxploitation film *Cleopatra Jones* (1973), starring African American actress

Tamara Dobson. Likewise in that film poster, the images of action scenes from the film are cut in angular frames around the center of the poster. The title character stands beside her car—in this case a black Corvette—with a film tagline that reads "6 feet 2" and all of it Dynamite! Jones." With her perfectly round afro, Dobson stands with her hand on her hip in a position of power with one high-heeled boot resting on the hood of the car. Her black pants flair at the bottom. The most significant difference between Rita Indiana's album cover and the film poster is the way that Cleopatra Jones resonates visually as a powerful Black woman. Rita Indiana's image does not claim its power from her Blackness but from her masculinity, conveyed by her stance and the suit she is wearing.

On the face of the *El juidero* CD is another image of Rita Indiana where she deploys what could be read as a masculine aesthetic. The photograph is angled slightly from above and as she is sitting in the infamous Cadillac. The door is wide open and she is turned as if exiting the driver's seat. Both her feet are planted on the ground as she turns her body away from the cigarette held between her slender fingers. The photograph has been digitally filtered to make it look as though her cheeks were painted with strokes of blush. Her white skin appears paler with this distortion; the artificial paint strokes highlight undertones of blue and pink. In this moment of contemplation, Rita sits knees bent, thin legs falling slightly apart. She has men's brown leather dress shoes on her feet, and is wearing a red polyester jumpsuit and jacket, as depicted in the first scene of the video. Rita Indiana's gender ambiguity here visually disrupts heteronormativity in her representations of dominicanidad. Rivera-Velazquez aptly describes her in this way: "If you can picture an androgynous person who one minute is asked to leave the gay bar for being misrecognized as a conceited straight-man infiltrator, and the next is welcomed to stay, owing to a tacit recognition of some unspoken femininities . . . then you are imagining Rita. Her work and persona embody the notion of fluidity."[48] But even though painting on a mustache to queer her gender performance and painting her face and body to shift her racial identity within the visual text are in line with the type of visual disruptions that Rita Indiana's work consistently provides, the two are not equivalent.

Rita Indiana's Brand

In her essay "The Importance of Being Rita Indiana Hernández," Celiany Rivera-Velasquez contends that "while hypervisuality and multimedia are characteristic of many of the mediated texts of these times, Rita is actively choosing how to represent herself through her artwork. Functioning at the periphery of first-world media conglomerates, Rita and others like her could be said to be not only the directors, producers, promoters, and marketers, but also the agents of their own voice."[49] Indeed, Rita Indiana's interview with faculty at Notre Dame reveals this as well as the ways that her exposure to US culture shaped her work as an artist, all informed by the privileges of her own upbringing, which was steeped in a transnational Dominican culture.[50] Like so many Dominicans of her generation, she attributes her fluency in English to the cable television she was able to view beginning in the 1980s, time spent living abroad, and her access to a transnational circulation of books in English and Spanish. Likewise her use of language is such that she moves back and forth between English and Dominican Spanish in the interview as necessary, demonstrating the lived reality of an everyday trans-national mixing of culture through word, sound, genre, and aesthetic.[51] Rita Indiana's particular "brand" also includes the Dominicanizations of English words; her novels and music reflect the ways Dominicans speak Spanish. It is an art of sampling, like that of a DJ. Jokes Rita, it is "a tricky way of steal-ing other people's work."[52]

Both Vera-Rojas and Hutchinson contend that the radical nature of Rita Indiana's creative work lies in the ways that she sutures together the borders of that which seem incompatible. Writes Hutchinson, Hernández's work is "transnational, trans racial, trans gender, and trans genre."[53] Vera-Rojas argues that her sampling creates an instability that "writes bodies of materiality that account for the instability and possibilities of resistance with which subjects operate and those corporalities that inhabit the drift of hegemonic discourse and the interstices of the devices of power."[54] Rita Indiana's work is a product of a neoliberal context and it is exciting because it is subversive, yet it exists in the form that it does not *in spite of* systems of race and gender, power, and privilege but rather *because of* those systems.

When Ríos Avila asked her how her work in marketing and publicity shaped her own creative work, Rita Indiana described the field as a place in which she encountered many creatives (visual artists, writers, musicians) because the work paid well. "You can do something that's kind of artsy and not that boring . . . it's fun," said the young creative in her early years. But, as she noted, "It drains you because you're working with the same tools you would use to develop your own project." She goes on to acknowledge that this is recognizable in the work she produces: "My work has definitely been influenced by seeing all that, by that [marketing] culture and seeing how things are sold, and seeing how you make a product, seeing what people expect, and what people believe and what people want to believe, and what you can make them believe. The whole language . . . at the beginning was a very intense creative workshop for me. In that sense it was good. But you're just making crap, 90% of the time, to sell."[55]

In her examination of Surrealist Salvador Dalí's commercial artwork—a series of department store windows—of the 1930s, Zalman argues, "Advertisers hailed Surrealism for its exotic color, considering that to be one of the prime aspects of its eye-catching associations. The Surrealist windows were instrumental in demonstrating new ways that color could be used disruptively, and that mundane objects could be invested with mystery."[56] The tradition of Surrealism influencing marketing to benefit capitalism precisely for its irreverence is controversial because of the radicalism that Surrealism had intended to represent; yet it certainly has precedent. Likewise, being shaped by the economy of Dominican advertising and even her experience in creating jingles to sell products may have given Rita Indiana an edge in knowing what sounds are catchy and what will sell. One example of this is her work in 2010 for Yokomo Sushi, an extremely well-marketed restaurant that capitalizes on Dominican hybrid culture, fusion foods—including sushi rolls with plantain—and the popularity of Japanese cuisine in Santo Domingo. The name of the restaurant is a play on the sentence in Spanish meaning "I eat sushi" and its slogan "Sushi Aplatona'o" suggests "Dominicanized sushi." Items on the menu include the Feisbuk Roll and the Twitter Roll. Yokomo Sushi had Rita Indiana y Los Misterios produce the ringtone "yo como sushi" as a fee-based download. On YouTube, the video for the jingle opens with the cartoon of a Dominican chef and a Japanese chef reviewing the restaurant's menu. However, the punchline of the anti-Asian humor deployed is that the Japanese chef is unintelligible—speaking a fake Asian language—while the Dominican chef translates for listeners menu items that include the Mr. Miyagi Roll (a reference to the classic 1980s film *Karate Kid*). A signature part of the Dominican restaurant's popular aesthetic online and off is a brightly colored mural of a Dominican woman wearing a head full of *rollos* (hair curlers) that are in fact sushi rolls—a depiction that is highly surreal. With this same celebration of fusion and inundation of global marketing, Rita Indiana's work resonates as authentic and representative of Dominican culture because of all that she habitually folds into the mix—though the sushi metaphor could be taken much further.

Racial Vacillations and the Epistemic Knowledge of Mixed Race

As I have written elsewhere, the possibility of shifting and changing of one's racial meaning is appealing under a capitalism that is seeking constantly to sell us something "new" and commodify the Other.[57] The racial fluctuation of representations of Dominican women who perform their multifaceted racial meaning for transnational audiences, functions as a provocation to look further. Rita Indiana's racial meaning fluctuates as desired by larger structures of power.

In Judith Butler's reading of Nella Larsen's novel *Passing*, she argues that the "vacillation" of Larsen's all-but-white character between Black and white functions as an "erotic lure" that attracts the protagonist to another Black woman who is also passing for white. This dynamic relationship to Blackness for these two fictional characters brings something to bear on my analysis of Dominican racial ambiguity and the appeal of the racially ambiguous Dominican body that wholly involves the act of looking. Butler's psychoanalytic reading of how vacillations of racial meaning might occur on the pages of a novel is useful to my analysis of how we see Dominican women's mixed-race bodies. Larsen, the American daughter of a Danish mother and a West Indian father of African descent, theorizes aspects of her own experiences with racial ambiguity in her 1929 text. The tension that she crafts between two Black women who are passing for white in New York City is produced initially through numerous knowing glances of discernment. Writes Larsen, "Clare had a trick of sliding down ivory lids over astounding black eyes, and then lifting them suddenly and turning on a caressing smile." Lori Harrison-Kahan argues that this moment can be read as "an optical illusion," that "enables two contradictory meanings," because not only do Clare's all-but-white eyelids cover the black of her eyes, they also lower to cover the *whites* of her eyes.[58] The notion of a mixed-race body as an optical illusion is useful to my readings of Dominican women's representations. However, I want to suggest that it is the seeking of visual confirmation that is most provocative in viewing the mixed-race body. We look harder, to discern racial signifiers and verify what we are seeing, even if what it means to us can change right in front of our eyes; my theory of the see/saw suggests that such vacillations in the act of seeing rely on a juxtaposition of bodies.

Racial vacillation also requires narrative and context for meaning, all factors that produce a pull toward ambiguous difference and Otherness.[59] In order to make meaning around what we might see between the two fair-skinned Black women, a visual hierarchy must already exist to make them legible in juxtaposition to one another. The ways that Larsen wrote of Irene seeking visual markers of authenticity around race is highly surrealist in the ways that as readers we become privy to her internal dialogue. Irene's observations when looking at her "rubia" friend Clare highlight the obsessive use of one's own eye to make a racial evaluation of the body of another—specifically seeking signs of Blackness—in order to confirm for oneself racial boundaries.[60] Larsen writes Irene's act of looking for racial confirmation beautifully:

> The face across the forehead and cheeks was a trifle too wide, but the ivory skin had a peculiar soft lustre. And the eyes were magnificent! Dark, sometimes absolutely black, always luminous, and set in long, black lashes. Arresting eyes, slowly and mesmeric, and with, for all their warmth, something withdrawn and secret about them.
>
> Ah! Surely! They were Negro eyes! Mysterious and concealing. And set in that ivory face under that bright hair, there was about them something exotic.[61]

We learn from this passage in Larsen's novel that race is something that one may encounter and reencounter. It is something we attempt to see and, like the use of color hierarchies and comments about color and language about color that Dominicans engage in, it must be constantly reencountered for it to be useful or sustained as a system of social organization. A constant reencountering of race is required in Santo Domingo in order to produce and define the border between white and black when racial boundaries are so often blurred.

Often, racial meaning does not "compute" for individuals when all of the preconceived notions about a racial identity do not line up and designated visual markers cannot be visually verified. White Dominicans defining their social location within a racial hierarchy in relation to blackness may be better understood by looking here at Larsen's theorizations of Black women passing for white. Butler also analyzes the power of Irene's husband's "white gaze": he does not *know* she is Black and therefore he does not *see* her as Black.[62] Furthermore race is associative. Accordingly, Butler notes, "If he associates with her, she cannot be Black. But if she associates with Blacks, she becomes Black. Where the sign of Blackness is contracted, as it were, through proximity, where 'race' itself is configured as a contagion transmissible through proximity."[63] As we see with the curiosity about Rita Indiana's sexuality and the danger and "taboo" of association with her Otherness, the risk of negative association both repels and also pulls the viewer back to better see the rupture of gender that Rita Indiana represents—and the spectacle.

Estrategias Raciales, Estrategias Cuir

In Rita Indiana y Los Misterios' 2011 music video for "Da' pa' lo' do," Rita can be seen dressed as the Virgin Mary, perched on the back of a motorcycle while traveling across the desert landscape of Hispaniola. Her voice, chanting the fast-paced lyrics of the song, can be heard well before she appears on screen as a vision in turquoise, draped from head to toe in a fuchsia-lined mantle; the satiny cloth ripples in the breeze. Only at the moment in which the *motorista* steers her past the camera does Rita Indiana reveal her face. It is in that moment that viewers register that she has darkened her face with makeup. Since Rita's many fans know her to be fair-skinned, it is a visually startling moment to see her "blackened up" on screen. For those of us familiar with the history of blackface performance and minstrelsy in the Americas and its role in dehumanizing Black people as well as appropriating Black culture, Rita Indiana's visual transformation is legible as such and is alarming, to say the least. My reading of the performance contrasts that of Dominican scholar Lorgia Garcia Peña, who suggests the performance reflects Rita's "embodiment of the mulata Madonna as an attempt to make Afro-Hispaniola religiosity an alternative way for understanding the islands cultures and histories."[64] Yet because there does exist a history of blackface performance in the Dominican Republic and the Caribbean more broadly, it is difficult to read Rita Indiana as not signifying this history in the context of the video.[65]

Although Rita Indiana and her team filmed the music video in 2010, they did not release "Da' pa' lo' do'" on YouTube until October of the following year.[66] The images in the video do far more than simply picturize the song's lyrics. While the story takes place on the island of Hispaniola, the narrative resists positioning Hispaniola within the dominant visual discourse of the Caribbean (past or present): there are no beaches or palm trees, or brown women in swimsuits. Rather, the central figures that carry the load of representation in the video are two black men crossing a desert. Their images are fixed within a hierarchy of color that produces visual meaning in terms of national belonging. Racial systems evoked in this music video easily serve as "a form of 'super-nationalism' refiguring notions of national heritage and culture into more powerful and virulent ideas of national inheritance, the national body, national purity, and aesthetic ideals of national men (and women)."[67]

Following Siobhan Somerville's approach in my queer reading of this cultural text, I "modulate my analysis from a singular focus on sexuality to one equally alert to the resonances of racialization."[68] Rita Indiana's performance in the "Da' pa' lo' do'" video is inextricable from her larger body of work, and therefore it is important to problematize the ways that she uses blackface and symbolic dress to evoke Dominican racial meaning. She chose to portray the Black Madonna, also recognizable as the Haitian goddess Erzulie Dantor, a *misterio* celebrated in syncretic religious practices and known for her blackness and nonheteronormative behaviors. At the end of the video, Rita's queer body comes to represent a mother to the nation. Her performance as such is a sort of floating signifier, left to circulate on global media (YouTube) across contexts well beyond the borders of the racial schema of the Dominican Republic.

Rita's tall, thin, white, and masculinized body and queer sexuality position her outside of dominant notions of la dominicana and what the Black Madonna might look like. Racial fluidity runs parallel to and intersects with her gender ambiguity and nonheteronormativity in performances such as this one in which she transgresses racial lines in ways that she had previously crossed hetero-patriarchal boundaries. At the same time, the video clarifies something about the privileges of whiteness in the Dominican Republic, and that which cannot be masked by brown makeup. Her "black" body in the music video is understood by Dominican viewers in the context of existing narratives of the Dominican nation. Her use of idiomatic signifiers and African sounds "darken" her at some moments, even though knowledge of her color and class background lighten her in others. Rita Indiana's queered body requires makeup to represent the Black Madonna but she also employs vernacular language to produce a discursive racialization of her Dominican-ness.

"Da' pa' lo' do'" presents a simple allegory of brotherhood between the two sides of the small island of Hispaniola and it brings attention to ongoing discord on the island that is so much a part of Dominican contemporary politics of identity. The music video seeks to counter Dominican xenophobia. In a 2009 interview for the magazine *Mujer Unica*, Rita Indiana states, "I know the horror that lives on this island, the violence that injustice and pride have generated, the racism and the passivity with which we react to hell, but what we need is major therapy to show us how beautiful and good we are and all that we have lost because we are not supportive of one another."[69] Like many Dominican elite, she is critical of the misogyny, homophobia, and anti-Haitianism that exists in the Dominican society in which she grew up.[70] The song's chorus, "Da' pa' lo' do' [there's enough for two]," serves as a mantra that the listener carries with her, to "extend the table" in the way that Dominicans do. The lyrics are about two poor little boys, but the visual narrative depicts two men of African descent traversing harsh terrain, through cacti and thorny brush. Two adult male black bodies, one a slightly lighter skin color than the other, symbolize the two sides of the island. These bodies visually signify a racial logic for Dominican viewers while simultaneously essentializing notions of race, color, and nation on Hispaniola that erase existing racial diversity across the populations of both countries.[71] Through her lyrics, Rita Indiana recites the physical attributes that each boy shares in common with one another, as brothers: two eyes, two feet, two hands. She sings, "Vinimos todos en el mismo bote," suggesting the shared history and shared African ancestry of the peoples on both sides of the island, "Siéntelo, el abrazo del mismo abuelo [Feel it, the embrace of the same grandparent]."

Although the lyrics never refer to color, we immediately see a marked difference between the two men in the video who represent the boys in the lyrics of the song. Their dark muscular bodies remind us that slave ships transported millions of stolen Africans to the New World. Rita Indiana's lyrics point to the north of the island: "Desde Juana Mendez hasta Maimón/Y de ahí a Dajabón/En bola e' bon." She again documents and plays with dominican-izations of language, which in this case is the transformation of the Haitian city of Ouanamenthe to "Juana Mendez" when she sings "From Juana Mendes to Maimón/and from there to Dajabón." The video was actually filmed in the Dominican border town of Dajabón (near Monte Cristi), an infamous and porous space between Haiti and the Dominican Republic. Dajabón is a site of tremendous historical violence, where Trujillo enacted a genocide against those who were identified as Haitian living in the borderlands; his troops killed tens of thousands *rayanos*, the people who inhabit the border territory.[72] In contrast, the two black men in the video peaceably carry weapons and various other accoutrements of the colonial era, which they shed on their journey, stripping away markers of nation as they remove clothing and shoes. The black man traveling from west to east across the screen represents Haiti, wearing a red and black jacket, evocative of the flag of Haitian independence—and he is shades darker in skin color than his counterpart. The brown-skinned man, traveling east to west, is wearing a blue jacket, a bright red bandana, and matching sash around his waist, representing the Dominican flag; he also has a Dominican *sombrero de caña* resting on his head.

Rita Indiana appears to the two wandering men in a "Marian apparition" as the Blessed Virgin Mary. According to Engel Leonardo, the Dominican graphic designer who conceived of and directed Rita Indiana's video: "The idea to use the Virgin we did not think of as at all controversial, really it was well intentioned and in a respectful manner, who else but a celestial figure to call attention to the two people and help change the course of their relationship."[73] Of course, the final work reads in much more nuanced ways than Leonardo suggests. We see that Rita Indiana is painted brown from head to toe as she towers over each man to offer her blessings and the colors and symbols that surround her inform the meaning of her blackface. Brightly colored, animated streaks appear on the dark faces of the two young men as they kneel before her—spirited lines of blue, fuchsia, and gold that dash across their cheeks and brows as they move toward each other and also suddenly appear on the left cheek of the Virgin and creep up and around her face. The lines approximate the two striations on the left cheek of Our Lady of Czestochowa, the Black Madonna brought to the island of Hispaniola by the Polish at the turn of the nineteenth century. Rather than a golden orb behind her head, Rita wears a wicker circle pinned there to reference to the religious iconography. A large gold *vevè*, shaped like the letter *M*, dangles on a chain around her neck; through digital effects, it glints once or twice in the sun.[74] The vevè is a symbol of Rita Indiana's band Los Misterios who are absent from the video, and it also associates her with Haitian vodou. The necklace charm's sparkle and the shine of her satin gown further reference the posh markers of the creole virgin, Erzulie.[75]

By placing herself in the role of Erzulie Dantor, a significant saint in the cultural traditions of Dominican vudú and Haitian vodou, Rita makes claims on these cultural traditions with African roots.[76] She removes racial whiteness from this performance of Dominican identity and repositions herself as of the island and of the people by making her body brown. The tall, thin, fair, and masculine-of-center Rita Indiana otherwise does little to evoke the bosomy goddess of femininity, Erzulie Dantor, so she darkens her skin color with paint. But Erzulie, a figure associated with whiteness and blackness alike, provokes questions of racial ambiguity.[77] In one iteration, she is known as Erzulie-Fréda, the fair mulata lover of the dark god Ogoun, and in other iterations she is known to carry symbols of Daballah and Agoué-Taroyo, male gods who are imagined as white.[78] The pale or even white Erzulie-Fréda traces onto the Catholic image of a white Mater Dolorosa while "the dark-skinned Erzulie Danto[r] becomes Mater Salvatores, depicted as a Black virgin holding a child, two scars on her right cheek, and a halo around her head."[79] Rita Indiana might easily have represented herself as the racially ambiguous spiritual figure of Erzulie-Fréda with white skin. But by putting on brown makeup she instead locates herself visually among the Dominican majority—while also portraying a powerful Haitian goddess. As it happens, Erzulie Dantor has her own erotic lure, based not only on the ambiguity of her racial identity but her vacillations between whom she desires.[80] She is known as the patron saint of all gays and lesbians, while simultaneously recognized in Haitian vodou as the mother of all Haitians. And although Rita never appears holding a child in the music video, in the concluding scene she is suddenly surrounded by dancing children.

In her reading of the musicality of Rita Indiana's creative work, Hutchinson has argued that the artist's engagement with black culture "is in line with the output of many progressive artists in the Dominican Republic and Puerto Rico today who seek to valorize African roots, whether or not those roots are part of the artists' own genetic heritage, and to forge links with Haiti."[81] Note, however, that valorizing blackness looks quite different than appropriating it. Blackness performed on Rita Indiana's white body—across the transnational media in which it circulates and for viewers worldwide—is not easily decontextualized from a long history of blackface minstrelsy in the United States.[82] Her blackening up, some may argue, is not the type of blackface performance by whites that serves to denigrate blackness. Yet blackface performance is a cultural phenomenon taken up throughout the Americas (and beyond) with the same consequences of dehumanization. Rita Indiana's blackface reflects an exotification of blackness as mythical and magical, which then supports an ideology of primitivism in order to, as Johnson argues, "justify the colonial and racist gaze."[83] That is to say, it reinforces the ways that Dominicans *see* black people (meaning Haitians) as foreign. Her desire to valorize Haitian identity and culture by performing it herself is a familiar trope and requires the belief or understanding that she can shed her own racial meaning. Her Dominican whiteness affords her the privilege of racial transformation while the black bodies in the video are fixed; they remain relegated to the childlike and even hyper-erotic.

When the two men in the "Da' pa' lo' do'" video eventually strip down to their tight white pants and reveal their bare muscular bodies, to my eye it is difficult to interpret the significance of their embrace as something other than homoerotic. We are primed to read the video for queerness simply because it is the work of Rita Indiana. Upon arriving in front of the tree of life that opens the video, each man drops his weapon—the Haitian man a rifle, the Dominican man a cutlass—and the two meet face-to-face. Each topless black man is then captured on camera in a moment of saintly repose, while wicker halos are set behind their heads as well. Their images juxtaposed, one after the other, further emphasize their difference in color. When shown again, they are standing face-to-face, each extending a right hand, until, glistening with sweat, the Dominican man pulls his Haitian brother into his arms. This lingering skin-to-skin contact flies in the face of existing constructions of masculinity in the Dominican Republic. The scene serves as a queer counternarrative to the type of fraternity promoted by forefathers of the Dominican nation.[84]

Brown children dancing around Rita Indiana as La Virgen in the final scene suggest the future of the Dominican Republic is brown—and perhaps also queer. Interviewer Carmen Imbert Brugal suggests that Rita Indiana's critique of the Dominican bourgeoisie inspires audiences on social media who are reminded of "*el can* [can-do]," by "a very fashionable white girl who speaks English and is a writer."[85] Yet as Rita Indiana does recognize, she is claimed as Dominican while able to distance herself from her home country, when Dominicans of Haitian descent and many other Dominicans on the island do not have that mobility. Notably, Rita Indiana's Virgin evokes the version of Erzulie whose "followers are mainly single working-class Black women who identify with her industrious nature and her struggles as a single mother."[86] The video marks a transition in Rita's work and identity as she moves away from the rebellious youth she was identified with through her early fiction and performances. In her own words: "I'm not a night creature anymore, I used to be when I was in my 20s. Now I'm a mom. I like hanging out with my family and friends at home, and the night gigs were boring and exhausting."[87] Rita's appearance as a mother in the video allows her to make this transformation. Ironically, her blackface is precisely what makes her legible in this role as mother because her darkened skin aligns with a racial logic in which the brown children around her look like her and might be her offspring—although this correlation is not a racial logic that necessarily holds true in the Dominican Republic, even if people want to believe it might.

In *A Queer Mother for the Nation: The State and Gabriela Mistral*, Licia Fiol-Mata clearly demonstrates how "queer desire is not immune to racialized constructions of eroticism or the lure of achieving national belonging through a collective exercise of racial fetishization."[88] Indeed, we find that Rita Indiana's visual productions provide "cronicas, viñetas urbanas con sonido, humor, descaro . . . es juglar posmoderna [chronicles, urban vignettes with sound, humor, impudence . . . she's a postmodern minstrel]."[89] It is just such "*juglaria*," or "minstrelsy," in Rita Indiana's performances that reinforces racial hierarchies and silences black voices. Scholar of blackface performance Eric Lott argues in *Love and Theft* that "minstrel devices (ventriloquized dialect, racial burlesque)" may appear to be benevolent in their celebration of blackness but nonetheless reinforce the dominant racial power structure that relies on the racialized Other to produce whiteness.[90] Performing blackness is no less problematic when it is done by white Dominican artists within a culture and nation-state that has long been associated with blackness. Claims on a belief in racial equity while replicating visual messages that romanticize blackness, and benefitting from its appropriation, ring false. But they do inform us about the ways that whiteness functions in the Dominican Republic and transnationally.

As both a cultural producer and cultural critic, Rita Indiana has enjoyed significant access to venues through which to share her critique of Dominican popular culture and society. Furthermore, her broad fan base among scholars and intellectuals has made it possible for her to speak at book festivals, on conference panels, and within universities. From a young age she has been given the opportunity to contextualize her own work and offer her own definitions for the public record. One such example is her writing on popular culture for the Dominican newspaper *El País* from 2014 to 2016, while she was living outside of the country. In a particularly impassioned essay she wrote, she commemorated the death of British musician David Bowie.[91] Rita eulogized, "In the Caribbean, where we know him for his hits of the 1980s, David Bowie was adored for his music, for his familiar tropical elegance with which at the time he embellished some of his videos and with which he determined the blackness of his maneuvers in pop."[92] Rita clearly draws on "the thin White Duke" as a style icon and her cultural productions employ a masculinity as genderfluid as Bowie's—something that a simple Google Images search of each artist reveals. Whiteness offered Bowie privileges throughout his career in the ways he was able to appropriate African American musical culture and make it more marketable than the work of Black people themselves.[93] Dominican whiteness seems to also provide Rita these privileges, along with access to a particular form of masculinity. Rita concludes, "In the small stage of the *Soul Train* program, Bowie sings and dances for a sea of youth of color, like the Black star that he is, like the beautiful cellophane that covered the gift that the descendants of slaves have given to the world, to the whole planet."[94] Whiteness like a translucent cellophane wrapper allows Rita Indiana to be seen as a new and different gift of popular culture, while suggesting that her blackness lies visible underneath. Her metaphor might also lead us to imagine a covering over of blackness with something that might contain it, while leaving it looking neat and shiny. Or it could be interpreted as a thin and impermeable packaging under which blackness is able to gleam, without one having to truly encounter blackness itself.

4

A Thorn in Her Foot

The Discomfort of Racism
and the Ethnographic Moment

> Growing up in the Dominican Republic, I experienced
> racism within my own family—though I didn't think of it
> as racism. But there was definitely a hierarchy of beauty,
> which was the main currency in our daughters-only
> family. It was not until years later, from the vantage point
> of this country and this education, that I realized that this
> hierarchy of beauty was dictated by our coloring. We were
> a progression of whitening, as if my mother were slowly
> bleaching the color out of her children.
>
> Julia Álvarez, "A White Woman of Color"

"We Dominicans are all black people, all of us," twenty-four-year-old Genesis (pronounced "Hennessy") explains to me in English. "Although you're white—you dye your hair blonde and have green eyes—you are black girl. I mean that's it. You can do nothing about it . . . all the people here who have power or money, by birth or because they worked a lot, those people can be very racist. People with a lot of money can be very racist." She repeats, "I mean if you are Dominican, you're black."

I have occasionally run into Genesis around Santo Domingo at film festivals and cultural events. She agrees to meet me for an interview at the advertising firm she works at on a street off Avenida Winston Churchill and we sit across from one another at her desk. She seems invested in helping me get the information I am looking for; however, the images I offer in my photo elicitation do little to spark conversation between us. Genesis describes Martha Heredia as "Dominicanyork" in her aesthetic: "she can be my cousin, who lives in New York, like in the Bronx" and she is certain that neither Zoe Saldaña nor Michelle Rodríguez are true dominicanas, regardless of the origins of their parents, but are merely Hollywood actresses. All of these women come back to the Dominican Republic, she says cynically, "to earn another public . . . to get more fans to their fan page." Rita Indiana, whose music Genesis likes, is too Puerto Rican for her taste, in culture and manner of speaking. "I don't like her at all . . . because she's Dominican but she behaves like she's not, she behaves, like, Puerto Rican."

"What does that mean?" I ask, surprised to hear this critique.

"You know, some Dominicans take other cultures and make them their own," Genesis explains, suggesting that it is an act of denial of Dominicanness to adopt this other Caribbean affect. "It's good music, but I don't like it. It's too much, like trying to get to popular music. She's a nice person but I don't like her music."

Our forty-five-minute interview is informative as I learn about who Genesis is: she attended to college at APEC; she went to an English immersion school through third grade but had no formal classes in English; her parents work in government and import-export; she reads books on metaphysics and loves the writing of Paolo Coelho, a popular author in the Dominican Republic. Genesis says she doesn't want to live permanently outside of the Dominican Republic because "It's paradise," even with its many challenges. She has family whom she enjoys visiting in Miami, New Jersey, and New York. We have a good laugh at her description of Washington Heights as "El Conde." Next week she is off to visit cousins in Germany.

We shift back and forth between Spanish and English, settling into English for the second half of the interview, and when I finish my list of questions, she asks, "That's it?" I tell her that I'm sure I'll see her around. But just before I pack up, I explain that I'm especially interested race and I ask her how she identifies.

"I'm black," she says without missing a beat. "I mean for me, people tell me that I'm not black because my skin is not black and my facial features are not black because I do not have a nose like this," she says pushing down her nose, "or this mouth or whatever," she says tugging on her lips, "but I consider myself black. Indian-black . . . or African American or whatever, I mean my blood is—not *black*," she says, her intonation in that moment clarifying that she is referring to the color of ink, not the color of skin. Then she changes back to referring to the identity: "but I feel black and it's sad because people here are—can be very racist. And what they don't remember is this saying that 'everyone has black [behind] his ear.'" In the moment, I find myself struggling with my own cognitive dissonance around the blackness that Genesis claims. What I see when looking at her does not align with how she describes herself to me, using the word "black," to suggest a political alignment with blackness in the diaspora. Her skin is fairer than many of my Dominican friends and lighter than my own (after a trip to the beach)—which is to say, she is lighter in color than Martha Heredia or Zoe Saldaña but darker in color than Rita Indiana and Michelle Rodriguez. Genesis's eyes are dark in color. Her straight hair falls to her shoulders and has a reddish tint. I do not ask whether she relies on the salon to keep her hair that straight, though she tells me her natural color is more of a chocolate brown.

To illustrate Dominican racism for me, Genesis recites a story that I had heard elsewhere about a black woman who was denied entrance to a Santo Domingo club by a bouncer because she was black yet, as the story goes, he himself was a black person. "He was *charcoal* black," Genesis tells me, using English to emphasize the bouncer's location on the color spectrum. A fight broke out, there were guns, she says, and the girl was killed. While the story could be interpreted as cautionary tale about not trying to enter spaces where one is excluded because of one's race, in this instance it seems to serve as an explanation of the fact that black Dominicans themselves are upholding these racial boundaries with one another. Genesis lets the story speak for itself.

"Your parents identify themselves as black?" I ask, circling back to something she mentioned.

"Yeah—of course," she responds, telling me she is identical-looking to her father. "You see me, you see my dad," she says. "We are exactly the same." Her words in English seem to be a translation from a Spanish expression I have heard before. It is a way of describing family similarity as much as it is a way of seeing. I switch over to Spanish in an effort to better understand some of the things she is saying about Dominican logics of race and color that get obscured in English. Genesis had first used "indio" to describe her father but then says (in Spanish) that "maybe his color doesn't exist—[or] maybe 'mulato' or 'moreno' is the right word for him." Neither of these color categories would I use to describe Genesis because of how I have heard them used elsewhere for my darker-skinned peers. "But I'm not morena," she says in Spanish, affirming in the moment what I also see, "They say indio [for me]." Possibly because of her gender, Genesis is perceived as fairer than her father, or is described as such, even if the two of them do in fact share the same features and are the same color.

"My mom is white as the white clouds of the sky, she's white white white white white," she tells me in English.

"So then how can she identify as black?" I am asking her in Spanish, because her confident use of the words "white" and "black" to talk about skin color have begun to confuse me. "Because she is from a town in the Dominican Republic" is Genesis's only explanation.

"I'm the only black person in her family, I think," she says chuckling; then she corrects herself: "me and my brother. Her grandparents of her grandmother came from Spain "and blah blah blah," she says capturing the way that it is so common for Dominicans to highlight their European heritage, it is almost cliché. She says, "They were born in Moca. Although there are white people in Constanza, La Vega . . ." Her brother identifies as indio in color, she says, suggesting that to her this is a category of blackness. But his features are "mucho más fino," she tells me. Then our conversation about color ends as abruptly as it began; we got far enough in to realize that we hold completely different frameworks of understanding. I had struggled to see her racial identity in the terms in which she understood it and this felt a bit awkward.

From the porous borders of public and private spaces, from streets to malls, from that which is deemed authentic to that which is deemed inauthentic, from the racial consciousness of afrodominicanas to that of "white" dominicanas—I aim to shed light on the ambiguities of Dominicanness within the Dominican Republic and the social structures in place necessary to produce and maintain the identity of la dominicana. In the chapter that follows, I consider a series of affective moments in the lives of the women I have interviewed—and in my own instructive experiences navigating Santo Domingo—that teach them about race and gender.

La Plaza and El Mall

At night, the streets in the Colonial Zone are still bustling with tourists and locals out enjoying the warm breezes of Santo Domingo at this hour. There is a calm. On this night, Clara pushes her cart towards the plaza. She is selling café, hot ginger tea, and slices of sweet cornmeal arepa with just a few raisins scattered in it. I press the soft warm ridges of the thin plastic cup between my fingers, just firmly enough to hold it without dropping it but not so tight as to bend it and spill the steaming liquid, and I take a sip.

On some weekend nights, Clara brings her granddaughter, a chubby eight-year-old girl with fair skin like her grandmother, round cheeks, and two thick braids down her back. She races around the shopping cart from which her grandmother sells late-night snacks. The child runs across the plaza with friends, and then sometimes back to the shopping cart, lacing her fingers in between the metal mesh, as Clara pumps hot liquid out of the large thermoses that hang off its sides. One pump, then two, fills my cup to the brim with syrupy tea that makes my fingers sticky as it cools enough to drink. This is how I remember Santo Domingo. And the murmur of people wandering in the plaza.

"How many?" Clara asks us, as my friends and I calculate the number of coins we have between us or whether one of us will break a bill to cover it all. Four teas, and we add a slice of arepa to share: "Keep the change." Each year, I go back and find Clara there, and the look of recognition on her face when I stroll up becomes as familiar as the sweetness of her ginger tea. The taste of our night complete, my friends and I wander on cobblestone streets and brick plazas. We find a bench to sit on and watch as people pass; we wait to see familiar faces of those out to enjoy the evening breeze and to rest in the shadows. The frustrations of the day are lost in the darkness and in plastic cups of beer that offer some relief from the heat. A toddler screeches under the yellow light of Catedral Isabel Católica, chasing after his ball beneath the shadow of the statue of Cristobal Colón. Every night we sit and drink right beneath the nose of empire and colonization.

In contrast to this outdoor public space, numerous malls fill the city, popular for their food courts with American chain restaurants and movie theaters showing American films. They are packed with families on outings and teenagers hanging out. It was a common occurrence in my life in Santo Domingo that I went to the mall. On any given day it was an opportunity to leave my apartment, where the power and water were irregular, and to sit in an air-conditioned public space. Sometimes I would take along one of the kids in my neighborhood who was bored and stuck at home. If they had already been to a new mall, they would go with me to show me around and enjoy an ice cream or some pizza. We would get there by guagua, through loud and dusty traffic, crammed in with many other bodies, to arrive at the elegant air-conditioned new facility.

When the luxurious, six-story Blue Mall opened right down the street from Acropolis Mall along Avenida Winston Churchill, like everyone else I went to investigate. Blue Mall had many of the same stores, they were just bigger, newer, and fancier. On any given afternoon, you could find the enormous food court filled with white Dominicans and foreigners like myself, and their children and their nannies dressed in uniforms. Clearing trays and emptying trash cans in the brightly lit food court are workers, visibly darker in color than those whom they serve. One can easily spend eight dollars on lunch at one of these malls, knowing full well that your neighbor budgets only twelve dollars a week to feed her whole family. From the balcony of Blue Mall there is a view of the growing city of Santo Domingo with all of its new *torres* (apartment towers) of blue glass and white concrete: canvas pulled taut across their railings makes them appear like ships ready to set sail. At Blue Mall, sometimes they open up the wide doors on the first floor to drive in a Lamborghini to display next to the Cartier watch store. There are shops inside that I do not enter, with price tags I am afraid to glance at, on items that I hesitate to touch. I feel underdressed there in my sweaty and sun-bleached cotton clothes and well-worn hiking sandals. Youthful salespeople sitting in each store look bored and hungry. They are all white upper-class Dominican youth who look much like Spanish teenagers: boys with polo shirts, skinny jeans, and shaggy tousled hair, sitting in quiet, brightly lit shops, heads bent over their BlackBerries.

As I exit Blue Mall, I walk past a large fountain spewing water nonstop and wonder whether a supreme irony is lost on these architects—each day, most of the city's population struggles to get water in their homes. Where I live just two miles away, we gather water in barrels in our bathrooms for the times when the city turns it off; while for those who live in rural communities on the small island, spaces unrecognized on maps, there has never been running water. I wonder if the fountains are guarded 24/7 or if kids I see on that block—Haitian and Dominican children washing windshields in traffic day in and day out—would be able to dip in that same water for a refreshing break or use it to wipe some of the dust off of their faces in the unforgiving midday sun. Like so many other details in the landscape of Santo Domingo, the shiny new fountain is a contradiction, a visual reminder of the uneven development of the city, like the shiny new cars I sometimes spot parked on the street in Barrio Chino beside beat-up pickup trucks—held together with rope and ingenuity—that spew black smoke. These daily disparities always remind me of a young medical student from the working-class neighborhood where I lived in Santo Domingo who fought her way to study medicine in Spain: "So I can have a BMW," she told me.

When a beat-up guagua drops me right in front of the Acropolis Mall, the most upscale mall that I knew of in the city at the time, I twist and clamber out of my seat. I recall that this mall is the third that has opened since I began living in Santo Domingo. It is a good place to steal away to a movie, but a ticket would be equivalent to American prices. I have entered Acropolis in order to pay a cell phone bill and get out of the heat, the noise, the crush of *la calle*. Acropolis Mall is shaped like a ship—and it feels as if I have boarded a cruise ship. It boasts Hooters, TGI Friday's, Benetton, Haagen-Dazs, and a two-level Zara. I have mostly seen its stores empty, but Zara is packed this Friday afternoon. The people shopping there are kids from the American school and upper-class families, buying clothes for the fall season, though there is no fall in Santo Domingo.

I step into the air-conditioned mall and head to the new food court. Unable to find something I want to eat at the Sbarro's, Wendy's, or Domino's, all familiar chain restaurants with Dominicanized menus, I go to the Dominican pizza place that sells *pasteles*. As I stand with food tray in hand, I find myself invited to share a table with a kind stranger who has singled me out for company. She waves me over, even though there are many empty tables around her. A fair-skinned woman maybe in her fifties, she says she is happy to chat while I eat, making small talk with me in English. She tells me all about why she is at the mall that day and offers her own unsolicited sociological study of the Dominican Republic. She is from Puerto Rico, she tells me.

"You aren't from here, are you? Are you Brazilian?" she asks. It is a question I have been asked elsewhere in Latin America, too, reflecting a racial imaginary of who is black in Latin America. The woman tells me all about why her daughter is here to study medicine, and the exams she will have to take later. The school that she is at—IberoAmerican, I think it was—is a private school. Then, she begins to tell me about how much she dislikes the Dominican Republic and lists her own observations about the problems with this place that I have been calling home, and why it is different from her beloved Puerto Rico. At the moment of our meeting, I had no point of comparison. They have big malls in Puerto Rico, too, she tells me. "But they also have police that you can call if there is a problem," she says. "And the men aren't so chauvinistic, and the traffic isn't so bad, and everything isn't so expensive . . . and the people aren't so racist as here in the Dominican Republic."

For a moment, I start to believe her because I have heard this many times from Dominicans and non-Dominicans alike: "Somos racistas [We're racists]," I am told matter-of-factly over and over again by Dominican activist friends in Santo Domingo. The assertion can at times be a welcome contrast to US "colorblindness," under which Americans of all backgrounds feel comfortable prefacing a generalized statement about a racialized group or an overtly racist sentiment with "I'm not racist but . . ." Meanwhile, Dominicans regularly declare that they aren't *as* racist as Cubans or North Americans. Puerto Ricans aren't as racist as North Americans either, this stranger assures me; though she seems to do so in order to reassure herself. But by then I have begun to feel angry about her criticisms of my newly adopted home, defensive and protective of this place that has so generously taken me in. Even when it mistreats me, I feel protective of its shortcomings and the problems I have seen that are part of life in Santo Domingo.

Patricia: Dominican German Feminism

"Did you learn more about mulata identity there or here?" I ask twenty-six-year-old Patricia, trying to draw out ideas about race that she had formed in the Dominican Republic and compare them to those she had developed while studying abroad in Europe for several years. I am audiorecording the interview in her second-floor apartment in the neighborhood of Bella Vista. We have located ourselves in her bedroom, away from wide-open balcony wrapping around her living room, to avoid some of the background noise. Since we met through a mutual friend in 2010, Patricia and I have become friends, and I have witnessed her relationship to her Dominican identity shift over the years that I have known her. I decide to finally interview her while I am in Santo Domingo for several weeks in 2014 and staying with her. Our conversation that day takes place primarily in English but we move back and forth.

Patricia returned to the Dominican Republic after completing university in Germany because, she told me, she was afraid of heading into adulthood. She had assimilated into German culture while living abroad and carried back with her to her family and friends in the Dominican Republic an outlook on life informed by her experiences in Europe over the previous seven years. Patricia is completely fluent in English and German; her stepfather is German. She explains her own cultural difference: "It already started here but I guess that it went deeper when I moved to Germany. That's where I was more interested in all of my identities and all that stuff. But I'd say it has to do with my age; I was eighteen when I left, so I was pretty young and that's kinda a phase where you get to know yourself better, you know, early twenties."

Patricia's education abroad is not unusual for Dominicans; however, out of my pool of interviewees, she may have had the most class and color privilege. Her color allowed her a particular level of assimilation abroad, even as she experienced being seen as the Other while in Europe, thus shaping her perspective and analysis of Dominican identity. "At the beginning it was a process, " she explains. "I was a foreigner, like anyone else. We were all foreigners, because who was learning German? All foreigners. It was in college that I actually had a German social circle. But ever since, it's just been like I'm one of them." Indeed, when I introduce Patricia to a German colleague of mine visiting Santo Domingo, he is shocked to learn that she is Dominican. She did not fit his conception of Dominican women, he told me, and she could easily pass as German because she has no detectable accent in her German. She is phenotypically white, one might say, with wavy brown hair.

"How do you feel you compare to the social construction of what it means to be a Dominican woman?" I asked Patricia. "Like, how do you feel like you fit? This is one of the things I am wrestling with in my research project. The stereotypes and then people's realities."

"Yeah, me too. Not in the project but in real life," she responds. "Well, it's very complex for me because when it comes to race, I feel very Dominican. I, like, I become a fan of finding out all of my identities and everything. And not from a purist perspective but acknowledging all the different identities that make me who I am." Patricia references the common practice in Dominican families of carefully tracing their family lineage in ways that highlight their European ancestry, as a point of pride. Other interviewees and friends have mentioned this to me as well. Afro-descendant relatives, on the other hand, are unmentioned or erased in these moments. Patricia's family on her father's side is from northern Spain.

"And, um, if we want to be simplistic about it they're just Spanish. All of them Spaniards, end of story. But even then, as we were talking about earlier, I always felt there was something else other than that and it turns out that there is part of the family, a Jewish part of the Spanish family. So there's that." She seemed to say this pointedly, excited to share this new information with me because she knows of my own Jewish heritage.

"Then, from the Dominican side of the family, which is my mom, I know that my grandmother's mother . . . had French family and African family, because they were from the Haitian side. So she was much darker but she had French grandparents or something, so I am assuming that you had the whole racial mix with the slaves and the Europeans and everything. Then my grandfather has a Spanish or Italian last name, so we assume that the family either came from Spain, Italy, or Portugal. So all of that got combined into *this*." She gestures to herself, her body, and she laughs. Patricia is eager to narrate for me this understanding of herself and her racial identity. In this and other contexts she has referred to herself as mulata, an identity shaped by the reality of her mixed racial heritage and her relationship to whiteness abroad. This identity doesn't translate effectively to the Afro-Dominican spaces I have inhabited. Yet, it is her truth. As critical mixed-race studies scholar Reginald Daniel has suggested, "For multiracial people, you live your racial narrative by creating it. . . . There is an element of fictionalizing to it, but it's not falseness. It is choosing the proportions and the proper fit of the various ethnic elements one possesses."[1] For Patricia, because of the racial ambiguity she has experienced, it is also this process of coming to know and then defining herself against the ways that others have read her racial identity and defined her.

All of the things that Patricia shares with me throughout our interview highlight how her color, gender, and transnational experience shape her everyday understanding of her Dominican identity. Aspects and details continue to shift over time. Like Michelle Ricardo, in chapter 2, I have gotten to know Patricia at the point of her return to the Dominican Republic, when she is negotiating her own home country as a transnational subject and as she comes understand her own identity in relation to home. After meeting both Michelle and Patricia in very separate circles in 2010, and finding each had returned home with newly formed feminist politics, I connected the two of them. Because of class differences, their social circles may otherwise never have intersected yet they became close friends—something they have each described to me as "lifesaving." Their friendship helped them survive the transition back to Santo Domingo and growing into adulthood after having come to see themselves and the world in new ways—ways that friends who had not left Santo Domingo could not.

"It's been a growing up journey, coming back. What I had imagined was that it would be difficult to adapt socially and I will do my thing and work like a grown up and be able to go to the beach on Sunday. But then it hit me . . . so many privileges I have had in Europe as a woman and they were gone in a minute. No more going out at night alone, no more walking down the street, no more riding my bicycle everywhere. [In Santo Domingo] I had to get a car. I absolutely despise driving [although] it was also cool because it gave me this other sense of independence but still I absolutely feel the loss of certain rights, or . . . things I took for granted. And that was a big bummer. You get used to it and that was the worst part that you actually get used to living like a little slave inside your four pretty walls. And then you try to fake it by moving on your own . . . and then you're happy you have your own place but economically it's a disaster. So you work and you work and you work but you don't really have much out of it, so you become this work slave. Then what? That's it. Then that's all you do. I understand now why the cultural offering is so limited, everything is so limited. Going out there are barely activities."

Patricia's complaint is that even though she is working to live in the city, it is hard to enjoy going out when prices are so high and one cannot afford much more than inexpensive restaurant meals. The demands of capitalism have her discouraged: "You have to work so much to maintain a level, and you're really tired. Then you don't want to go out. All you want to do is go to sleep." Still, I find myself uncomfortable with her use of the word "slave" in her description of the economic pressures on middle-class Dominicans in a neoliberal economy, as it seems dismissive of the history of chattel slavery on the island and disregards some of the grueling working conditions that many Dominicans experience today. Moreover, after having enjoyed so many film festivals, book fairs, and theater festivals while living in Santo Domingo I am skeptical of the idea that cultural offerings do not exist. I am sympathetic, however, to her frustration with the range in quality of local arts programming that can make going out hit or miss, but I know that there are many arts and social spaces she does not enter because of her class background and social network. Patricia's close friends in Santo Domingo generally relate to her worldview, based in transnational perspective on life on the island and a sense of the world beyond it. She shares an apartment with her friend from high school, a Venezuelan-Dominican who returned to Santo Domingo after studying in Mexico.

"Most of my friends did master's programs abroad, most went to Spain or the US and then came back. But they never left to live in another country," she says. Likewise, Patricia came home and worked to make a life on the island. She worked at the Dominican embassy, then taught at a private school, then nannied, and then taught behavioral psychology to families, and finally has been working with people with disabilities: "My experience in Santo Domingo . . . is that it has been a lot of change in a short period of time."

"What are things that you have seen since you have been back?" I ask.

"I see a lot of new buildings and no planning whatsoever. So it's a lot more chaotic. I feel like the city has become this horrible big city in a small city. The city's not so big, if you compare it to other places, but it's this busy, busy place . . . I wanna move to the countryside!"

I have heard Patricia referring to Germany as home so often that I was not entirely surprised when ultimately she decided to move back there: "I've always felt that that's my home. It's more of a gut feeling, so that's home for me. . . . Now after four years here—five years here, and trying and fighting the system and everything, I went back and I was like, 'Oh my god, wait a second,' I can also have this? So why, why keep dealing with that." Like her family and friends in the Dominican Republic, I eventually watch her life in Germany play out in pictures on social media.

"What are the things you've been fighting since you came back [to the Dominican Republic]?"

"My liberties, expression, finding and meeting people. I learned how to portray myself, and all the change, and going through depression. It was really cool for me that it happened here and I got to be close to my family again, and I am aware that grandmas don't last forever. . . . Now I am back to 'So what about me?' I've always thought I wanted to have a family at some point and when I think about that I think, 'Yeah, do I want to give this to my kids?' If I ever have kids, and who am I gonna have kids with? Because no, I'm not changing my life. I cannot imagine having to fight over basic stuff with a partner, specifically gender stuff, like how to raise a boy or a girl. Because what I see is, I see a lot of very smart independent women getting married and then having to compromise a lot of their belief for their husbands or for their families. I am lucky enough to have a family who is very accepting of who I am—after a lot of fights."

"So you haven't encountered any non-sexist men [in the DR]?" I ask.

"No, no, believe me I've tried. Dating here has been a joyride." She says in English, perhaps meaning "roller-coaster." She says, "It has been really interesting from one sexist level to the next. I'm still open, but I know what I'm up against." What Patricia is up against, as she and other Dominican women have explained to me, is a dominant culture of patriarchal sexism, machismo, and homophobia that reinforces gendered social hierarchies in overt and covert ways. Women learn to navigate it daily, and sometimes, when they can, they leave the country in order to distance themselves from it.

Returning to Santo Domingo after university, Patricia arrived at several conclusions about the structure of the society she entered back into in terms of race and gender and how it limits her opportunities for her own identity and construction of self: "It's definitely not the life that I want. Most certainly not. And I almost convinced myself that no matter where I went this was going to be my life and now, I was like, no wait a second. No it's not. There is something else. And I can actually have a different life and I can be in a place where I can just ride my bicycle and meet my friends anytime I want and ride the bus at night . . . by myself, and you know, without having to be so afraid. It's not that . . . it doesn't end. Women, we're always managing ourselves within this concept of possible violence all the time. That doesn't change the core. Here or in Germany, I will watch out when I go out at night, who I'm with, who's around me . . . so that doesn't change. But there is more room, to breathe, I guess."

"And then the men, oh my god." Patricia and I have often had discussions about Dominican masculinity and her challenges navigating it in the dating scene. She frequently found herself initiating relationships with foreigners who were visiting the island rather than Dominican men. When she got serious with Dominican men, she explained to me, she bumped up against aspects of Dominican masculinity in which they were invested—everything from pushing for unprotected sex, to being unable to share their feelings, to fragile masculinity—things she says she could not tolerate. German men "are open to each other. Receptive to the love that they give and receive within the friendship. And you don't see men doing that here—'That's gay, so gay,'" she says, mimicking how homophobic discourse discourages Dominican men's emotional attachments to one another.

"So much anxiety about gayness," I say, reacting to my friend's comment, while thinking about the cultural shifts I have witnessed over the last decade in how Dominicans talk about LGBTQ+ identities and the spaces queer people inhabit.

"You don't have that there, I mean you do, but not to the same degree." Patricia says about men's fear of showing emotion. She joins me in thinking about gender crossculturally in order to better see the present context. Her transnational experience in Europe shapes her critique and her epistemic knowledge of the nuanced ways that gender is informed by culture. Patricia has also studied gender studies in and out of the classroom and we have swapped references and resources, in both Spanish and English. She is well informed about the cultural legacies of each of the countries she has called home, and the impact of colonialism on broader perceptions of the Dominican Republic. Like some of my other Dominican friends, she reads Michel Foucault and Judith Butler for pleasure. PDFs of their work in Spanish circulate online.

"I think it's interesting though, how 'they' portray us, and by 'they' I mean specifically Europeans when they come here. And if they are really educated and they are . . . self-reflective, they still have this Eurocentrism within them, right? And it's so difficult for them to get away from that and even see that they are being that way. So they start talking about us in ways like, 'If you did this or you did that you could do so much better.' And I'm like, 'But you're not here. What are you talking about?' I could also go to Germany and tell them if you would get the stick out of your ass and be more open emotionally to people then you would be happier people but I don't go and say that to them because that's just the way that their culture works. And that's perfectly fine." In these moments, Patricia draws on firsthand knowledge of Dominican society and German culture and experiences a feeling of insider-outsider-ness that has never seemed to leave her in the years I have known her. On the one hand, she finds herself defending her own place of origin from the critique of foreigners, on the other she has chosen to live outside of the Dominican Republic for some of the very things that others criticize. From each vantage point, she can better see the strengths and weaknesses of the cultures of which she is a part. She recognizes how closed Germans can be to foreigners initially and that this can result in their leading very lonely lives. In contrast, Dominicans value being with people and family, she explains, though it isn't something that Dominicans then go tell Germans that they ought to value.

Patricia also articulates in our conversation the ways that Dominicans are unable to say "no" to people. They put pressure on one another to maintain the social contract, to borrow money, to fulfill their needs and desires. Unlike in Germany, Patricia explains, Dominicans see no problem with always dropping by your house without any sense of intrusion. "Mix that with sexism and see what you get," she says. Her observation corroborates my own experiences of family dynamics in the Dominican Republic and particularly the ways that men pressure women and girls.

"So, what do you think people should know about Dominican women in Santo Domingo?" I ask Patricia, seeking her insights as a collaborator in this research and contributor to the project I have been developing over the years I have known her.

"*Is* there a Dominican woman?" Patricia asks. In her world, among many more white friends who attended private schools, she has experienced a different type of policing of her performance of gender and femininity defined by whiteness and class privilege.

"Do you get a lot of comments on skin color?" I ask.

"Well, the thing is that when I go to the beach my color doesn't change that much. But people automatically assume that I have money, because I am lighter skinned. Or they directly assume that I'm white. I always have so much fun explaining to people that I'm not white or *why* I'm not white. And what the concept of 'mulatto' is or mixed race or something. So that's really funny. It depends more on their level of education, but even then it's funny. When I tell my Spanish friend, she doesn't want to recognize that it's true." Patricia views the situation as humorous, irrational even, finding that others cannot see on her body a racial narrative she knows to be true. Her mixed racial heritage is not legible to others so she must inform them about it. Still, what is at stake for her in terms of her claims on a mulatto identity are quite different from Dominican women who are visibly mixed race of African descent.

Patricia and I have had several conversations about instances in her life abroad in which she realized that people were identifying her race differently than she identified in the Dominican Republic. I have not pushed her further on how she understands her own nonwhite status in relation to the Afro-Dominican women she has met through me. I am aware of only one friend in her social circle who is a dark-skinned dominicana, the friend who introduced us, suggesting that she has limited exposure to the ideas and experiences of afrodominicanas. Social media images also bely the whiteness of her social networks and community, made up of fair-skinned Dominicans and German friends abroad, and it is in this space too that her racial identity and Dominican identity is both produced and contextualized. Like so many Dominicans, Patricia's Dominicanness can exist at arm's length from blackness, even though she is inclined to lay claim to her Afro-Dominican racial heritage.

Who Is Afrodominicana?

My interview with theater actress Robelitza Pérez captured an experience *not* of being marked by an ambiguous Otherness because of skin color but of being seen as decidedly black abroad—and decidedly Dominican within a Spanish racial hierarchy. The color of her skin meant that Robelitza experienced overt racism in Europe. I decided to interview her about her role in Teatro Maleducadas' 2013 production of *La Casa de Bernarda Alba*, which I discuss in-depth in chapter 5. We had not met before, but we get to know each other over a simple breakfast of *mangú* and *un café* one morning in the cafeteria section of Supermercado Nacional on Churchill, where she buys me breakfast.[2]

"I studied in Spain, in Madrid for nine months," Robelitza tells me. But when I ask her how the experience was, she laughs nervously. She seems eager to share while also reaching for the words to articulate it, as if she has not spoken about it often. "Spain, I think, is the country with the second most Dominican immigrants. Although I went under special conditions as a student, I felt that I was very, very marked by the situation of . . . ¿cómo decirlo [how do I explain it]? of Dominicans, not only los *negros*-negros, but of [all] Dominicans." Robelitza reinforces the dividing line between her and the "*black*-black" Dominicans who have immigrated to Spain. Due to her privilege as a student abroad, she had thought she might not be seen in the same racial terms as other Dominican immigrants but she could not exempt herself from racist social structures in Europe. She explains: "There was a very white girl, very tall, very *lacia*—with fine hair—she said at one point . . . about the computer software that was not working, '¿No funciona o es que soy *negra?* [Is this not working or is it that I am black?]' She said it and I was there and *la única negra era yo* [the only black was me]. For me this was like, she didn't do it with bad intentions, they are like questions that were already in the language—it was not in the heart, but in the language, in the culture, it's like you say here *'ya, todo el negro e' Haitiano* [all blacks are Haitians]'—it's not that you have bad intentions or are a bad person but it becomes part of your culture, like, if you are black you are a brute, that was what she meant. *'¿El gestor no funciona o es que soy negra?'* So, that's something I am never going to forget because, you know, like, there I am in a place with so many freedoms but in reality there is this whole perception associated with my skin color of ignorance and brutality."

While she seemed to have come to some understanding of how anti-blackness was part of everyday discourse in Spain, it didn't sting any less. In another experience she wanted to share with me, Robelitza described an interaction with the "white woman with straight hair," who coordinated her degree, and how she came to understand the way that woman saw her through a racist and essentializing lens: "I have always had my hair just like I have it now. Not so *rizado* [curly] but my normal hair . . . and," Robelitza laughs as if to shake off the discomfort, "[the woman] says, 'I like your wild hair.'" Laughing much harder then, at the horror of this when it comes out of her mouth, she says the woman used the word *"salvaje* to say that hair like . . . natural hair is wild [or savage]." Robelitza's disbelief stems from the realization that she is seen in ways that she does not see herself and that she cannot control. I understood quite well, having had just such an experience with a Spaniard in Texas; the comment stung for me as well.

In the first fifteen minutes of our conversation, Robelitza shared with me many examples of anti-blackness that she experienced in her nine months abroad and each sent her a very clear message about how she was perceived as a black woman. She says, "There are people, too, white people, who treat black people with privilege, to make amends," but this is also *feo* [disgusting], she says, because it is another form of differential treatment. Our conversation allowed me to affirm what she had experienced, and we connected quickly over a mutual understanding of anti-black racism in its many forms.

Robelitza also described an experience in the theater group she joined while in Spain. She tells me, "I was not Dominican to them because the perception that they had of Dominicans is something else, which I understood later. [T]hey told me that I was Colombian, that I was Venezuelan, but not Dominican, because they are not used to meeting a Dominican woman in that context, you understand? *Entonces, nada."* She laughs. The awkward transition signifies for me an underlying shame in being cast in such a light. What is unarticulated are the negative stereotypes that her Spanish classmates held about Dominican women, and Afro-Latin American immigrants more broadly who are perceived as sex workers. It was a perception so deeply held that they told Robelitza she was not Dominican because *they* did not see her as such. They felt empowered to decide for her on their terms how she should see herself—that she should transform her presumably malleable identity into something else—in order that they be able to maintain their racist belief system intact. How she was viewed by others as a Dominican in Spain was relational to the bodies and narratives about other women from Latin America, and so she see/sawed in the social hierarchy, balanced in contrast to the Colombians and Venezuelans her colleagues had known. They could not make sense of her darker skin color or who she was as a Dominican so she would see/saw in their vision of her until they could let go of what they initially saw, even if only for a short time. She has no interest in living abroad again, Robelitza tells me.

Of course, it has gotten easier not to look for answers abroad. "In the past, there was less technology through which *el globalización* arrived," twenty-one year old Lisette tells me.[3] She says her younger brother has even more influences from the United States than she did: Nickelodeon, The Jonas brothers, skinny jeans, and the dance moves of US rappers.[4] "When I was in New York in December, which was the last time I went there," Lisette says, "I watched videos with my cousin . . . and when I came back here, I was surprised to see these boys doing the same things. ¡*Ven acá* [Come on now]! That's what I saw them doing there."

Yessica y Ambar: Different *Razas*

I meet Yessica at her house, around the corner from where I lived when I first moved to Santo Domingo. Having known Yessica's family for a few years, I am aware that her extended family members are occasionally startled by the "mature" manner in which she chooses to dress, but her parents seem to support and encourage it. I have seen her at ages sixteen, seventeen, and eighteen dressed in tight jeans with bare midriffs, plunging necklines, and tight dresses that are so short they inadvertently "ride up." I remember when she got her bellybutton pierced at eighteen. Her typical choice of attire starkly contrasts with what the majority of the young women I interviewed were wearing (skinny jeans and T-shirts, with sandals) so I was eager to talk with her. She agreed to do the interview with me because we had known each other for some time. Yessica later suggested that her friend Ambar, whom she had recently introduced me to, might also be interested in being part of the conversation. We sit in the living room area of Yessica's home, on the sofa and chairs squeezed in beside a large wooden coffee table. Yessica has her hair up, wrapped around her head with a net cap over it that is held in place with several bobby pins. This temporary styling will keep her hair straight until she takes it down to go out. Her long, thick hair requires weekly trips to the salon in order to keep it straight the way she likes it, as well as a monthly chemical treatment (which sometimes takes place in her backyard). On the day of our interview, she is wearing jeans and a blue T-shirt covered in silver studs. In her casual dress, she does not look particularly feminine, reminding me of the considerable effort she puts into her public presentation.

Ambar calls Yessica a bit after our conversation is under way to let her know that she is on her way over to join us. She shows up complaining that her hair has turned out badly after her mother straightened it at home. Yessica brings Ambar into the conversation explaining to me that she was an example of someone who is "clarita," or light in color, almost white. Eighteen-year-old Yessica, in contrast, is dark in color. In Dominican society, this difference alone separates the two young women and, among other things, shapes their perceptions of the world in which they live. Their mothers were childhood friends and they are now neighborhood friends in Los Jardines del Norte. The neighborhood is just north of Avenida de la Kennedy, across from the Rica juice and milk factory. The two friends are my youngest interviewees.

At nineteen, Ambar is more talkative and appears more self-assured than Yessica. She is studying business administration at la UASD. As soon as Ambar joins us, the tenor of the conversation shifts. Ambar is not nervous about answering my questions and quickly feels at ease, while Yessica appears uncomfortable being recorded and remains aware of my little red digital voice recorder up until nearly the end of our conversation. She even shoos her parents out of the room at one point, telling them that we are recording. Since neither of the two young women immediately understand what I mean when I use the word *estereotipo* (stereotype), I try to explain. After I reformulate my question, I find they have much to say on the topic.

The teens are armed with as clear a sense of what it means to be a Dominican woman as they have of what an "American" signifies to them—a category that they do not think I fit well. Most people I meet in the Dominican Republic are surprised when I tell them I am American because I do not look like what they think (with their narrative eye) Americans look like. I say as much to Ambar and Yessica, and Yessica exclaims in agreement. According to Ambar, "Ameri*cana*-Americana," means a blonde female, making clear that "American" is understood to be white.

"There are Americano-morenos, but . . . ," Ambar drifts off.

"Of course," Yessica jumps in, "the President!" she says, referring to Barack Obama.

Yessica is earning a degree in tourism from Universidad Pedro Henrique Ureña, known as UNPHU. She tells me she would like to work in resort hotels in Bávaro or Samaná, where they pay in dollars and tourism is more developed than in the capital. She hopes to have a job working at the front desk. In her field of study, what she wears and how she presents herself has significant consequences. Undoubtedly, she constructs a femininity that responds to social beliefs about her dark color that would assume her sexual availability, particularly in the field of tourism.

Yessica says her mother helps her with her style. "There are no ugly women, only unkempt women," Yessica advises. I learn that she reads magazines such as *Mujer Única* and *Cosmopolitan* (in Spanish) at the salon each week. Although she compliments me on my natural hairstyle, she says that her own hair has curls that are too tiny, what is referred to as "pelo malo," she explains. Straightening her type of hair, she tells me, is "*obligaó* [required]." "For me, the mujer dominicana is very cheerful. . . . Physically, they are more like this, morenita of my color, with *pelo crespo* [kinky hair]. . . . I am very typical, very cheerful," Yessica adds. She identifies herself as a "typical" Dominican woman, in both her physical appearance and personality.

Ambar further complicates my inherently essentializing question: "I can't identify a Dominican woman by her style of clothes, because this is global. . . . One can copy what people are wearing in New York. You can only identify a Dominican woman by her way of life in *la RD*." Thus, she identifies directly the ways that a global popular culture influences Dominican youth and that what they are participating in is, in fact, a transnational mainstream culture. She reflexively points to New York City, because indeed it is common for Dominican styles to come straight from that central location in the Dominican diaspora. People in the Dominican Republic who are unfamiliar with the geography of North America commonly refer to the United States as "New York"—for generations that was where their relatives lived abroad.

"But you can identify them by their physical appearance too, right?" Yessica asks her friend, regarding Dominican women. She is correct that there is far more to the cultural construction of the Dominican woman than style or way of life. There is the matter of physical appearance and what Dominicans believe a Dominican woman should look like. "I think that the Dominican woman always has a lot of everything . . . a lot of ass, a lot of tits," said Yessica. Having "a lot" of these physical features is generally deemed most desirable and typically associated with Blackness.

"Straightened hair, a little brusque," Ambar added. "I identify with the mujer dominicana who picks the first fight, tries to get everything she wants. When she has it she wants to castrate everyone . . . when she has it all, she wants to escape." Ambar describes a particular type of *tigueraje*, or Dominican street smarts or aggressiveness that although attributed to Dominican men is recognizable in Dominican women as well.[5] Her statement suggests that while there are many ways to be a Dominican woman, this aggressiveness is one of the particularly recognizable personality attributes. Yessica says, "Before, too, it was like, they had been . . . the mujer dominicana identified more as being the *ama de casa* [homemaker]. I don't know . . . she always had to be. The husband always worked. So, it's been at least ten years since the [Dominican] woman has developed herself as an educated person." Yessica's measurement of a decade is a long time for an eighteen-year-old, suggesting that she is aware of the changes in gendered expectations for Dominican women during her lifetime.

"It's more than that," Ambar jumps in. "It's since the Mirabal sisters fought Trujillo to make him recognize the value of women and the rights that women have. You know, everything changed. Now women have a voice, and vote, now women can rise above men." Ambar uses a common example of the Mirabal sisters to explain the rights that women have gained in the Dominican Republic. Her narrative of gender activism, while oversimplified, represents a common explanation of women's "freedom" in Dominican society. Her ideas about the freedom of women also reflect her own privileges and access as a young, light-skinned, well-educated, working-class Dominican woman.

When Ambar confidently shares her views about race and gender, they echo underlying rhetoric regarding social identity constructs pervasive in many circles in the Dominican Republic, both educated and undereducated. Her racial privilege reveals itself: "There are women who are tough, there are women who are weak," Ambar explains matter-of-factly. "This also depends on race." In the Dominican Republic, the meaning of the term *raza*, which typically translates into English as "race," is further blurred by our conversation when Ambar goes on to describe these tough women, while connecting the term *raza* with *rústica* and yet another term. She says, "Hay una raza rústica, como fuerte—moyeta, fuerte . . . ," meaning there is a less refined race of people. She uses the term *fuerte* to mean "strong" but by adding the term *moyeta* she is also referring to color. Moyeta is a Dominican term that describes a woman who is both brawny and morena, or dark brown in color. I had not heard the term before this conversation. Yessica's mother later explains to me that there is no such thing as a white woman who is moyeta. With this language, Ambar was differentiating herself from her friend.

With Yessica and me, Ambar is outspoken with her opinions about racialized difference—and open about the logic behind her opinions. She states assuredly, "There are women that can plant to harvest, drive a crane, that are a race that is strong and rough. The others are women who are *una raza empresarial* [an entrepreneurial race], they don't know how to cook dinner, they only know their mathematics or physics. There are many kinds of women." Her logic reveals a racial bias that perhaps confirms her own trajectory in getting a business degree. "There are women who are Dominican and they don't have the same strength, or structure of their body. I think that Yessica is stronger than I am," Ambar tells me. Her delineation between herself and Yessica points to their difference in color, and perhaps other aspects of their phenotype, even as the two women are around the same age and same size.

"Ay no," says Yessica emphatically. It becomes clear that being a female and a race apart that is stronger and tougher—"fuerte y áspera," as Ambar describes it—is in no way a compliment. Ambar's description undermines the femininity that Yessica works daily to produce, through her femme and sexually provocative clothing and trips to the salon to straighten her hair and polish her nails.

"Why?" I ask Ambar about what she has said about her friend.

"*Porque sí* [Because yes]. She is stronger than me—you don't think so?" She turns to ask Yessica.

"It's because I eat a lot, and she doesn't eat meat," Yessica tries to explain, attempting to distance herself from this categorization; she seems to laugh off some embarrassment. There is something uncomfortable about Ambar's assertion regarding the difference between the two young women, one light and one dark: "For example, there are Dominican women who play basketball. Domini*cana*-Dominicana, therefore these are games of *gente rustica* [unrefined people] . . . I am much weaker, she isn't; she is much stronger. It could be because of nutrition but also it's also a hardiness they have . . . it's because they are strong women—¿*Tú me entiendes*? [You get me?]—that they can do that." Ambar's reference to the unrefined is clearly tied to color in this instance. And her use of "they" suggests that she sees Afro-Dominican women as Other. When she speaks about color and the difference between herself and her friend, her use of the term *raza* seems to reflect a true slippage in meaning. It cannot convey the same meaning of the term "race" as it is understood in the United States. I have heard the word *raza* used in referring to different breeds of dogs. The difference that Ambar describes, an investment in meaning that is signified by color, is a window into the ways that color categorizes Dominican women differently and consequently shapes their lives. It is also a very uncomfortable ethnographic moment in which one childhood friend articulates in front of another the beliefs she holds which, even if she has not parsed them out entirely, denigrate blackness.

Ambar goes on to further explain this difference to me: "I say that by race there is differentiation . . . the style of being, the strength, or what they believe in, because it also depends on upbringing." Ambar's explanation, as she tries to sort out the differences between two groups that she sees as innately dissimilar, winds its way from a nature to nurture argument. As is the case with race, there is no clear line and yet she is in that moment certain that a fundamental difference does exist. In the very moment of articulating their identities, Ambar and Yessica establish themselves in juxtaposition to one another just as Hazel Carby has argued in her close engagement with the work of Stuart Hall: "the racialized self is invented in the process of an encounter, produced, in other words, as a subject dialogically constituted in and through its relation to an other or others."[6] It is in this encounter, Hall reminds us, that unequal power dynamics are established.

Throughout our conversation, Yessica and Ambar make an effort to point to specific physical markers of Dominican women, possibly for my benefit, as they pick up on my steering the conversation in that direction. At the same time, their precise observations about phenotype and demonstrated awareness of the significance of body type, hair type, and color all exist within a larger framework of understanding and visual discourse that I attempted to tease out. After presenting Yessica with the set of four pictures of transnationally recognized Dominican women that I am using in my study, I ask her the same research questions: "Which are the most dominicana from this group?"

"Martha [Heredia] more than the rest, for her way of being and because of her color, and her hair too . . . the way she speaks, also, it's distinct." Through popular support that involved endless text messages from Dominican viewers in the United States and the Dominican Republic, Martha Heredia won the 2009 *Latin American Idol*. Some women I spoke with identified her as having a working-class background and so her self-presentation was to them most dominicana, or "Dominicanyork." Though many of my interviewees thought of her as having grown up in the diaspora, YouTube videos capture the privileges of her middle-class upbringing partially in Santiago de los Caballeros, the Dominican Republic's other major city.

"Did you call or send a text in support of Martha?" I ask Yessica about the singer's win.

"Of course, everyone did!" she exclaims, confirming what I had heard. "Martha, she's not from here, she's from Miami but she . . . yeah . . . [Zoe Saldaña] looks more Dominican . . . and Martha too, they look the most dominicana . . . because of the physical form of her face, and her haircut." Both Martha and Zoe are brown in color while Michelle Rodriguez and Rita Indiana are not. When I showed Ambar the four photos I had selected she, like Yessica, does not recognize Michelle Rodriguez. If I had had an image of Rodriguez as her character, Letty, in *The Fast and the Furious* and its sequels with Vin Diesel, she might have been more familiar. Ambar recognized Saldaña as being an actress, though Yessica initially confused her with a past Dominican Miss Universe winner, presumably Amelia Vega from 2003. Vega is much lighter in color than Saldaña, though both have the requisite straight dark hair that falls past her shoulders. Says Ambar, "Yes, Michelle has it, she looks dominicana . . ."

"But she looks *cibaoeña*, or *santiaguera*, right?" adds Yessica, making sense of the star's color by associating her with a particular region of the country (Cibao and its capital, Santiago); she looks to Ambar for confirmation. When Ambar declares that a hairstyle is something that can be a "global" style, it is Yessica who reminds her that no Dominican would choose a woman with pelo crespo to represent them. The Miss Universe Dominican Republic competition is one barometer of this, in which each of the contestants is expected to have bone-straight hair for the competition—their headshots posted on Facebook capture this convention.[7] The sole contestant in 2012 who wore her hair natural for the shoot faced extensive criticism online and off. She was apparently interpreted as denigrating her own beauty by presenting her natural hair. Neither was she appropriately participating in a gendered performance and conventional efforts to conform.

"A lot of traditions have changed in the last six years," says Yessica, "Look at the celebration of Semana Santa [Holy Week], there were many different rules that people do not follow now." She goes on, "How women dress has changed a lot." Certainly young girls in the street are wearing short skirts when they used to wear skirts that fell below the knee. More often than not they are wearing jeans. "There is a lot more *dilenquencia*," she says.

When I delicately ask Ambar and Yessica about the prevalence of prostitution in the Dominican Republic, Yessica talks freely about the topic. I am especially curious about her thoughts on the subject because of her choice to pursue a career in tourism. "There are a lot of Dominicans that prostitute themselves," she says, referring to both men and women. Her body language shifts as she talks about it—she hugs a pillow from the sofa in front of her stomach.

"You learn about this and discuss it in your classes?" I ask.

"I have learned a lot about it in my classes. The professors did a debate with us about it." Her teachers tell them stories about women in administrative positions who are pressured for sex by the men who work above them and risk losing their jobs if they do not acquiesce.

"We are taught to respect ourselves," she says. But there is a lot of gray area in this and not only can women make a lot of money by sleeping with male suitors but there is also a lot at stake if they refuse: their job, their future in the career of their choice, salary increases—and they may subsequently face ongoing sexual harassment.

"There are many women who want to improve their lives, but they have these options in front of them to make money more easily," Yessica adds.

At some point, Yessica's mom gets on the phone to call the colmado. Not long after, the delivery guy from the corner store walked in with a cold beer and small plastic cups on top. Later, we smell food frying in the kitchen, and by the end of our conversation, Yessica's mother presented us with a plate piled high with *tostones* and fried salami.

"So, do you think you are very Dominican?" I ask Yessica.

"Yes, I think of myself as very Dominican and I love my country."

Ambar says she feels less Dominican than Yessica, with her taste for cornflakes and other things introduced from abroad. "*El cornfla*' comes from over there, it's something from America," she says. "I don't like *habichuelas* [red beans] . . . these are things of my culture."

"Yes, but you like *sancocho*, and *mofongo*!" Yessica assures her.

"But there are other things about my culture that I don't like. And people tell me, 'Look, but you don't seem dominicana.'" This is a theme for many of the women I spoke with, that others tell them that in some way they are not Dominican enough. Ambar does not seem to perform the kind of Dominican femininity that her friend Yessica does. Nevertheless, she does describe herself as "domini*cana*-dominicana." Like Yessica, she consumes a lot of US popular culture.

"I like the movies a lot." Yessica tells me. "Action movies, of Vin Diesel, Will Smith, a morenito that I can't remember the name of." The "morenito" whom she cannot recall turns out to be Denzel Washington, whose name I hear repeatedly from his many female fans in Santo Domingo. Like so many teenagers across the globe, Yessica views plenty of Hollywood films. She can watch them at home thanks to bootleg copies sold throughout the country by young men on the street or illegally streamlined online. Vin Diesel films are in high demand and his racially mixed appearance seems to appeal to a broad Dominican public. Yessica continues, "I like Julia Roberts . . . and the one married to Marc Anthony . . . and the actress in *Fast and Furious*." She does not immediately recall the names of Latina actresses Jennifer Lopez or Michelle Rodriguez, nor does she recognize Rodriguez in the picture that I show her. Ambar tells me she listens to music and watches videos online, "Honestly, I don't like to read. That's why I am studying administration, it's more mathematical." She lists just a few stars that she likes by name, including Angelina Jolie.

"Why do you like Angelina Jolie?" I ask, curious.

"She is in action films, but she doesn't look like a strong woman. Yet she does her action roles. That's a good actress." With this comment, Ambar further highlights the appeal of *looking* feminine, while being tough. She also finds appealing a white actress whose racial identity is played up as ambiguous. Jolie's phenotype (including broad lips and tawny skin) allowed her to play the role of Mariane Pearl, the French, Dutch, Cuban wife of Daniel Pearl in the film *A Mighty Heart*—a role for which her skin had to be "browned up" a bit.

"Vin Diesel, I like," Ambar adds.

La Nigüenta

Contemporary cultural references and images embedded in this hierarchy of color relentlessly inform dominicanas of their place in society. The dynamic conversation and interwoven insights of Yessica and Ambar highlight the ways that their individual understandings of self are informed by privileges and expectations that their phenotype dictates—even when their interpretation emerges through narratives of la dominicana.

One iconic image of white girlhood that circulates widely throughout the Dominican Republic permeates Dominican consciousness as well. Like the ubiquitous muñeca sin rostro, one can see an image of *La nigüenta* hanging on the wall in homes around the country. But *La nigüenta* is a cherubic white child sitting on a grassy hill and plucking something from her toe. Believed to originate in Europe, *La nigüenta* is presumably a variation of the sculpture *Spinario*, or "Boy with Thorn," a Greco-Roman Hellenistic bronze of a young man removing a thorn from his foot. In the Dominican Republic, the figure, reinterpreted as a girl, is understood to be removing a chigger (a small insect from the grassy rural areas of the island). Dominican filmmaker Leticia Tonos remarks on the pervasiveness of this image—and its irony—by including it in a scene from her film *La hija natural* (2011). Tonos's placement of *La nigüenta* on the wall of a poor family's home gestures to the details of rural Dominican life and superstition as much as to the visual culture that informs that reality. While the image is thought to bring good things into the home, it also bestows the domestic sphere with symbolic white femininity combined with the innocence of (white) girlhood that might be far out of reach for Dominican women and girls. In response to this visual dominance of whiteness in a country in which the majority of the population is mixed race of African descent, one unnamed artist produced a black version of the very same child to sharpen the contradiction: *La nigüenta* with brown skin has a thick round head of curly black hair. Highlighting the differences between the fiction and the reality in the Caribbean, the work of the artist online is surrealist in form.

Both the presumed innocence of girlhood and the ubiquity of whiteness in such a racially mixed context are important themes throughout my reading of Dominican women's identities in contemporary Santo Domingo. Metaphorically, *La nigüenta*'s chigger has dug itself deep beneath her skin, causing increasing discomfort while viewers visually consume and come to desire or align themselves with the cherished image of her white innocence. The white girlchild attempting to remove a buried pest (or past) is a reminder of the discomfort of racism that lies just below the surface. It is also a useful metaphor for thinking through surrealist cultural production in my examination of whiteness in the chapter that follows.

5

The Camera Obscura
Teatro Maleducadas' Production of
La Casa de Bernarda Alba

"Who are YOU?" said the Caterpillar.
This was not an encouraging opening for a
conversation.
Alice replied, rather shyly, "I—I hardly know,
sir, just at present—at least I know who I WAS
when I got up this morning, but I think I must
have been changed several times since then."
Lewis Carroll, *Alice in Wonderland*

A black-and-white digital photograph shared on Teatro Maleducadas' Facebook page memorializes a moment from the theater collective's 2013 production of Federico Lorca's *La Casa de Bernarda Alba*. The image captures a scene in which three sisters in the play are sitting side-by-side, topless, with their backs to the audience as they pantomime bathing in the candlelight. Only two of the women are visible in the photograph, yet the slow movements of the scene and its shadows are captured. In translating the narrative from the live Dominican performance into black-and-white photographs shared online, what remains visible is the eroticism of the moment, various symbols of identity, and the ways the young women's sexuality is repressed and restrained. The Spanish lace fans the young women are waving in many of the photographs are symbolic of early twentieth-century Spain, while their presence as props simultaneously remarks on the growing heat and stifled sexuality within the household. During the live performance, each young woman sits straddling a wooden box on the stage, while slowly drawing her hands across her body in the dim light. Each is wearing a black lace skirt that reveals the outline of her lower half and the low lighting penetrates the gauzy material to highlight her curves.[1]

Figure 6. Photographs of Teatro Maleducadas' 2013 production of *La Casa de Bernarda Alba* were circulated on social media. Photos by Fran Afonso.

The scene is titillating, as the sisters sit and caress themselves in silence and each actress withholds turning her body toward viewers enough that she might expose her nudity; in every small gesture the audience observes a fire being stoked in each of them. Immured in their household for the last seven years as part of a mourning ritual for their late father, the sisters are as controlled in their movements as they are in their sexuality. This theatrical production, and its translation into a visual archive online, sits squarely within a history of the black female body and we are informed in our reading of what we see by a present weighed down by Santo Domingo's history of colonialism, slavery, genocide, and gender-based violence, factors that remain foundational to the contemporary social dynamics that I examine in the Dominican Republic.

"Race becomes a way of seeing" asserts Coco Fusco, in regards to American racial politics in the world of art and photography.[2] In fact, race and gender combine to become a way of seeing. According to Deborah Willis and Carla Williams, "Photography is the perfect medium for revisiting and re-interrogating the black female body, for tracing a history coded in images bound by fear and desire."[3] The photographic moment that Las Maleducas captured is "colored" for viewers by an already imagined exoticization of Caribbean women's racially mixed bodies.

La Mulata al Revés

Las Maleducadas' production of Lorca's play opened to a packed house in Santo Domingo in June 2013 as part of the third annual Festival de Teatro.[4] Audience members jammed into the small theater at the back of Casa de Teatro to view the play. Interpreted by an all-female Afro-Dominican theater troupe, the contemporary production of this Spanish play newly locates Caribbean women's bodies in a work that has long shaped perceptions of early twentieth-century Spanish womanhood. Themes central to Lorca's Surrealist script, like the photographic, containment, insanity, and death, transform under the vision and emotional engagement of Dominican women artists in the cultural context of contemporary Santo Domingo. Lorca's celebrated work, published posthumously in 1936, presents audiences with the wrath of a steel-armed matriarch, who rules over the lives of her five daughters. In form, *Bernarda Alba* is patently Surrealist; freeing itself from the rational, many of the lines delivered in the play reflect the characters' subconscious and engage with eroticism and destruction.[5] Lorca skillfully weaves an overarching tale of

Figure 7. Selfie by actress Cindy Galán (*left*) as Adela, with Karina Valdez, who plays her mother, Bernarda.

unmet desire among a group of Spanish women. Their longings—a yearning to be self-actualized—are familiar to Dominican women in Santo Domingo. In Las Maleducadas' production, Adela looks like an Alice in Wonderland, in a bright dress and perfectly coiffed red hair tied back with a bow placed at the top of her head. She is the girl-child, the Surrealist's *femme-enfant*—existing as the central object around which society's messages swirl; she becomes increasingly contrary and rageful act by act.

Lorca was attuned to the impact of the visual image in an era of technological advancement in photography and this likely influenced how he crafted his Surrealist writing in multilayered and visual ways. He opens the text of the play with a very specific author's note that states: "These three acts are intended as a photographic document." Analyzing Las Maleducadas' production, attendant to race, color, patriarchy, and transnationalism, as I am here, reveals layers of significance around seeing and being seen for women in a patriarchal society, both for the Dominican actresses in this production and the characters in the play itself.

Because of *Bernarda Alba*'s universal appeal it has had numerous iterations worldwide: from Ghanaian students performing it as part of their Spanish studies, to Mexican actors in a nationally televised film production, to an all-male cast in Saõ Paolo, Brazil, and an all–East Asian Canadian performance.[6] Yet the Dominican actresses of Las Maleducadas uniquely compliment Lorca's vision for the original work by expanding its visual significance and symbolic register. Their brown bodies in varying shades force "a different seeing, a different ordering of the visible."[7] The production also reveals Las Maleducadas' awareness of the visual currency of the contemporary moment and its impact. The ongoing social media presence of the production disrupts the white supremacist act of erasing black and brown bodies from "classical theater," the Spanish cultural productions embraced by Dominican elite. Classical theater is part and parcel of the same scopic regime (and political economy) that works to erase black bodies from the Dominican national identity and imaginary. Just as Nicole Fleetwood argues that "the visual sphere is a performative field where seeing race is not a transparent act; it is itself a 'doing,'" Stuart Hall has argued for our understanding of racial construction as an act and sustained action.[8] In viewing a performance of Dominican theater, we are participating in the construction of new racial meanings. Therefore in this chapter I ask, How do we see Dominican women "doing race," and in particular mixed race, through the production of this Surrealist Spanish play? And how does the photographic matter in these performances?

José Esteban Muñoz in his writing on Latinx performance reminds us that "performance functions as socially symbolic acts that serve as powerful theoretical lenses through which to view the social sphere."[9] Not only does performance capture something about a culture, but as a theoretical intervention it helps us to better understand Dominican identity. Visual details specific to Las Maleducadas' decidedly *afrocaribeña* version of the play leads audience members to interpret the narrative in new ways. Isabel Spencer, the play's director tells me, "We haven't stuck so much with the stereotypes of the white, blonde woman with blue eyes and such. How the classics are usually interpreted, you know?" My initial short interview with Isabel in 2013 and follow-up interviews in 2014 and 2016 inform my analysis of the play and related efforts by Las Maleducadas to make more visible the creative work of Caribbean women artists. Further insights from two of the actresses in the collective, Johanna González and Robelitza Pérez, contribute to my readings of race and color in the production and in the Dominican Republic more broadly. As dominicanas, the actresses undoubtedly also identify with aspects of the Spanishness of the play. "However," says Isabel, "one way or another what we did was find a way to inject a bit of the Caribbean into this classic, in order to make it a little bit more from here."

Although language about race and color are absent from Lorca's script, other codes of the visual underscore the significance of class differences that map onto color.[10] Las Maleducadas' arrestingly intimate scenes of relationship dynamics among this group of women cannot be interpreted without an eye for hierarchies of color in the Dominican context. The production is embedded in a contemporary visual discourse of racialized beliefs about the hypersexuality of brown and black bodies in the Caribbean, visual knowledge that is essential for viewing the layered meaning of the play live and in photographs online. The actresses' bodies—in a range of shades of color—produce a visual narrative that disrupts notions of who gets to be imagined as Spanish as well as what narratives get to be claimed as Dominican. Drawing on my own observations of this live performance, in this chapter I also consider Las Maleducadas' presentation of this production online through professional photographs (both in color and in black and white) circulated via Facebook and Instagram. This archive offers additional clues about how skin color carries meaning based on ingrained narratives that help us see race.

Throughout this chapter, I question how we *see* Dominican womanhood in the context of this contemporary theatrical performances of hispanicity combined with dominicanidad. The Dominican actresses' bodies are presented within "a racially saturated field of visibility," in which the racial meaning of the black body is already circumscribed.[11] Hierarchies of color embodied in the contemporary performance and its visual archive on Facebook inform meanings in the play that reverberate across time and space. Fleetwood's notion of "rendering" is useful here in considering how the black body is produced through and within this visual discourse.[12] For these Afro-Caribbean actresses, rendering not only signifies an active becoming and production of a specific type of blackness, it also gestures to the digital formation of an image and the act of constituting that image's racial meaning. At the same time, the gaze repeatedly shapes interactions between the women in *La Casa de Bernarda Alba.* "In the case of the daughters," writes Nina M. Scott, "seeing and being seen is also crucial, principally because in their type of society the entire system of courtship is based on visual contacts."[13] Yet much more occurs in the space between what Dominican viewers see on stage and how they interpret race and gender being presented to them within a Dominican scopic regime. It is the case that, as Norman Bryson writes, "Between the subject and the world is inserted the entire sum of discourses which make up visuality, that cultural construct, and make visuality different from vision, the notion of unmediated visual experience."[14] Consequently, each viewer's experience of the theater is unique, in the same ways that Dominican women's bodies shift in racial meaning from context to context.

Bernarda Alba presents Dominican audiences with a narrative that resonates within a specific hierarchy of color to which they are attuned, by drawing on a Dominican awareness of the coded differences between the women on stage, that justify class narratives and characters' social positioning. Simultaneously, the production disrupts viewer expectations around color as it critiques the gendered circumstances of women. Las Maleducadas' version/vision of *Bernarda Alba* makes profound suggestions about the meaning of difference as it is read on the body. The actresses reflect a broad range of Dominican phenotypes; prior knowledge of the context of the Dominican Republic informs how we view the women in this Caribbeanized performance. Their phenotypic differences require that we use our imaginations in observing the significance of different moments of interaction between characters in the play, witnessing the said and the unsaid. Dominican hierarchies of color are a way of seeing just as seeing shades of difference is a mode of seeing. Whether in live performance or in the photographs of the theatrical work circulated well after its conclusion, race, and, with it, color are an inescapable frame of analysis for understanding gender in this performance.

A Looking-Glass World

Bernarda Alba tells the story of a tyrannical Spanish matriarch and the isolated world of women over which she rules: her daughters, her servants, and her own aged mother. Central to this narrative is the social value of women—particularly the significance of a daughter's purity within a patriarchal society—and women's own consciousness about the precariousness of their social positions. In Spanish society of the 1930s, out of which this work emerged, women were consigned to marriage, childrearing, and childbearing.[15] Following the death of Bernarda's second husband, she has imposed a traditional mourning period of nine years on her household, sequestering her five unmarried daughters, ages twenty to thirty-nine.

Like many of the Dominican women I focus on in this book, Lorca was a queer transnational subject whose work was influenced by visual culture and experiences living abroad. He spent several formative years of his life in New York City, roaming the streets of Harlem at the turn of the twentieth century. His experience peering into another world—a world of Black culture at that—is reflected in the poetry he produced during that period of his life.[16] The way his writing addresses universal human themes sustains its transnational appeal. As Christopher Maurer notes, these include "different figures of desire: the sexual urge, homoerotic love; longing for marriage or maternity; the yearning for social justice; the drive toward personal fulfillment of one sort or another."[17] Lorca "looks beyond the 'here and now' and sees what is present as a symbol of what is absent. No matter where one opens his work, its theme is *the impossible*; the melancholy conviction that all of us have certain indefinable longings that cannot be satisfied by anything around us."[18] It was a truth Lorca understood living under Franco's dictatorship and one that resonates profoundly in today's post-Trujillo neoliberal Santo Domingo.

As Lorca's story goes, Bernarda's oldest daughter from her first marriage, Angustias, has inherited a significant amount of money from her father. Meanwhile, Bernarda's second husband left only small amounts to each of his four daughters. Angustias (with her dowry) attracts the attention of a young suitor from the village named Pepe El Romano. Angustia's sisters are envious of her since her dowry symbolizes the possibility of her freedom from their mother's authoritarian rule. Bernarda's youngest daughter, Adela (played by Cindy Galán), is especially jealous of her oldest sister for, as it turns out, she has also fallen in love with Pepe and is having a secret affair with him. An off-stage whistle from Pepe each time he comes to see the sisters is recognizable to Dominican audiences, according to Isabel: "This is very caribeño too. . . . Suitors could not go to the house of the girls so they had a whistle and then she knew they were there. They still use these a lot," she says, and then makes the sharp high-pitched sound.

Says Isabel about the 2013 production, "The costumes that the actresses use are emblematic of the era, with some modern touches proposed by the young designer Renata Cruz."[19] Cruz worked with lace, ruffles, and collars to construct contemporary costumes for the characters that echo Lorca's era. They are aesthetically referencing early twentieth-century Spain, at the moment when women wave their lace fans, but there is something more Caribbean that we see when they don black lace bodysuits over black bustiers, accentuating and sexualizing their bodies, rather than covering themselves from head to toe as in other productions of the play.[20] I come to the visual images of this play by way of Las Maleducadas' social media presence—specifically looking at how they articulate the work they do as a collective while also disseminating staged professional photographs on Facebook and later Instagram. The photographic stylization periodizes the performance as representative of women at the turn of the twentieth century. Minimalist sets and costumes used in the play were produced as if for black-and-white photography and highlighting sharp contrasts between white walls and black chairs, or white aprons and black lace. In one photograph, the women are wrapped in black lace and tulle, and the look is menacing. Even their dark painted lips speak to a rebellious sexuality that will not be restrained. Meanwhile, the chains and bars used in the set to convey the women's entrapment are captured at the corners of each photograph, making the scenes appear to take place not in a home but in a dungeon of torture, as the young women experience it to be.

Lorca's work, with its contrasts between black and white in the script and staging, was written during and inspired by the era of early photographic technology.[21] In her 1976 essay, "Sight and Insight in *La Casa de Bernarda Alba*," N. M. Scott articulates the significance of the optical experience as a central metaphor in this particular work, interpreting it in the original Spanish: "Throughout the play there are constant references to the verb 'ver' and the associated concepts: 'vista,' 'visión,' 'mirar,' etc. Lorca does not limit himself to that meaning of 'ver' which denotes the physiological act of seeing, but also uses 'seeing' in the metaphorical sense of 'comprehending.' Thus, we are dealing with variations of outward and inward vision, or of sight and insight" on all levels of the play."[22] Las Maleducadas' production constantly alludes to the visual differences that help us to better comprehend the narrative—Martirio's body contorted with a hump on her back; Adela marked by her impossibly bright red hair. Hierarchies of color are one more layer of the narrative.

When Fusco argues, "Photography generates a distinct *mise en scéne* and provides material that is visually reminiscent of but phenomenologically distinct from reality, for voyeuristic engagement," she seems to suggest that photography produces the surreal as it draws us away from what is rational and what is real.[23] This is true for Lorca's theatrical narrative, into which we peer to see black contrast white, on objects and on bodies, and in language. "Whereas white symbolizes the unlived, subliminal, aerated, and unreal world," writes Bettina Knapp about *Bernarda Alba*, "black represents primordial, undifferentiated, chthonian darkness."[24] Furthermore, black bodies hold a unique relationship to being seen and to the technologies made for viewing them.[25] Ocular technologies "are seen as hostile and violent forces that render blackness as aberration, given the long and brutal history of black subjugation through various technologies, visual apparatus among them."[26] An analysis of the technology of the visual is therefore essential in reading this production by Dominican women, because the work reveals how "optical technologies have been used to discipline racialized bodies."[27] However, in this instance Afro-Caribbean women as subjects of the gaze have agency in representing themselves in this production, online and off, not so much despite but because of their being under the "inescapability of racial marking."[28]

Scott and others have suggested that the experience of viewing this particular Lorca play is not unlike that of being trapped within a camera obscura, a dark box that one looks into to see an image projected onto a screen or wall. The language of the photographic reminds us that we are looking through a lens into this family dynamic in which Bernarda fears being "exposed." In the camera obscura, the lens that the light travels through turns the image entirely on its head when it is projected. Likewise, Dominican women's bodies effectively "flip the script" and turn Lorca's story on its head, forcing us to see different meanings in this narrative.

"*Es otra cara*," says actress Johanna González about the production, "it's the flipside." By placing Afro-Caribbean women's bodies in Lorca's text, and crafting the work so that it reflects who they are as women artists and performers, Las Maleducadas have offered an alternate vision for how Lorca's world might be seen. When their production includes scenes in which the actresses are showered in red light, all dressed in form-fitting black lace, they are eroticized in ways that the collective identified as true to their vision as afrocaribeñas. A photograph of the daughters standing behind Bernarda captures this moment. The color of the light shining on them suggests their growing rage about their own captivity, yet it cannot be read outside of the Caribbean industry of sex work and notions of a red-light district in which brown-skinned women have sex to sell. Because of the context in which we view it and the Dominican cultural details added to the work, we no longer experience Lorca's *Bernarda Alba* as bound by the context of Spain.

Other Worlds Are Possible

Award-winning actor and director Isabel Spencer has built a decades-long career producing theater and performance art in and beyond the Dominican Republic. Isabel's theatrical productions address issues of women's rights, violence against women, immigration, anti-Haitianism, and gender and sexuality, topics that often go overlooked and underfunded.[29] I attended no less than five productions in Santo Domingo in which she was involved, three of which she directed. Isabel moved away to Mexico for a few years when the opportunity arose and then returned with new and important stories to tell in her work about who Dominicans are, a new urgency and a comparative cultural analysis. A skillful character actor, on several occasions I have witnessed her transform herself for an audience by merely channeling a range of Dominican regional accents—on stage, on the street, and in community with friends. When we met in 2010, Isabel was a member of an Afro-Dominican feminist collective that was committed to reading and discussing black feminist theory. For some time she wore a head of thick locks, an uncommon sight in Santo Domingo. In a measure of time passing, I have seen her cut those locks, begin to grow them out again, and shave her head once more. She has also since been nominated for and won some of the Dominican Republic's most prestigious awards for her work.[30]

In 2013, I was able to steal a bit of Isabel's time sitting outside in Parque Duarte in the Colonial Zone. I ask her a few pointed questions about her vision for the *Bernarda Alba* production and audiorecorded her response; it is the closest I can get to an interview at that moment, having tried and failed previously. The periodic growl of a motorbike passing by punctuates, more than disrupts, our conversation. I work to keep up with Isabel's Spanish, as her accent from Puerta Plata keeps me feeling uncertain about my own fluency in the language.[31] Her friends pass by and she greets them; a few folks we know sit down beside us on the park's steel benches, listening in to the conversation.

"We dropped the [Castilian] Spanish," says Isabel, describing a shift in the language in the performance, "and brought it down to the level of *el Caribe.*" She makes clear that this action was a political move to bring art to the people so that they might see themselves in it: "[It contains] the cadence of the Caribbean and that really worked. It also works because of the mixture, the diversity of the women on one hand . . . At the heart of the theater collective is the work of women—[our goal is] to make visible the art of women through theater, but also to make visible the art of Afro-Caribbean women in theater." She goes on, "We try to preserve a little of the aesthetic that the author had planned, but . . . we have not stuck to it. . . . We worked on the aesthetic a little, but were little daring. I don't know if you noticed, the bolder aspects of the piece?" It was also to "free us from this *jartadura y esa vaina* that the classics have," says Isabel, using dominicanisms that emphasize their frustrations with the text. Las Maleducadas took the classic and ran with it.

I manage to conduct a follow-up interview with Isabel in 2014 at the home of our mutual friend Yaneris.[32] "It's one of the first all-woman collectives in existence here," Isabel tells me about Teatro Maleducadas. At the time, they had only been working together for two years. According to Isabel, "The object of the collective is to make a bit more visible the art of women, our way of seeing things, the way we see the world . . . how we see it, how we feel it." I ask whether everyone in the group identified as *"mujeres afros,"* a term she uses in our interview, or *"mujeres negras,"* a term I have heard her use with friends. "We identify as *"mujeres afrocaribeñas . . . Afrocaribeñas,* actually," she responds.

"We are pursuing the portrayal of who and what we are as *mujeres dominicanas,* as *caribeñas,* as *mujeres afro.* So the group basically has that characteristic of what you saw, that diversity of women of African descent and those women who are on similar journeys in relation to negritude." The group concentrates on the work of Dominican women, making visible their art—specifically the art of afrocaribeñas in theater—thereby pushing back against dominant narratives of Dominican women's identities. One issue the collective has faced is finding works that might be performed by an all-female cast and for which they can access the rights: "There are four classics that we worked with. We are all women, the group has enough depth, it has a certain gendered focus in our work too. And I think that where women gather to work, out of necessity there has be a gendered focus," Isabel explains. She seems to echo the Dominican media's preoccupations about the performance. *El Caribe* online suggested, for example, that "the independent theater collective Maleducadas, which is formed entirely by women, is betting on a new female generation in the world of Dominican theater."[33] In an article in the Dominican paper *Listín Diario* online promoting the production, journalist Roxanna Cruz Betances felt the need to assure readers that although the production was by and about women it would still appeal to broad audiences.[34] Notably, the race and color hierarchy that I have observed within the production go unmentioned in media reviews of the play, revealing some of the limitations of popular discourse on theater in the Dominican Republic. A lack of discussion of color also speaks to the unremarkable nature of a diversity of phenotypes among the family of Bernarda Alba in the play; while Bernarda is relatively dark in color, her daughters are varying shades of brown and even "Dominican white," with a range of other features beyond skin color that suggest the mixture of the Caribbean.

Figure 8. Isabel Spencer (*front*) with cast of *La Casa de Bernarda Alba*. Photo by Fran Afonso.

Las Maleducadas intended to portray with its production of *Bernarda Alba* the familiar dynamic of competition among women in the Dominican Republic. Says Isabel, "The system always puts women to compete with each other . . . compete, compete, compete." As she describes it, aside from Bernarda, who wields a power that "crushes these women," throughout the play you come to understand the desire on the part of her daughters for "liberation, freedom from oppression, to liberate their bodies, freedom of speech, to free themselves." The narrative resonates with Isabel and so many other Dominican women fighting against patriarchal oppression within their families, and by the state and the Catholic Church. The story aptly parallels the life experiences Dominican women tell me about and those I have witnessed firsthand: a matriarch who upholds and replicates a patriarchal system that benefits her at great cost to women and girls around her; a society in which young women's purity is a central preoccupation.

For Bernarda, "her family becomes the main source of her power."[35] Adela's fight to become independent of her controlling mother is a familiar experience to many Dominican women. Violence, notions of purity, and the pressures of social expectations around young women's reputations serve effectively to keep Bernarda's daughters prisoners in their own home, bound by an economic system that has their worth tied to their marriageability.

According to Isabel, the play is a clear analogy of everyday reality and it "makes quite visible the theme of the power games that go on among women that do not necessarily occur among men because the world is built for men, truly designed for them so that they can be in power. Sometimes if women do not tread carefully, we can . . . be used by this same power play." Isabel has explained to Dominican media that "as the women realize their fate, they compete for their survival, they show how power and authoritarianism exerted over women, prevents them from making decisions and keeps them crushed so they are without agency."[36] She laments that it is women who reproduce patriarchal violence themselves, "therefore, it is this that we must get rid of so that women see what is happening in society, right now." A century after Lorca wrote his play, set an ocean away, women are still fighting to wrest themselves from their family home only to position themselves under the control of their husbands: "*y ese construction hace feria de lo que es*, like a family that is cool, very central to one's life, but sometimes it is *muy castrante*. It's very oppressive." It is common in the Dominican Republic to see older women in an economically vulnerable position because they are devalued by men and unwanted when they reach a certain age, yet they can rule families as the matriarch in a society in which mothers are revered. Bernarda, however, is a distorted version of the loyal and self-sacrificing Dominican ama de la casa (mistress of the house) that I discussed earlier.

In my initial interview at the park, I had asked her about collective focus around afrodominicanidad: "Did you come up with this idea about identity by reading texts together?" I imagined some sort of consciousness-raising group like the one I knew Isabel to be a part of previously.

"No, look, *fíjate*. I'm going to be honest with you. Some are a little more into it than others. I'm the one who has a bit more experience with these things and they go into it with me . . . becoming a bit more conscious of racial issues and through theater, too." The collective's identification with blackness does not necessarily define the work they choose to present but, Isabel explains, "this awareness exists in the group. We're not seeking that blonde, out of the box, and posed actress, we are working from our reality. I won't say they already had a super deep discourse about racial construction but we are on a journey. On this front we are growing."

"How powerful art is," I say during our conversation at the park, recalling a theater program I had heard about in another part of the country, and also the impact of street theater on so many folks I know in Santo Domingo.

"Yes, I think art is what is going to save this ship," she says to me in her characteristically scratchy voice.

"You think?"

"Yes, I believe a lot in art, really for me in particular I am talking about myself, because it has saved my life. If I hadn't made art, things would have been very bad for me." The other women sitting with us in the park that day sigh and smile in agreement.[37]

When I follow-up with her in 2014, Isabel tells me that that as a director she had a vision of what she wanted to see after a deep engagement with the text and she developed with the collective a vision for where they wanted the work to go. "Part of our objective is to do work with political content, with a focus on gender," she explains. While she wouldn't necessarily describe the theater collective as a feminist project, "it touches on the topic of gender and that is one of the discussions on the table, as we discuss the characters we portray because everyone has their own very particular opinion within the collective." Isabel's reticence in speaking for others in the collective about the significance of the work they are doing, and her clear sense about the specificities of identity based in experience, could be attributed to her own engagement in feminist organizing in Santo Domingo. The black feminist knowledges that she has engaged with in transnational collective work among Dominican feminists likely informs her desire not to speak for others around the nuances of their racial experiences.

Las Maleducadas' intention was to come together as a group of revolutionary women artists, "Because, we really have a lot to say and if we have a space like the theater where one can say it is a rebellious art, it is an art of revolution, an art of transformation, then grab on to that tool. I think that . . . I won't tell you we are going to change the world but really transform things; we teach the people another way to see the world through theater and that there are other things that exist there, other worlds that are possible, you know?" Therefore, it is not surprising that the theater collective crafted an eleven-point manifesto, shared on Facebook, that reflects the work that they are engaged in.[38] Radical in the feminist organizing that their work implies, and with a commitment to social justice, they named themselves "*las maleducadas*" in critique of the society in which they live, identifying themselves as women who do not do as they are told, who are poorly behaved.

Their guiding vision is not unlike that of Lorca's generation of Surrealists, who stood against "white supremacy, patriotism, religion, colonialism, prudish morality, and respect for the law," resisting the culture of the bourgeoisie and that of commercialism.[39] Las Maleducadas also articulate feminist values without naming them as such. In the opening of their

Figure 9. Selfie by actress Cindy Galán (*center*) with the cast of *La Casa de Bernarda Alba*. *Left to right*: Johanna González, Karina Valdez, Cindy Galán, Paloma Palacios, Indiana Brito, and Robelitza Pérez.

manifesto they assert: "A shadow continues to hang over WOMEN. This shadow is to be educated but negating one's voice. As dramatists, we call ourselves MALEDUCADAS and claim women's expression in all of its fullness. We name ourselves this in order to reject the indoctrination that turn us into unhappy human beings." Through the manifesto they celebrate their differences, demand their right to education as a liberatory tool, and reject the idea that as women they might be in competition with one another. Although the idea of "women" is used as a unifying identity in their manifesto, and "difference" as a theoretical point of engagement, they do not mention color or phenotype as informing their perspectives. Through the manifesto they have crafted an anticolonial statement that suggests that they are not only a collective of artists but also a group with political aims; art is necessarily political in the context of the Dominican Republic. Their assertion of choosing "theater as a mode of expression through which to be a woman in support of the construction of a just society" reflects the time they have spent building collectivity and theorizing their own experiences. Their fifth tenet in the manifesto, "*Maleducada* because I question," parallels the type of Dominican women I have focused on in my research, those who are critical of the world around them and bring this critique to their cultural productions, as they, like Lorca's characters, question the role to which women are relegated in society.

Although she is the director, according to Isabel there is no hierarchy in which she is "put on a pedestal." Rather she is part of a team of organizers: "This is why we are a collective and each person has her contribution in her area [of expertise]." She explains when I interview her a third time in 2016, "We try to create a sort of horizontality that each person in her own can do what she wants to do, you know? Because it is also a way of breaking out of a pattern of stale leadership." It is also a feminist organizing technique. With this rotation of leadership, members of the collective are able to experience growth, she explains. "And for me, really to collaborate with women, we could not have encountered this level of professionalism [another] way. You see? We feel comfortable working together and we love each other and there is respect . . . We care for and love one another and we do the work." Isabel sees this community of shared growth and learning among women as a once in a lifetime experience, even as she goes on to try to replicate with theater groups elsewhere. A subsequent production of the play takes place in Mexico City, with dramatists there.

"What happened is three of Las Maleducadas, the collective, went to study abroad—China, France, Spain—and this is nice because they go and they return, for example, now the first one coming back is Robelitza, she is back again." Isabel explains that it is the intention of the collective to have a "flow of women coming who can come and go," each leaving their mark. The group of young women grow in the experience at the moment that they are part of the collective. "It isn't just eight women in the collective," she explains, "because there are always women circulating in and out." At times there are men like the musician involved in the group, Isabel explains, "but the force is the women." She says, "for this collective to function, every person carries a key part," and without this, "*no camina* [it won't go]."

"I feel like every day we are advancing a little more," she says. "I didn't learn [to work this way] from my professors because they weren't ever like this," she tells me. " . . . One has to start out by looking for another way to relate to others, that isn't this power and authoritarianism, you know?" In fact, socialism and leftist political organizing, and her own involvement in the feminist movement in the Dominican Republic, inform her extensive training in theater and shape Isabel's work.

"To my professors I am very grateful for lot of the theater training. You see, what they have taught me the most is the work, pure labor, a way of structuring a work, and certain other things. . . . But . . . the consciousness that I have about some things, I owe to my circle, in which I came up, with black women, my *compañeras*, my friends, partners, that influence, yes. . . . You know, it's a mix of all of it."

Seeing Gender, Seeing Race

To broaden my understanding, Isabel encouraged me to interview actress Johanna González, who played the role of Poncia the maid in the 2013 production. By the time I interviewed her, however, years had passed since I had viewed and written about the play. By then I had also seen Johanna perform in *Hasta el abismo* in 2015, another outstanding Teatro Maleducadas production, for which Isabel would win a "Dominican Oscar" for her directing.[40]

Johanna and I are able to meet in summer of 2016 for a forty-minute interview. I find her at her work in the Palacio de Bellas Artes in Santo Domingo and we use the seating area just outside of the theater's main office. Occasionally a phone rings, an office staff member passes through, and we raise our voices over conversations taking place right on the other side of the door. We twist toward each other, squeaking in our faux-leather waiting room chairs, and laughing uncomfortably as we get to know one another. Not only are Johanna and I complete strangers at the start of the interview, but her acting has been so skillful in the two productions in which I have seen her perform that I do not know exactly whom to expect when we meet.[41] I am not prepared for her unfamiliar mannerisms and her rather introverted nature, which contrast with the confident, angry, and outlandish women she transforms into on stage. Since graduating from the Escuela de Teatro Nacional, Johanna tells me, she has been a part of numerous productions and theater collectives. It was in theater school where she encountered Isabel. I try to ask her about race and what she thinks of the theater collective casting an Afro-Dominican actress (Karina Valdez), in the role of Bernarda Alba.

"Let me see if I understand what you are asking," she responds a bit nervously. When I ask more generally what she made of the production of *Bernarda Alba* in light of the different shades of Dominican actresses who made up the cast, she responds without hesitation: "Well, it totally goes against what is socially established, where the white [person] is rich and the black [person] is poor. It goes against what they sell us in society."

"Did you have the opportunity to choose your role?" I ask, stumbling through Spanish that had become rusty over my years away and unprepared with a vocabulary to talk about theater. I am just getting warmed up and slow to pick up on Johanna's use of *personaje* when referring to the many roles she has played rather than my attempt to use the cognate *carácter*.

"Would you have wanted to play Bernarda?" I ask her. She tells me that Isabel decided on her role but she actually liked playing Poncia more than Bernarda: "La Poncia carries everything, she is aware of what is going on, nothing is hidden from her." Moreover, Johanna affirms, making Bernarda the darkest one in this production upends many Dominican ideas about color and class: The matriarch is black; the maid is white. And yet, within Dominican racial logic it is also no surprise to see Bernarda, the character most invested in distancing herself from others through class, portrayed as dark-skinned. Her strong desire for social attainment seems to make sense. She is desperate to resist others seeing her as socially inferior because of her gender, class, and color. Even though Johanna plays the role of La Poncia, the maid, she is, as she says, "más clarita," a more fair-skinned dominicana, making the casting a visual contradiction of racial logic. In fact, under the bright stage lights her skin is pale, her blonde hair gold in color.

"I'm not white," Johanna informs me. "Como dicen, tengo el negro detrás de la oreja [As they say, I have black behind the ear]," she interjects swiftly. "I'm just lighter but not of the white race." Although I was not seeking an explanation, Johanna seeks to clarify this for me, as if she has been misinterpreted before. The Dominican Republic has a long history of census-takers determining the racial identity of those they are surveying and the producers of the national identification card selecting the racial identity for that person.[42] Johanna tells me that she would not be cast as Bernarda in this instance, because as she says, "Soy lo más clara" and the production "es otra cara," showing another side of things in which "*el negro* is not bad, is not ugly, is not poor." Casting a darker-skinned Dominican woman in the role of Bernarda is disruptive of the status quo.

"Somos del Caribe . . . it's otro energia, no es la misma Bernarda de los españoles. Su energia es diferente, tiene cultura diferente. . . . [We are from the Caribbean, it's a different energy, it's not the same Bernarda of the Spanish. Her energy is different, she has a different culture]."

"What else can you see that is different?" I probe.

"Bueno, el fuego, el calor [Well, the fire, the heat] . . . wao!" she says excitedly, reflecting on the tension that builds among the women in Bernarda's house.

"I saw you as a white woman in *Hasta el abismo*," I confess to Johanna, remembering the disparate range of Dominican women characters in that production as well. The darkest in color wore her natural hair in an afro. Johanna's character worked at the front desk of the psychiatrist's office, while a series of patients called and entered and tensions build. Not only because of her being *mas clara* but because of the office job that Johanna's character holds in that play, it seems feasible to me that the audience interpreted her as white, as I did.

"Yes, there is a racial hierarchy," Johanna tells me, "but I don't see it this way . . . I see everyone as human beings with the same capacity and right to exist. I have the same rights as you to be in this place." The language that Johanna uses and her framework for discussing race is common in the Dominican Republic, one that centers human rights. It is only at the end of our conversation that I further describe my interest in the ambiguities of racial identity in the Dominican Republic, and Johanna shares a bit more.

"Sí, aquí yo soy blanca. Pero no soy blanca [Yes, here I'm white. But I'm not white]," she laughs. I know exactly what she means and by now I understand the ways she holds these seemingly opposing realities of Dominican racial identity. It is possible to represent multiple racial meanings at one time, something hard to understand for those whose racial identity matches how they see themselves. While I explain that I am also looking at the symbols that inform how we interpret someone's racial meaning that go beyond color, Johanna is reiterating what I have been told in so many ways by Dominicans before, both verbally and nonverbally: "For example here, a black from Haiti and a [Dominican] black . . . they are different."

When I interviewed Isabel the week before, I had asked her about the "optics" of this production of *Bernard Alba*, or what she thinks the casting might look like to an outsider. It is only when I nudge her further, explaining my politics and the questions that I want to engage with her about her experience and knowledge of race—mentioning the black feminist writing of Combahee River Collective, bell hooks, and Audre Lorde that I know she is familiar with—that she begins to understand what I want to talk about.

Inevitably, as an outsider, I am frequently misreading race in Las Maleducadas' production even as I am reading for color: "Claro, Johanna es una mujer negra [of course, Johanna is a black woman]," Isabel tells me. "Claro que sí [of course she is]."

"Yes, here [in the Dominican Republic] we have a problem in this sense because Johanna is a black woman. What happened is the theme of *la negritude* here is a theme *muy fuerte* because it is a thing that the people understand as limited to skin color and la negritude is all of a system of power, you understand?" I do understand. Though in the moment I realize the differences in my own thinking about racialization and dominicanidad. Isabel's explanation is decidedly more nuanced than my own when Dominican women who are "black behind the ears" identify with and mobilize their blackness in collaboration with other Afro-Dominican women who, because of their darkness in color, are experiencing their blackness quite differently. I had assumed Isabel would be more critical of an all-inclusive notion of who is black, as several of my other Afro-Dominican friends have been, but she points to a politics of blackness in her collective.

"Like, what *la negritude* implies is a political system and the way the people understand it is very basic by color because they have invested in '*el negro pobre, el negro malo, el negro este*' [the poor black, the bad black, the black who is this or that]." It is the same stereotype that Johanna references.

Isabel explains, "Johanna is a black woman. All of us Caribbean women are black. You see? But I imagine this is a very personal thing as well." Isabel says that she tries to work with actresses who have this political understanding and that there are many who do not or are not interested in this topic. She says of her colleague, "Yes, well, Johanna has skin that is a little lighter but she doesn't *not* say she is a black woman from the Caribbean, and situations happen but in relation to us she has the *privilege* of having the lightest skin within the group [her emphasis]." It is within Teatro Maleducadas that Johanna's political identity as a black woman is sharpened. This is not unlike Karma Chavez's assertion in her reading of Chela Sandoval's notion of differential consciousness among women of color: "Who someone is, is constructed by where they already belong and where they choose to belong. Differential belonging also compels us to *be* longing, to desire relations across lines of difference [emphasis in original]."[43] Johanna's racial background shapes her politics even when her phenotype may not reveal much of this "truth" about her racial identity.

It is the misrecognition of visual cues, something that often occurs when we move across scopic regimes, that causes problems. Those instances of misreading race as it aligns with context—when an individual identifies herself on racial terms that are different from how others in society identify her, for example—are interpreted as mistakes of an irrational mind. Spinning into madness, it seems, is something that inevitably happens to young women like Adela who have begun to see the world in other ways, or as Isabel suggests, recognize "other worlds that are possible."

My questioning of Isabel, hesitant at first and then more assertive, seems to provoke in her another level of engagement with the production. She recalls the production of *Bernarda Alba* anew, likely drawing on emotions surrounding it as well as the photographic images that exist as part of an online archive.

"Very interesting," says Isabel. "Now here's what I'm thinking. Bernarda is blacker than La Poncia and La Poncia is the servant of Bernarda. They are also doing this power play, breaking from the established power structure because Bernarda is a black woman and *la dueña* and La Poncia is under her; her servant is white. Of course, it isn't supposed to be like this because the idea is that these hierarchies of power don't exist between women put in competition with one another. But now I am thinking about this phenomenon that I hadn't seen. Talking with you I realized it." In reality, it is more like Isabel is reencountering this detail of the production, rather than not having thought of it. I had asked her these questions about race and color after I had first seen the play. Our interaction in this ethnographic encounter (many years later) demonstrates the dialogical nature of the interview and my ongoing presence as vocal observer of her work: Isabel shapes my thinking on her cultural production while I also shape hers.

Whiteness as Metaphor

Introduced in the previous chapter, Robelitza is one of several actresses in Teatro Maleducadas who Isabel mentioned had traveled abroad and then rejoined the collective when she returned to the island. She had much to share with me about her experiences of racism in Europe, which had put a finer point on how she understood her own identity as caribeña and how she talked about Dominican hierarchies of color. Robelitza's skin color has clearly shaped how she experiences her own identity in terms of race. Her hair type, which she brings up in the conversation, is long, dark, and wavy. She is the closest in color to Karina, whom I saw play Bernarda, but with different hair texture. At some point during the banter of our back-and-forth conversation Robelitza casually remarks, "Eres mulata, more or less, you are mestiza" in an effort to place me within an existing Dominican scopic regime that, according to her, would categorize me as mulata or mestiza. It is in no way an unusual comment for me to hear from someone I have just met. I have already read Robelitza as only the slightest bit darker than I am,

yet I realize there is something I overlook about facial features in my calculations, including how she might interpret my identity. These interactions that
define our racial observations of one another happen in the flash of an eye.

Our interview takes place at the *cafetería* of the Supermercado Nacional on
Churchill. At times we are shouting in lively conversation with one another
over the din of people having breakfast. A man with a deep voice offers a
lengthy explanation of something to his companion at the table behind us,
and the loudspeaker of the supermarket occasionally crackles on over music
being piped in. It is the average level of sound in Santo Domingo. We are
seated beside windows that face the parking lot. Robelitza is interested in
my work on gender but it is clear that she has not resolved her thoughts on
the subject to the degree that she has about the race and the racism she has
experienced as a Dominican woman. More than once in our conversation
she relegates something she is about to say to being "off the record," mainly
because it is not fully formed as an opinion that I should include in my research, or it is the anecdotal personal experience of someone else. She pa-
tiently corrects me as I work to pronounce the word *misogénia* (misogyny)
in Spanish with my emphasis on the correct syllable.

"Yo soy—yo era, muy introvertida [I am—I was very introverted],"
Robelitza confesses, laughing in a way that cuts through my own nervousness
about asking yet another stranger personal questions about their experiences
of race and gender. She says, "I have been much more so than I am right now,
but I studied theater since I was very little. I don't know if you could tell, but I
am another person on stage."[44] I have in fact seen this level of transformation
in *all* of Las Maleducadas, a true testament to their training and expertise.

"I have always had the good fortune to be directed by women and to
work with other women," she tells me. "We all have in common this question, this restlessness to always do things and we are very, one should say
. . . we are very authentic. There's no question of wanting to pretend, no, . . .
let alone around being Dominican. And the other thing I can confirm is being *caribeño*—or rather caribeña. Many times they want to you to highlight
your African heritage only but there are all kinds of things that you come
from, including, for example, I'm from a town where there is a lot of Arab
influence, there are many, many Lebanese immigrants, Turkish too. I mean,
I can't separate that from my culture, you know? Because in some way that
influences you." For Robelitza this mixture is very much what it means to
be caribeña, which she describes as an entire world of cultures including the
language and influences of the Taíno. "Yo soy de [I am from] San Juan de la
Maguana," she explains.

"When did you begin to use this term *caribeña* over others?" I ask and she shares with me a story about the complexity of her identity development. "My father helped me a lot. He gave me many books. He told me that he did not want me to be raised like a little girl who was waiting for her prince to save her, none of that." Her father expected Robelitza and her sisters to work hard and become self-sufficient. It was as an adolescent that she came to understand her identity further: "In high school, I worried about my future ... because I am a black woman, I am from the Caribbean, I am poor, I am a woman." She could see the ways that her intersecting identities marginalized her and made her a minority of a minority so, she said, she worked harder. In college at la UASD, Robelitza joined cultural groups in which she was able to read the works of those, including Lorca, who were equally marginalized yet able to find their voice. While she studied journalism and communication, she continued to participate in theater where there was also space to talk about and use the term *caribeña*.

In the 2013 production of *Bernarda Alba*, Robelitza's role was Maria Josefa, "la vieja," the sequestered "lunatic" mother of Bernarda. In a scene late in the play, Maria Josefa turns up with a little white lamb in her arms that she coos to as if it were her child. Her stream-of-consciousness rants emphasize the smothering nature of the family's extended mourning period but also bring into our awareness the overwhelmingness of whiteness in Lorca's story and how it serves as a critical metaphor throughout the play. Lorca describes the setting for Act One as an "extremely white inner room"; Bernarda commands her servants to whitewash the courtyard; a white stallion appears near the house like an apparition. While implying purity and the sterility of the home, the whiteness that surrounds the women becomes oppressive.[45] It is even more obvious when the actresses delivering these ruminations, metaphors, and even euphemisms about whiteness are themselves not white as they reference whiteness throughout the production. Words that a dark-skinned Robelitza delivers in the role of Maria Josefa will be understood differently, then, in the Dominican racial context: "It's true. Everything is too dark. You think I can't have children because my hair is white, but I can. I can have children, children, and more children. This child will have white hair, and there will be another child and another and they will all have snow-white hair, and we will be like the waves of the sea, and we will all have white hair and we will be foam."

Robelitza's empassioned performance as la vieja can easily be interpreted as a desire for and preoccupation with whiteness within the family line, not unfamiliar in a culture in which "*mejorando la raza* [improving the race]" or producing fairer children is encouraged. In this racial context, the text resonates with this Dominican preoccupation, paralleling Bernarda's deep desire to improve her social standing. Through Robelitza's portrayal of Maria Josefa, the whole family's insecure relationship to whiteness is revealed.

The Wrath of Bernarda

Dressed all in black—with dark skin and black eyes and her thick black hair pinned up in a bun on top of her head—Bernarda is a force to be feared. She has rigid ideas about the role of women and men and limited perceptions of her role as a mother.[46] She is ambiguous in her gender performance because of the power that she claims as the master of her domain, in a society in which women do not typically hold that level of power: "As the hermaphroditic high priestess of her own religious cult, Bernarda Alba is convinced that she is carrying out inherited patriarchal obligations."[47] In fact, she is masculinized by her desire for and attainment of power over women.[48] By the same token, her character's blackness in this production leads us to read her as less feminine. Bernarda's aspirations for social attainment ring true in Lorca's text, across time and space, as does Bernarda's misogynistic rage. Her servant Poncia describes her as a "tyrant of all she surveys. She could sit on your heart and watch you die slowly for a year and not once unfix that cold smile from her damn face!"[49]

From Bernarda's perspective, Adela and her sisters are goods to be sold within a capitalist system. Lorca was as critical of the narrow expectations placed on Spanish women as I am on those placed on Dominican women to be either "saints and martyrs," or "whores worthy of hell and damnation, torture and burning."[50] His characters reflect three different generations of Spanish women: Romanticism in Maria Josefa (early to mid-nineteenth century), Realism/Naturalism (late nineteenth century) in Bernarda, and the Generation of 1898 that are Bernarda's daughters, representative of Surrealism and the early twentieth-century ethos of Spain.[51] According to Lorca, argues Knapp, "To idealize such moral absolute, women as sacrificial victim—as the Spanish masses did and as Bernarda Alba does—is to permit one's self and being to exist only through projection."[52] Indeed, Bernarda remains preoccupied with her reputation; worried what people will say about her mother's insanity or her daughters' purity. She keeps her mother and her daughters locked up, not out of concern for their well-being but for fear of what others might think. *¿Qué dirían?* she obsesses, "What will they say?"

She is representative of the oppressive messages of the broader society that can easily turn to paranoia.

Throughout, Bernarda's daughters direct their anger at their captor, rather than the society from which they have been removed, and she metes out a punishment on them for daring to be young women; like the dictatorship, the patriarchy reproduces itself. Rather than maintaining a home, Bernarda seems to rule over an estate, or a prison even, pacing the grounds and keeping an eye on all that enter her territory. Because of her blackness, her hold on economic power can be read as precarious and it seems to confirm for viewers that her anxieties about society are not unfounded. Racial discrimination and policy in the Dominican Republic have regularly led to the reappropriation of land owned by black and Haitian farmers in rural communities.

"The men around here are not of their class," says Bernarda, seeking to justify her daughters' captivity. Yet with men literally invisible in this narrative and its performance, we come to see that it is the matriarch who has driven her daughters' distress rather than society's violence. What Bernarda is willing to do to maintain the patriarchal order allows those who benefit most from the patriarchy to not even have to be involved. Men assume the role of an invisible hand. Bernarda is dedicated to maintaining systems of oppression in which she—in this case as a visibly black woman—is most vulnerable. She becomes the problem of patriarchy as an actor who maintains it; her five daughters are each merely an extension of her property.

"You have no right but to obey," Bernarda says to Angustias. "A disobedient daughter stops being your daughter and instead becomes an enemy."[53] At another point, Martirio tells her sister, "I do things without believing in them, but I do them anyway, like a clock."[54] The comments capture something of the mechanisms of identity and patriarchy under which independence is not rewarded. For women who do not fall in line, there is a high a cost. Throughout *Bernarda Alba*, Lorca offers a lesson in what happens to women who rebel, women who dare have their own desires. Three other women in Lorca's narrative fall from grace as a warning or perhaps a foreshadowing of Adela's fate. First, in town an unmarried woman—referred to only as "Librada's daughter"—had a child and then killed it to avoid disgrace within the community, but word traveled quickly about her actions. When the townspeople call for her to be killed, Bernarda is one of those who supports this violent response. She states, "Let the woman who tramples on her virtue pay the price," going further to state, "Finish her off before the police arrive! Place a burning coal where her sin lies!"[55] Secondly, Paca La Roseta, a foreigner whose story unfolds throughout the play, has a reputation as a "loose woman" to contrast with the purity of Bernarda's own daughters. Third, an unhappily married woman named Adelaide invokes the colonies; her parents met in Cuba, we come to learn. It is through this last tale that Martirio implies that the Caribbean is a wild and lawless place of violence.

Seeing and Policing Bodies

"Leave me alone!" says Adela. "Asleep or awake, what I do is my business! I'll do what I like with my body. . . . I wish I were invisible so I could walk through these rooms without you asking me where I'm going!" Adela is overwhelmed by life in her mother's house for she cannot escape constant surveilling of her every action by other women around her. "Martirio's eyes, Poncia's, are heterotopic: They function on all parts of her body—fingers, head, arms. These women see everywhere, into the most sacred and shaded areas of the household. Hunted down and haunted by Martirio's gaze, Adela can find no refuge, no place within the home that she can call her own; she feels hounded," Knapp explains.[56]

In an exercise of power, Martirio (Paloma Palacios) stares obsessively at her sister, policing her every movement. The interaction emphasizes the mere power and control of gazing at the body, through which the human eye—and later photographic technology—has long-served to produce (and reproduce) racial logics, write Maurice O. Wallace and Shawn Michelle Smith, thereby reinforcing a "desire for classification, an obsession with recognizing the body as the essential teller not only of racial status but of racial difference."[57] As viewers of the play, we are likewise complicit in the surveilling of Adela. When she shouts at Martirio "Stop looking at me!" she is in fact shouting it at all of us watching her on the stage. We are trapped into seeing.[58] It is as if we have our eyes pressed into a stereograph. As we witness the violence against the girl-child and her subsequent unraveling, there is no clear action for us to take so we become nothing more than complicit voyeurs, peering into the camera obscura that Lorca has constructed.

"She follows me everywhere. Sometimes she looks into my room to see if I'm sleeping," Adela's complaint continues. "She doesn't let me breathe. And she's always saying: 'What a shame about that face! What a shame about that body that no one will ever see!' She's wrong about that. My body will be for whomever I want!"[59] Adela talks back to the bodily policing that her sister perpetuates. Martirio bullies her sister in this way because she, too, wants to possess Pepe. When she steals a photograph of him away from her sister Angustias, to whom

Figure 10. The Facebook page of Teatro Maleducadas, with Karina Valdez as Bernarda. Screenshot by author.

he is betrothed, he is transformed into an object. As such, the photograph of Pepe becomes a good for transaction; with it she holds hostage the love of one for another.[60] As Susan Sontag recognized, "Photographs give mock forms of possession: of the past, of the present, even the future."[61] The technology of the photograph that haunts Lorca's work uniquely translates in today's use of social media, representing evolving social constructions of gender, race, color, and class. These online and offline visual representations refract a distant Spanish past into a contemporary Dominican transnational present.

While Bernarda cares a great deal about *how* others see her, Adela, at twenty years old, is merely desperate to be seen by others. Adela is coming into her own identity; she seeks freedom at all costs. Although Bernarda demands that all of her daughters wear black in mourning, Adela appears wearing an emerald green dress. Under bright stage lights, the color dramatically contrasts her pale skin and candy apple red hair, making her stand out. Color matters here and she is shockingly provocative with red hair and a dress that is the color of her own jealousy, as her sister Angustias suggests. It also contrasts the rest of the staging. Writes Stephen M. Hart, "The greenness of Adela's dress, itself ostensibly an image of life versus the death imagery of white/black, however, is ambiguous, since green, in Lorca's private world of symbols, invariably contains the seed of its own death."[62] It becomes another foreshadowing and when no one is there to see Adela and confirm her life and her beauty, she begs the hens in the hen house to bear witness to her.

Adela appears almost a decontextualized object at the center of the play where she stands out from the rest. Her existence seems symbolic of the Surrealist moment: we hear a cacophony of voices around her feeding her subconscious.[63] For example, in a scene in which Adela is speaking with Poncia, she tries to turn off her chastising voice:

> ADELA: Be quiet!
> PONCIA: (*Loudly*) Do you think I haven't noticed?
> ADELA: Lower your voice!
> PONCIA: You should kill all those thoughts in your head!
> ADELA: What do you know?
> PONCIA: Old women can see through walls. Where do you go at night when you get up?
> ADELA: You should be blind!
> PONCIA: My head and my hands are full of eyes when it comes to such things. No matter how much I think about it, I still don't know what you're up to . . . [64]

The scene depicts how intensely the older woman is seeking to control the body of Adela, while both of them are trapped in Bernarda's home. Though she tries desperately, Adela is unable to silence Poncia's voice and we witness the lines blur between what she is truly experiencing and what are actually voices her head: "Be quiet!" shouts Adela.

"I will not be quiet!" snaps Poncia.

"Mind your own business. You're nothing but a nosy, treacherous creature!" Adela screams back at the old woman.

"I shall be your shadow!" Is Poncia's response.

In contrast to Adela's, Martirio's body is different. Her spine is twisted and she declares that this malformation has spared her: "It's better never to look at a man. Ever since I was a child I have been frightened of them. I would see them in the stable yard, yoking the oxen and lifting the sacks of wheat, shouting and stamping their feet, and I was always afraid to grow up and find myself suddenly in one of their arms. God has made me weak and ugly and has kept them away from me forever." Her sentiments reflect her own interpretation of herself as an object to be "manhandled" like animals or sacks of grain. Yet Martirio does not see her bodily difference as determining her lot in life, or so she tells Adela: "What's ugliness to them? All they care about is land, oxen, and to have a submissive bitch to feed them." She teaches her younger sister about a value system in which she has come to understand her social position.

"That's what it means to be a woman," Bernarda explains as Adela suffers emotionally from her confinement. Poncia responds: "Cursed be all women." Another of Adela's sisters, Amelia, proclaims: "To be born a woman is the greatest punishment." This punishment is often meted out by Bernarda with physical violence. After Martirio steals her sister's photograph of Pepe she faces her mother's rage and threat of violence. "May you be cut to pieces, you little good-for-nothing! Always making trouble in this house!" Martirio responds to the violence with anger: "Don't you hit me, Mother!"

"I'll hit you as many times as I want!" Bernarda asserts with great confidence about her ownership of the body of her girl-child.

"If I let you! Do you hear? Get away from me!" Martirio says, attempting to reclaim her body.[65]

Adela finds strength in her sexuality, that which causes fear in her mother. Bernarda says of her youngest daughter, "She takes after her aunts: white and dripping sweet and making goo-goo eyes at any common barber's least bit of flattery. How we have to suffer and struggle to make sure people behave decently and don't run wild!"[66] Ultimately, Bernarda's daughters contend with one another for the chance to be governed by a man, rather than a matriarch. The irony of Adela's quest for freedom is exactly this: "There will be an end to the warden's voice here! (Adela seizes her mother's walking stick and breaks it in half) This is what I do with the tyrant's rod. Do not take another step. No one but Pepe governs me!" Her action can also be read as a powerful metaphor for the transition from one dictatorship to the next. As Jeffrey Oxford writes, "Bernarda's daughters represent the philosophical underpinnings of early twentieth-century Spain. As a unit, their search for identity and a meaningful future, while being hemmed up in a restraining environment bound by the traditions of the past, corresponds closely to what is commonly called the second wave of the Generation of 98; i.e. the Generation of 27, or the *avant-garde* to which Lorca himself is often tied."[67]

Likewise, Isabel explained to me in 2014, "[Lorca] uses the character of Bernarda, I think, as a small protest against Franquismo [Franco's fascism] that was happening at the time. . . . As it happens, the women here in the Dominican Republic feel very cornered by many past events, you know? I made an analogy between that moment and this moment to contextualize the work."[68] Isabel's analogy is a powerful and effective one—these echoes of past dictatorships emerge in the psyches of this generation of Dominicans.[69]

As viewers of the play, we are the ones who bear witness to Adela spinning into madness. In the end, Lorca weaves a tragedy. Adela takes her own life when she believes her mother has shot and killed the man she loves. After Bernarda pursues Pepe with a gun, shooting at him and later declaring that she has killed him, Adela runs to her room and hangs herself, thus suggesting that she felt she had no other recourse and nothing left to live for. She frees herself from her mother's grasp only through death. For Bernarda, only her family's reputation matters in that moment.

Immediately testifying to Adela's virginity, she emphasizes her daughter's purity in death—what allegorically seems to underscore Adela's "whiteness"— rather than acknowledge the loss of life. Adela's death happens off stage, and audiences only witness her mother's response. In an alternate reading of Lorca's work through this Dominican production, such a denouement could easily be read as the resolution to a "tragic mulatto" narrative of early twentieth-century US literature in which the all-but-white daughter of a black mother takes her own life because she cannot live in a world where she does not fit into a racial binary. Often queer narratives end up with the same conclusion: a character who dares to challenge existing social categories must be eradicated in order for the larger social system to be maintained.

In the end, this focus on death reflects Lorca's understanding of the *duende*, a deep-seated passion he felt was required of the finest artists (particularly in southern Spain) in order that they be moved to create: "great art—art with *duende* can only occur when the creator is acutely aware of death."[70] However, we might best understand *Bernarda Alba* as a "record of absence from being but also as an *extended process that outlines the fragmentation of subjectivity*, a consequence of the paralysis of the imaginative vision by de-structive forces [emphasis in original]."[71] Adela, like her sisters, is trapped in a system in which she has little agency or autonomy. Along with her growing consciousness about the trap that she is in comes Adela's tragic demise.[72]

6

Feminist Rage and the Right to Life for Women in the Dominican Republic

Part of my anger is always libation for my fallen sisters.
Audre Lorde, "Uses of Anger: Women Responding to Racism"

"Those fears are over my child, they are over. . . . These times are different. It's not so dangerous now," says Dedé Mirabal in an early scene in the Dominican film *Trópico de sangre* (2010). She places her hand on the shoulder of a brown-skinned adolescent girl who appears startled by the narrative she sees unfolding as she steps into the childhood home of Las Hermanas Mirabal. Now a museum, it is a shrine to the murdered Mirabal sisters, Minerva, Patria, and María Theresa. Their younger sister Dedé, the only one to survive Rafael Leonidas Trujillo's dictatorship, greets guests at the museum. Now elderly, she has an arresting white streak in her black hair that seems to mark her trauma. We don't have to worry about such persecution from the government any longer, Dedé assures the unnamed girl, while also seeming to assure viewers that Dominicans can now live free from the terror perpetrated by Trujillo.

Although Dominicans no longer live under a brutal dictatorship, communities nevertheless contend with state and interpersonal violence and its rippling effects. This book would be incomplete without a more explicit discussion of violence and particularly the ongoing gender-based violence that permeates life in the Dominican Republic. This final chapter is a meditation on the ways that representations of Dominican women signify and how their identities consistently see/saw in meaning within existing structures of power. These structures of power sustain violence. When I began my research for what would become this book, I expected to focus on questions of race that had mainly been engaged historically in the field of Dominican studies.

I was curious about the "racial exceptionalism" narrative in the African diaspora, and interested in how Dominican national identity was produced in relation to Haitian identity—a focus of much scholarship in Dominican studies at the turn of the twenty-first century.[1] Living in Santo Domingo, however, I developed a range of relationships with many different Dominican women—interviewees, informants, neighbors, friends, host mothers, teachers, students, and even romantic partners. Based on these intimacies, I was motivated to consider the impact of patriarchal structural violence on how dominicanas live their lives. Intimate partner violence is one of the leading causes of death among Dominican women ages twenty to thirty-four.[2]

A surrealist lens on the contemporary moment in Santo Domingo encourages one to pay close attention to the morbidity of life; I would have had to make an effort to ignore the specter of death created by an epidemic of femicides. Like anthropologist Aimee Cox writing about Black girls in Detroit, it is with a sense of urgency and social obligation that I write about the "shapeshifting" that Dominican women do under the pressures of "globalized neocolonial realities" in the urban environments in which they grow up.[3] Cox argues that "understanding the ways in which every day Black women make sense of their lives by theorizing the present and imagining the future is essential for supporting ways of living that resist the dehumanization implied in normative scripts."[4] I am also interested in the acts of resistance.

When Audre Lorde spoke about the uses of anger, she was clear about the origins of women's rage: "We operate in the teeth of a system for which racism and sexism are primary, established, and necessary props of profit."[5] It is the cost of capitalism, many scholars have argued. Calculated risks taken and costs assessed by the powers that be during structural adjustment in the Caribbean in the 1980s are not unlike the impact of austerity measures today. The price paid, according to black feminist ethnographer Faye Harrison, is structural violence, which "relies upon constructions of masculinity and femininity that help produce and reproduce the mobility and accumulation of transnational capital."[6] Dominican feminists Magaly Pineda, Marta Olga García, and Laura Faxas suggest that to truly achieve "*liberación femenina*" and usher in new ways of thinking about gender, there must be a cultural revolution across all social classes in the Dominican Republic, or else capitalist modes of production will continue to inform a hegemonic structure that marginalizes women.[7]

Patriarchal oppression as a legacy of colonialism in the Dominican Republic is undergirded by a constant threat of violence, real acts of violence, as well as a long history of colonial violence integral to systems of slavery. Intersecting oppressions faced by Dominican women include their objectification as commodities within a neoliberal economy, particularly one based on tourism, and this reality shapes how Dominican women understand and perform their identities. As Paula Moya writes, "Identities are evaluable theoretical claims that have epistemic consequences. Who we understand ourselves to be will have consequences for how we experience and understand the world. Our conception of who we are as social beings (our identities) influence—and in turn are influenced by—our understandings of how our society is structured and what our particular experiences in that society are likely to be."[8]

This last chapter necessarily serves as a cry of rage in response to multiple examples of violence against women and girls that testify to the ways that Dominican women are seen as expendable within a hierarchy of class and color in which they have been "taught that [their] lives depended upon the good will of patriarchal power."[9] In interviews I rarely invited conversations about violence directly because it was not the focus of my project, nor was it something I had permission from the Institutional Research Board of my university to investigate. Yet violence against women was always present through daily street harassment, stories of community violence, or the high rates of sexual assaults that friends had experienced as part of daily life. Friends and acquaintances might hint at their own stories of sexual violence or abuse, but it was more common that they shared the stories of others: one friend spouted off two gang rape stories she had heard that involved two young girls in her neighborhood.

"It's often a band of tigueres," she tells me, to describe the behaviors of men moving in gangs on the street at night, acting above and beyond the law. Having heard this term often in the Dominican Republic, I interpreted my friend's use of it to refer to poor and working-class men, who act as "opportunists."[10] Of course she and I also know that it is often family members and neighbors who, under the cover of close-knit community, perpetrate sexual violence against children around them and blame is perpetually displaced. Dominican women learn at a young age that they are unsafe in their own bodies. The daily paper and news media publish story after story about men who have killed their wives, daughters, or girlfriends, frequently in acts of murder-suicide. Flimsy explanations for these brutal murders regularly accompany grim images of a crime scene or photos of the victim taken from social media: "she cheated on him," or "she tried to leave him," or "she didn't have his food ready for him when he came home."[11] Many of the young women I interviewed or spoke with informally had friends and family members who experienced the types of gender-based violence narrated and documented in the numerous studies funded by the United Nations, Amnesty International, local NGOs, and news media.

I begin this chapter by examining visual representations of gender, sexuality, power, and la dominicana in the 2010 film *Trópico de sangre*. Specifically, I interrogate Dominican American actress Michelle Rodriguez's performance of Minerva Mirabal, the main protagonist in this most recent retelling of the heroine's life. As a Dominican production created by writer/director Juan Delancer for Dominican audiences and funded by the Dominican cellphone corporation Orange (now Altices), the film is as an excellent concluding cultural text to consider. Not only does it affirm my broader argument about existing stereotypes of Dominican women within Dominican popular culture, but it also provides examples of how racial meaning is produced relationally through longstanding narratives about who Dominican women are.

Since at least the 1980s, the Mirabal sisters have been transnationally celebrated as icons of resistance, and their stories exist as enduring representations of la dominicana. When I asked my interviewees where they had read about Dominican women, many could name only one text: Julia Álvarez's novel *In the Time of the Butterflies*, based on the life and death of the Mirabal sisters. In 2010, Minerva's face could be seen on murals, T-shirts, movie posters, and protest signs throughout the country, and her photograph circulated widely online. Casting Rodriguez in the role of Minerva, I argue, reinforces a highly conventional representation of the Dominican heroine as white, while at the same time the actress's queered body inserted into the text disrupts the traditional narrative. A queer reading of this text is yet another way to explore the stories we tell ourselves about what we see when we see Dominican women's bodies. Moreover, symbols of different aspects of Minerva's identity and her shift from adolescence into adulthood determine how we view Rodriguez at different moments, watching her see/saw in meaning. In addition, one final ethnographic moment in this chapter provides instructive insights from two young women about how they view their gendered position within Dominican society in relation to others.

Finally and above all, transnational political organizing has been part of a legacy of Dominican feminist mobilization since the early twentieth century.[12] Dominican feminist activists have sustained decades of protest against anti-abortion laws, lack of separation of church and state, gender-based violence, and more recently LGBTQ+ rights. Today, increasing numbers of Dominicans are taking to the streets in protest. In 2017, the Dominican Republic saw unprecedented engagement during the Marcha Verde protests against government corruption—it would lead to elections that ousted the ruling

Figure 11. Feminist activists in Santo Domingo protest against violence against women as part of the Marcha de las Mariposas, November 24, 2019. Photo by Lorena Espinoza Peña.

party in 2020.[13] Preceding this, Ni Una Menos, a global movement against femicide that originated in Argentina, fomented numerous marches in the streets of Santo Domingo. In recent years, Dominican feminist activists mobilized to bring transnational attention to the deaths of two adolescent girls, killed because they were pregnant: one at the hands of the state when she was denied medical care and the other murdered by her lover. I consider their stories here, and how they were taken up by popular media, in order to reflect on the ways that the personhood of young Dominican women is differently imagined based on class and color. How these deaths were mobilized around and understood within the recent present in Santo Domingo has much to do with the young women's identities that, while seemingly fixed, remained malleable in the narratives that followed their deaths. I see these popular representations of Dominican women in the dominant culture as wholly connected and determined by race, color, class, and gender performance.

Fictions of Identity in *Trópico de Sangre*

Trópico de sangre retells a well-known Dominican story about the life and death of the Mirabal sisters, also known as "las mariposas."[14] The film made visualizable (and audible) for Dominican viewers some of the violence experienced during the Trujillo era. In yet another reminder of the horrors of the Dominican past that perhaps make the present reality look less terrifying, Delancer's film also reproduces notions of the respectable Dominican woman. Although Dominican viewers know the outcome of this story, the tense narrative of a young girl following her dreams while being pursued by a powerful man carries us through the film. I went to see the historical drama the week of its release in Santo Domingo at the Cinemacentro Malecón on the waterfront. Its opening scene places viewers in the recent present, in which a busload of Dominican middle schoolers travel to the town of Salcedo to tour Casa Museo Hermanas Mirabal. The museum serves as an entry point for a trip back in time, with a Dominican youth as our guide. We view the home through the eyes of a brown-skinned adolescent girl who explores the displays of remaining artifacts, as she learns the history of the Mirabal sisters for the very first time. When she finally pulls her headphones from her ears, it seems to mark her awakening from a technological stupor to truly see what is in front of her: the museum has framed the blood-stained cloth used to clean the three sisters' corpses. Viewers witness the child's recognition of this macabre history, though we never hear her speak.

When the camera pans across a black-and-white photograph of María Teresa, the youngest Mirabal sister murdered, we see her beaming with pride as she shows off her long, wavy hair that hangs down her back. In the most surreal of fashions, the brown-skinned Dominican girl of the contemporary moment takes in this image of the fair-skinned María Theresa and all that remains of her now: a tight braid of hair, salvaged after her death. The rope of hair, now separated from the innocent girlchild's body and displayed in a plexiglass case, is extraordinary. Now a detached object, María Theresa's braid still serves to racialize and feminize her by providing physical "proof" of a European ancestry, thereby distancing her from an African one. It contrasts with the curly, dark hair of the girl we have followed on this tour, whose *pajón* makes her stand out from her peers and tells us she is one to challenge the status quo, much like Minerva.

We are first introduced to Minerva in the film as she dances around in a shop making faces in front of some mirrors as she tries on hats. Rodriguez plays the protagonist youthfully. She first tries on a feminine pink hat that matches her dress and two women in the shop remark to a salesclerk, "What a pretty girl." In the next moment, however, Minerva places on her head a black beret, like that of Che Guevarra, and gives herself a good look in the mirror. When she hears the shouts of protesters in the street, she steps out of the shop to witness state violence against protesting workers and we infer her own moment of adolescent awakening. She is abruptly interrupted, however, when her older sister Patria whisks her away moments before Trujillo's henchmen jump out and bloody the crowd of protestors.[15]

Trópico de sangre's central narrative begins in 1947, seventeen years into the dictatorship of Trujillo and a decade after the massacre of thousands of Dominicans and Haitians at the northern border. Periodization in the film is conveyed through American-made cars of the era and black-and-white photographs of Trujillo that are hung in every home. Shots of banana plantations remind us of our location in the Caribbean. The rural landscape is dotted with brown bodies worn from labor, while the Mirabal family—all of them white Dominicans—is depicted as a pillar of the community, generously sharing their resources. We see young Minerva enamored of her country, as she gazes out of the window of her new American automobile that her father has given her for her birthday; she lovingly surveys the landscape and its workers assuming her status as part of the elite class of Dominicans. Class details reinforce for the viewer the idea that the Mirabals are a valued part of the managerial class.[16] In fact, the focus and vantage point of the entire film is that of a landowning class of Dominicans who, it suggests, offer potential for the future of the nation.

Across the collapsed timeline of the film, Rodriguez is able to transform Minerva from an innocent young girl to a rebellious college student, to a young mother, all while seeming to keep the protagonist's reputation untarnished. Minerva's feminine purity is protected, in my opinion, because of her whiteness, which is produced and confirmed throughout the film always in contrast to unnamed, sexualized, brown-skinned women around her. Part of Rodriguez's ability to transform also relies on her Dominican-ness, and the narrative of her background that warrants her presence in the film.

Queering Minerva

In many ways, Rodriguez was a good fit for the role of Minerva because she physically resembles her. But it was the Hollywood actress's reputation that most needed to transform. She was a controversial choice to play the venerated Minerva, a national heroine and representative of the nation. Carlos Leiter, president of New York–based Fundación Minerva Mirabal, made a public complaint in 2008 about Rodriguez's casting in the Dominican film.[17] Yet she indicated her enthusiasm for the part in an interview with the online Mexican paper *El Mundial*: "Tengo mucho fuego, inteligencia, no soy rastrera y tengo lo necesario para enseñarle al mundo aspectos de una mujer respetuosa como fue Minerva."[18] She uses Dominican colloquialisms to assert her identity and capacity to play one of the country's most respected female figures, while the paper makes a point of remarking on Rodriguez's fluency in Spanish, as if affirming her authenticity. In fact, the Texas-born actress had spent some years of her childhood growing up in the Dominican Republic and then Puerto Rico, eventually moving to Jersey City in high school. Regarding this childhood and her own formation of identity, Rodriguez articulates an experience of fracture: "I was split in two, kind of like a brain. But growing up in Jersey City was interesting. I got to learn a lot about different cultures: I had Hindu friends, Middle Eastern friends, black friends, Spanish friends. I spent the beginning of my life in Texas, and then my parents got divorced and I went to the Dominican Republic, learned Spanish, forgot every word of English I knew, and then, when I was about 11, 12, we moved to Jersey City. Everywhere I go I'm an outsider."[19] Her transnational identity and experience, through which she is often in the process of uniting different parts of herself and in a negotiation with her own dominicanidad, is analogous to the experiences of Dominican women I interviewed.

Yet, Rodriguez was not identified by any of my interviewees as "authentically" Dominican, based either in how she looked or what they knew of her identity. Viewed as a "bad girl," she did not appear to have much of a following in Dominican media, even though the *Fast and Furious* films she stars in are extremely popular with Dominican audiences. She plays a "tough girl" as Letty not only in those films, but also in earlier roles as Diana in *Girl Fight*, Eden in *Blue Crush*, Lou in *Battle in Seattle*, and later Trudy in *Avatar* and Ana in the TV show *Lost*, to name a few. Writes Milla Jovovich, Rodriguez's costar in *Resident Evil*, "[She is] known for being kick-ass, for being the strong woman and representing female empowerment."[20] Rodriguez explains: "At school, I was this tomboy kid who just loved to hang out with her friends and learn curse words, trying to fit in with the cool kids and defending all the kids who got picked on. . . . Nobody thought of me as a tough kid, except for the kids I beat up. [*laughs*] Not the real tough kids."[21]

A perception of Rodriguez as masculine in her gender performance has stuck to her so tightly that a recent film in which she starred had the working title *Tomboy*; movie posters depicted Rodriguez dressed as an assassin, her legs spread wide as she crouches above the film's title. Subsequently released only online in the United States with the title *The Assignment* (2017), the film tells the dark and violent story of Frank Kitchen (Rodriguez), a secret agent unwittingly forced to have "gender reassignment" surgery for the purpose of enacting a revenge. The role of a hypermasculine man trapped in a woman's body is the epitome of the way that Rodriguez is typecast. In her own derogatory terms, she had stated: "I play a butchy girl all the time, so they assume I'm a lesbo."[22] While denying or resisting a queered sexual orientation, Rodriguez has also racially essentialized herself when presenting heteronormatively by asserting a preference for hypermasculine men: "That's the Latina in me. It's in my construct, it's the way my DNA is just built for that alpha male kind of chemistry."[23] However, in general, the characters she portrays have consistently reinforced popular perceptions of her as queer: her deep scratchy voice, leather jackets, muscular build, the way she walks, how she takes up physical space as a woman, a visible awkwardness in hyperfeminine attire. These ways of being in her body are legible as nonnormative and nonheterosexual.

Rodriguez, in response to fans' interest in her sexual orientation—a lesbian fan following that claimed to have seen her with women in queer clubs from Hawaii to New York—laughed it off, saying, "Eh, they're not too far off. . . . I've gone both ways. I do as I please. I am too fucking curious to sit here and not try when I can. Men are intriguing. So are chicks."[24] Of course, it has long been the case that lesbians live under pressure to pass as heterosexual in order to survive in a patriarchal society.[25] When Rodriguez came out as bisexual in 2013, it was essentially to affirm an "open secret," as with Rita Indiana. She said of the media, "I don't talk about what I do with my vagina, and they're all intrigued. I've never walked the carpet with anyone, so they wonder: What does she do with her vagina?" When asked her opinion about the sexual prowess of her character Letty in the *Fast and Furious* films, she deploys the same misogynist language that the patriarchal system has likely used against her: "Yeah, she's a whore. [*laughs*] But you know what it is? People don't like talking about it, but if you're Spanish, you feel a weight. I don't have much history—I've got Rosie Perez, Jennifer Lopez, Rita Moreno. That's it. That's the history of Latin women in Hollywood, really." Rodriguez is aware of her own predicament in terms of the burden of representation in the film industry, that the sexism she experiences intersects with racism, nevertheless she seems to embrace a discourse that sustains it. In her own ways she resists the racialized gendered expectations of the film industry in the United States. Says Rodriguez, "I don't have the freedom to just do anything, because I have the political weight of having this last name and my heritage. . . . So when I looked at Letty, I told them, 'You can't do the stereotype thing. . . . Either you *don't* make her slut . . . and you respect her, or you're going to lose me.'"[26]

In *Trópico de sangre*, Minerva's resistance to proscribed gender norms and to being "put in her place" as a dominicana also appears to queer Rodriguez—or vice versa. "That woman is a man," a general tells another high-ranking official when he cannot persuade Minerva to have coffee with *el presidente*. In another scene, angered by her unwillingness to submit to him, Trujillo chastises his subordinates for not subduing her: "The one who organized this is not wearing pants. . . . She wears skirts!" Minerva—here, seemingly transformed by her clothing—disrupts his gendered ordering of the world. As it turns out, Minerva wearing pants during the film marks her shift out of girlhood. When we first see her in pants, she has just been denied reenrollment to the university and must write a letter to Trujillo pleading for her access to education. Conspicuously, in that same moment she is also wearing a large pink bow in her hair that, much like the action required of her, reduces her to childlike dependency like the *femme-enfant* of the Surrealist imagination. Minerva's childish bow, reminiscent of one worn by Adela in *La Casa de Bernarda Alba* (or even Alice in Wonderland), visually juxtaposes her agency and growing independence.

Color and Its Consequences

Trujillo views women as his property—he expects to have immediate access to them, the film suggests, and this includes the wives and daughters of his subordinates. After one of his speeches, he proclaims to a young brown-skinned woman in the audience, while looking her up and down: "You are very beautiful. Whose daughter are you?" Trujillo questions her social position in relation to another man, never even asking her name. He also pressures Minerva's family to bring her to a social event so that he might pursue her. Dressed in white, young Minerva resists the dictator's advances. When he eyes yet another brown-skinned girl at a party he has orchestrated, he takes the time to introduce himself to her. Publicly, Trujillo dances with fair-skinned young women, but he asks his henchmen to bring la morena back to his room that night.[27] When the unnamed woman obliges Trujillo's sexual desires—seemingly of her own accord—we, too, witness her disrobing. She is the mulata foil for Minerva's purity.

The fair-skinned Minerva remains chaste and clothed throughout the film, and only at the moment in which she runs off on a date with Manolo Tavárez and they pass by a *fiesta de palos*, an Afro-Dominican circle of drumming and dance, does she become sexualized. Kicking off her high heels, or symbolically discarding her class and the politics of respectability, she joins the dark-skinned Dominican couples dancing under a wooden structure. The pulse of Minerva's dancing seems to gesture to some deep connection she holds with the common people—and blackness. A closeup shot of Minerva's bare feet on wooden boards imply that those African rhythms beat inside her as well. We glimpse a wild look in her eye as if she is, in the moment, transformed. Her brush with a pulsing Otherness in the film eroticizes her, as blackness is mobilized to make her sexually desirable to Manolo, the man she will marry.

Actor Juan Fernández, who is famous for his portrayal of villains, plays the role of Trujillo in this film. He can be seen throughout covered in a fine layer of white dusting powder, something the dictator was known to do.[28] By transforming himself in terms of color and telling a different story about his family heritage as a Dominican of Haitian descent, Trujillo sought to access the privileges of whiteness. However, this required that those around him go along with the masquerade. His use of face powder in the film effectively makes Fernández's eyes look dark and beady; they convey Trujillo's desire to consume the bodies of the young women he sets his sights on. In a scene in which Trujillo powders his face while one of his attendants informs him about Minerva's beauty, the dictator licks his lips. The gesture echoes what Minerva's mother had warned her of—that El Jefe is known to "eat women with his eyes" and is "capable of eating one a day." When forced to dance with the dictator, she tells him that she is a little old for his tastes and he responds to her dig by asserting that a friend of his once said, "Que no hay mujeres terquas, si no hombres flojos [There are no stubborn women, just weak men]." His gross remark resonates with what Dominican men are taught at an early age about masculinity and their presumed power over women within a machista culture.[29] The "problem of patriarchy" that Minerva faces is not depicted as systemic, rather the story suggests that violence against Dominican women stems from the machismo of a megalomaniac.

"I didn't do anything wrong, why should I have to apologize to Trujillo?" she asks her father after rejecting the dictator's advances at a party. She is literally questioning the patriarchy about why the dictatorship has become such an obstacle for her and what the injustice of her gendered social position means for her life. It is her father who gently explains to her that she misunderstands the terms of their world. While it is a lesson for Minerva, it also becomes a paternalist warning to contemporary viewers about the dangers of Dominican women's advancement. As with Lorca's *Casa de Bernarda Alba*, death becomes the inevitable consequence for women whose worldview is not compatible with the iron hand of patriarchy (no matter who enforces it). We see toxic masculinity attributed to Trujillo alone, while other men in Minerva's life are portrayed as benevolent and well-meaning. Her father, for example, has a change of heart and allows her to study in the capital.

When Minerva's love interest is introduced in the film, he is immediately seen by Trujillo as competition. But Manolo Tavárez is shown as progressive in terms of gender. When he suggests that one day he and Minerva might have their own law practice and call it "Tavárez y Mirabal," Minerva's immediate response is "Why not Mirabal y Tavárez?" When we finally see the shingle hung it does indeed have her name listed first. The film is full of such moments, suggesting Minerva is a different kind of woman, as when she throws her law degree on the kitchen fire after realizing that Trujillo will never license her to practice her profession; she is furious about being relegated to the domestic sphere.

Minerva's rage is apparent through the visual shorthand that the film deploys: the camera focuses in on her tapping foot to convey her impatience as she waits to meet with el Jefe. In *Trópico de sangre*, we do not witness Minerva constantly batting off suitors, catcalls, or the sexual advances of men besides the dictator. The historical narrative does not align with Dominican women's knowledges of how they experience their gender today, each and every time they travel throughout the country, when they get in and out of a taxi, or sit by the road waiting for a guagua, or attempt to take up public space. While at no moment do we as viewers feel that the Mirabal sisters should have stayed at home instead of heading out to fight the dictatorship, we still take away from a story like this the lesson that Dominican men are unable to protect Dominican women from the brutality of other Dominican men.

Films such as this one that traffic in visual images of violence against women do little more than reinforce the martyrdom of the Mirabal sisters, without challenging dominant narratives around masculinity and gender roles. They do not "flip the script" but rather capitalize on the familiarity of stories of violence against women, and naturalize the aggressive pursuit of young woman and girls by older men. Because we know Minerva and her sisters will pay with their lives for their resistance to the dictatorship, one views the entire film with a sense of foreboding. In the film's final scene, the three sisters are driven off the road and attacked by Trujillo's henchmen. The violence against them is depicted in part from the perspectives of the male perpetrators, who stand over the young women beating and strangling them to death. In a scene that I consider to be pornographic in its glorification of the violence committed against the young women, they are murdered over the course of one and a half minutes of film. Viewers watch as the Mirabal sisters are beaten while crying for help, with no one to come to their rescue; then we see their bloodied bodies stacked in the back seat of the vehicle they dared to travel so freely in. So gratuitous is the scene that when one of the sisters coughs in the back seat, the thug stops the car to go and bludgeon her once more, spattering her blood on the glass of the window. The death scene remains a standalone video on YouTube, where viewers can rewatch it. Comments there lament the Mirabal sisters' brutal end, blaming the dictator for the brutality of his regime. Absent is a critique of what his henchmen were willing to commit in his name. In this way, violence against women in Dominican society is portrayed as an isolated event during a dark period in the nation's history.

Paradoxically, following this scene, in the last frames of the film the concluding text points to the observance of November 25, the day the sisters were killed, as El Día Internacional de la Eliminación de la Violencia contra la Mujer. The anniversary was established by the United Nations in 1999.[30] Feminists have long used Minerva's story and image as an inspiration for women's fight for democracy and resistance to patriarchal violence. The November 2011 issue of Centro de Investigación para la Acción Femenina (CIPAF)'s publication *Que Haceres* informed readers that "Minerva endured many years of being held hostage by the Trujillo Regime: the imprisonment of her father, revocation of her master's degree, her own imprisonment and being captive in her home."[31] While Minerva, Patria, and María Theresa remain universal symbols of Dominican womanhood today, they are decidedly white, heteronormative, and middle class.

Albania and Inez: "Niña No Esposa"

One evening in 2010, I conduct an interview with two friends, Albania and Inez, who have agreed to meet me at Café el Conde, a popular spot in the heart of the Colonial Zone. We are sitting outside on the corner of Parque de Colón just before dusk, surrounded by upscale tourist shops filled with jewelry made from Dominican amber and the pale blue stone larimar, specific to the Dominican Republic. Sitting in this spot, as each of us has done numerous times, we see mutual friends and acquaintances pass by and they stop to greet us. One could sit here all day and late into the night watching tourists and locals move past, witnessing myriad exchanges. Groups of tour guides sit waiting in the park, hoping some new arrival to Santo Domingo will hire them for a few hours work. Schoolchildren feed the pigeons in front of the Catedral Isabel la Católica on the plaza. Families take an evening stroll. Middle- and upper-class Dominicans turn up in shiny and expensive clothing and extravagant shoes. We can also see older European men with their young Dominican girlfriends or wives, sometimes with little children in tow.[32] As darkness arrives, so do women in tight dresses, low-cut tops, even an ill-fitting bustier. They introduce themselves to the foreign men they see loitering on the plaza; identifying them by their whiteness, they offer companionship and hope at the very least to be invited for a drink.[33] I watch as a mother pushes her toddler in a stroller, and then stops to ask a stranger for spare change. People sit on park benches texting, drinking beer from plastic cups, eating Yogenfrüz. The National Police and the Tourist Police in the area wander about with little to do.

Albania and Inez drink cafecitos and smoke Marlboro cigarettes (those manufactured in the Dominican Republic), as they have likely done in this spot a thousand times before. They each wear dark eye make-up and black clothing that contrasts with their relatively pale skin. Twenty-two-year-old Inez identifies herself as a goth poet. She tells me, "For me the stereotype of the perfect Dominican female is a mulata woman, voluptuous, with hair that is very long and well-straightened, who knows how to keep house and is always pretty. This is all that comes to mind . . . a woman who takes care of everything in the home and you don't see how she does it because she is always well put together." Her friend Albania responds, "For me, the stereotype is of a young woman. Because to be the stereotype, the woman would be young but a homemaker with children. There are many in this country who marry very young. Physically, I can't say that there is a specific stereotype of the Dominican woman because we are all very different." Yet in an effort to answer my question, she describes for me a class of women of which she is not a part, referring to the imagined Other. The average Dominican woman in her mind is morena, a darker color than her own: "Sometimes extravagant in her way of dressing," Albania goes on, "sometimes not. The Dominican woman really likes to express her sensuality a lot in her way of dressing."

"It's too much," says Inez.

"Too much," repeats Albania. "The more sensuality they show, the more they feel. I don't agree with this but most do."

Inez tells me that Dominican men like to have a woman on their arm who draws the attention of other men. She is quick to offer another example of how women are hypersexualized in Dominican society: "The women who work on television are not a representation of the women on the street who go every day to their work, you understand? But it's what the media projects, that they must be a woman with an exaggerated bust line, with extra-long [hair] extensions . . ." The two are in agreement about this.

"Very made up, very snug clothes, very short [hemline], normally very little clothing," Albania contributes. She says that in the middle of the day you see women on TV dressed up like they are going out at night: "They show a lot, considering the hour." These young women's comments capture the many contradictory social expectations for Dominican women. Ideas about respectability passed down from their grandmothers conflict with contemporary media messages and social pressures that encourage hypersexuality and women's accessibility to men. Rather than interrogate a history of colonialism based on rape and violence and narratives that reinforce a virgin/whore dichotomy in Latin America—a history I know Albania and Inez to be familiar with—they blame contemporary media for its negative influence on young girls today. Says Inez, "I asked my little nieces sometimes to dance for me and they dance in a way that isn't for children. I say 'where did you learn to dance like that?' 'On the program on television in the afternoon, or midday.'—Ay, what an example! Then, in the paper, the same people [upper-class people who program what is on the television] are saying they are very concerned about teen pregnancy. But if you give an example to a girl that they have to dress in whatever, to dress in a short little thing, showing everything, flirting, before they are of age, this is what they are going to do."

"No, girls don't dress like children," Albania chimes in. In public spaces, young girls and women receive both wanted and unwanted attention for dressing in ways that Albania describes as "sensual."

"Little women," says Inez. "The same way the mothers dress themselves, they dress their little girls: miniature women. When I was little you didn't see this. I had my big dresses and stockings." The two young women make a common assumption about there being a correlation between children's dress and young girls' sexual promiscuity, and they, like the broader society, blame the children's mothers for setting poor examples for their daughters. What is repeatedly omitted from public discourse around adolescent pregnancies, however, is the fact that Dominican girls are often impregnated by adult men who insistently pursue them to demonstrate their own virility. Neither are men challenged for sexually desiring young girls—particularly if those girls are poor and black, for whom existing narratives hypersexualize them and determine them as unnamed, and devalued. Today, though, I see (via my Facebook stream) on the shirts and banners of protesters in Santo Domingo the feminist campaign slogan "Niña No Esposa [Girl Not Wife]" from a global campaign that calls for a stand against child marriage, and it has unique resonance in the Caribbean. Today, the bodily autonomy of pregnant Dominican adolescent girls is an urgent site of contestation—and narrative instability.

"E'tamos fea pa' la foto"

According to the United Nations Population Fund program on Gender Equality, at the turn of the twenty-first century one in five Dominican women ages fifteen to forty-nine reported experiencing physical violence, one in ten experienced sexual violence, and nearly a third of married women reported emotional and physical violence from their partners as a regular part of their relationship.[34] It was only in 2010 that the UN's Gender Equality Observatory for Latin America and the Caribbean began to measure intimate partner violence; initially just four countries in the region used the classification of femicide.[35] In 2014, the Dominican Republic enacted Law 550/14 under the Dominican Criminal Code, to officially categorize the murders of women as femicides. Adriana Quiñones, past UN regional advisor on ending violence against women in Latin America and the Caribbean, relates the present-day attention to femicides in Latin American and the Caribbean to the horrific Juarez, Mexico, murders of the 1990s. "Gender-related killings are the last act—a culmination—in a series of violent acts," she explains in an interview for UN Women on their website.[36] She also wants readers to understand that violence against women is taking place in public spaces such as parks, buses, schools, and workplaces.[37] These other moments in which nonwhite, nonheterosexual, nonmale bodies are disciplined through violence regularly go unreported. Additionally, other forms of patriarchal violence not measured by national and international statistics include mothers who keep silent about sexual abuse in the family because they are dependent on an abuser as breadwinner, or who force their young daughters to give birth to babies born of sexual assault.

Along with El Salvador, the Dominican Republic is known for having the highest rate of femicides in the region, reporting an average of at least two hundred a year. Something the two countries also share in common is having some of the world's most stringent anti-abortion laws. In 2016 Amnesty International published an article that opened with the line, "Ser mujer o niña en República Dominicana es como ser una máquina reproductora [To be a woman or girl in the Dominican Republic is to be a reproductive machine]." In it, the international human rights organization goes on to name the many instances deemed not reason enough for an exception under existing Dominican abortion laws: pregnancy from rape or incest; fetal abnormalities that would lead to the death of the fetus; cases in which the pregnancy would result in the woman's death.

Dominican women at the first Encuentro Feminista Latinoamericano more than forty years ago pledged to make visible violence against women and bring it to the attention of the Dominican government as an issue of public concern: "la violencia contra las mujeres emerge como un problema central que se agravaba por el silencio de las víctimas y la indiferencia y/o complicidad de las autoridades y de la sociedad."[38] Writes Elizabeth Manley, Dominican feminists past and present "focused on local conditions yet sought out a transnational exchange of ideas, solidarity, and best practices." And while they "may not have described their own efforts as 'transnational,' they often creatively thought across the national boundaries such leaders sought to solidify."[39] Like many other local NGOs, CIPAF has been able to rely on international funding to produce and circulate research publications on violence against women in the region over the last several decades. The United Nations International Research and Training Institute for the Advancement of Women (UN-INSTRAW), a global project charged with addressing the human rights concerns of women worldwide, has been based in Santo Domingo since 1983. For decades UN-INSTRAW has worked alongside local organizations such as CIPAF, ProFamilia, La Collective Mujer y Salud, and the degree-granting gender studies program at the Instituto Tecnológico de Santo Domingo (INTEC), bolstering their work with a revolving door of UN interns and short-term contracts, a trademark of their presence.[40] While they have influenced public discourse and created jobs for feminist activists in Santo Domingo, it remains to be seen whether UN-INSTRAW has done more than articulate extensive recommendations for policy change to curb structural violence within a neoliberal economy.

Numerous agency reports point to young women and girls as an example of the rights that their globally funded organizations seek to protect. In their November 2018 report, "'It's Your Decision, It's Your Life': The Total Criminalization of Abortion in the Dominican Republic," Human Rights Watch interviewed fifty women of reproductive age about the negative impact that consecutive pregnancies and the inability to terminate unwanted pregnancies was having on them and highlighted these concerns in a documentary on their website.[41] Although in the public imagination the prohibition of abortion is in part an effort to discourage sexual activity among adolescents, this research shows that many of the women and adolescents impacted are already mothers. The last twenty-four years of abortion research data worldwide (now available from the Guttmacher Institute) clearly demonstrate that in countries such as the Dominican Republic, where abortion access is restricted and contraception is equally unavailable, rates of unwanted pregnancy have increased and subsequently so have the number of abortions.[42]

Upon reaching puberty, Dominican youth are forced to navigate their reproductive health with limited information, due to the influence of the Catholic Church in both culture and politics.[43] Dominican abortion laws exist as extensions of state power over the bodies of women and girls—disproportionately those with limited material resources—as an exercise in paternalism. Those in power see themselves as the best arbiters of these rights, while unable to see women as full human beings or fully formed subjects. As we have seen across this text, Dominican girls are imagined as either appealingly innocent and pure in their whiteness (la nigüenta) or unnamed and startlingly indeterminable in their brownness (la muñeca sin rostro). Within the neoliberal imagination, anti-abortion policies built on patriarchal demands and conflicting desires also simultaneously blur the lines of who is a girl and who is a woman. When Dominican adolescents are pregnant, it requires an ideological shift to imagine them simultaneously embodying the virginal *femme-enfant* and the hypersexualized young mulata who struggles to be seen as a mother-to-be.

Girlhood Interrupted

On August 17, 2012, sixteen-year-old Rosaura Almonte Hernández died due to complications from leukemia because she was denied treatment by her doctors since she was three weeks pregnant when admitted to the hospital. For twenty days, Rosaura's mother, Rosa, pleaded with the medical system to value the life of her daughter over that of an embryo. Media attention around Rosaura excluded the minor's name until after her death; she was known only as "Esperanza" or "Esperancita" (little hope). Her death at the hands of the state was a public legal test of the penal code that enforces a full and total abortion ban. With newer legislation criminalizing anyone who assists with an abortion, the country has become a battleground for issues of reproductive justice with a global audience. In this fight worldwide, abortion advocates are frequently asked to accept that notions of bodily autonomy do not extend to black and brown women.[44] Black feminist scholar Dorothy Roberts argued decades ago in *Killing the Black Body* that the right to reproductive freedom is inherently racialized and uniquely tied to the rights of Black women, acknowledging the ties between Black women's processes of self-definition as counter to the denial of personhood as experienced under slavery. Roberts writes, "This affirmation of personhood is especially suited for challenging the devaluation of Black motherhood underlying the regulation of Black reproduction."[45] Black women and girls worldwide do not get to become valued in society as mothers.

In the case of Esperanza, the transnational media messaging portrays her as an innocent girl, long before we know her name or see her image, and we must imagine her as a child whose life should be saved. When she is identified and her image is circulated online, the picture is of her in a white lacy dress, a tiara on her head, presumably a quinceañera photo. This portrait can be seen on protest banners and captured in the frame of a photograph taken for a Human Rights Watch article where her image is mounted on the wall above her mother's head.[46] Esperanza was a brown-skinned Dominican girl, and as the stories about her case make clear, she did not have the class privileges of private medical care that so often determine who can safely terminate a pregnancy. No longer a child, but not yet transitioned into adulthood, Esperanza's identity was ambiguous because of her pregnancy, for which she lost her personhood in the eyes of the state. Because of abortion laws that

Figure 12. Rosa Hernández (*left*) holding up a banner with an image of her daughter Rosaura Almonte Hernández. Photo by Lorena Espinoza Peña.

determined the embryo's right to life as greater than her own, the young girl was denied the opportunity to become a mother in Dominican society. Her mother, Rosa, was left behind to serve as the venerable spokesperson who would testify to the injustice that cut her daughter's life short.

#TodosSomosEmely

In her long-form article for the global media outlet BuzzFeed, journalist Rossalyn Warren crafts a compelling story about the murder of pregnant teen Emely Peguero Polanco and the "horrors faced by young women in the Dominican Republic."[47] While Emely's family struggled to get by, her boyfriend Marlon Martínez was raised in a big house enjoying relative privilege: he was born in New York and attended private school. The story of star-crossed lovers in the town of Cenoví, however, comes to a violent end with an unwanted pregnancy and an adolescent girl murdered. Warren's article reveals how class tensions and gender dynamics in this story were shaped by cultural values and impacted by Dominican laws. She notes that it is Dominican anti-abortion laws that endanger the life of young women like Emely; laws that criminalize assisting with an abortion carry a twenty-year minimum sentence. Warren writes, "The logic of Dominican law made it seem a better idea for Marlon to kill his girlfriend, and remove any trace of her altogether. After all, who would go looking for a poor missing girl?" Taking Emely to the hospital after she suffered internal bleeding from a botched abortion would be too great a risk to his own freedom, he may have calculated. In weighing his options, the value of Emely's life could not add up to the value of his own (or his class-based potential), so he left Emely to bleed to death; she would not get to be a mother. Later he called his own mother to come help him cover up the murder.

Warren's story is published with a photograph of Emely's empty bedroom and of her best friend now sitting alone in the school yard, highlighting the young girl's absence. For the families negotiating these cases and their after-effects—and for those who enacted the violence—how these young women's deaths were understood in popular media reflected how their raced and classed bodies are perceived in Dominican society. Dominican activists today use social media to mobilize transnational networks and bring attention to violence against the most marginalized Dominicans, those who are young, who are poor, and who are non-gender-conforming. When Emely initially disappeared, a campaign mobilized across the Dominican Republic and its diaspora. #TodosSomosEmely (#WeAreAllEmely) the internet movement asserted, reminiscent of #WeAreAllTrayvon following the murder of African American youth Trayvon Martin in 2012. The hashtag worked to name this brown-skinned young adolescent girl rather than let her disappearance cast her as expendable. Images of Emely were posted everywhere throughout Cenoví, on the news, and across the internet. Her story was circulated on Twitter worldwide and eventually received global media attention when Dominican American rap artist Cardi B amplified the call for justice. "What would you do to keep a clean image and reputation?" she asked her 23 million Twitter followers. "Make a 5 months pregnant sixteen year old girl get an abortion then kill her, put her in a luggage and throw her in the garbage so they don't find out your 19 year old son got a minor pregnant?" Wishing for Emely to rest in peace, the *rapera* concludes, "As [*sic*] traido el país Junto [you have brought the country together]." Notably, the "country" that Cardi B evokes includes the Dominican Republic and its diaspora, bound as one via its transnational digital networks.

A press conference organized by Marlon and his mother Marlin, in which they claim innocence, incites tremendous backlash. The public responds to unfolding information in the case with rioting and a particular hatred toward Marlin, who was an elected official. On camera, she initially denies her knowledge of the murder and calls for the safe return of Emely; she keeps up the charade for nine days. Her social status as a mother does not make her more empathetic toward the parents of Emely. Dominicans seem to interpret Marlin's actions as a mother's desperate attempt to maintain class privilege for her son and protect him from any consequences for fathering a child with a poor brown girl from the neighborhood. According to Amanda Alcantara of the popular online magazine *La Galería*, some of the furor around the senior Martínez's involvement was due to her government position; she was seen as yet another deceitful government official in a time of significant backlash against ongoing corruption. Outrage against Marlin's involvement in Emely's murder was so intense that when she went to court, she was obliged to wear a helmet and bulletproof vest. Marlin was likely also a target because her actions upend the archetype of the benevolent Dominican mother—one that the mothers of murdered daughters regularly exemplify.

Throughout the court case that followed, a range of familiar power dynamics within Dominican society were projected onto participants in the case, and onto the narrative itself, making the story look like any popular Spanish telenovela in which an evil mother seeks to protect her son from the designs of a poor and perhaps conniving neighborhood girl. Perceptions of Marlin contrast with those of Adalgisa Polanco, Emely's mother, who continues to be asked to publicly testify to the news media about the loss of her child. On November 7, 2018, the court handed down a sentence to Marlon Martínez of thirty years in prison and his mother five years. Following the ruling, riot police surrounded the courthouse and used tear gas to disperse the crowd. Marlin was convicted for corpse concealment and abduction of a minor; however, her sentence was later reduced to two years. There had been riots in the street when Emely's body was located. She had been packed into a suitcase and thrown away at the dump, in the most literal display of disposability.

Emely's image, notes Warren, haunted her hometown long after her death: "Her face is plastered on several billboards, on the front pages of newspapers, and on car stickers. Girls at her school say her murder was a reminder of just how dangerous it is to be a girl or a woman in the Dominican Republic." Equally haunting is the horrific reality that in the search for Emely's body, the bodies of two other teenage girls were found, dumped after a stepfather and a boyfriend had killed them.[48] Several of the Dominican women I spoke with in my research sought freedom from patriarchal oppression by leaving the Dominican Republic, packing their bags and going elsewhere. Instead, for Emely the suitcase became a casket: an ending place rather than a starting point, it could no longer symbolize travel abroad and freedom to cross national borders. Others, like Jessica Rubi Mori, a trans sex worker and activist in nearby La Romana whom I met in late 2010, did not have the means and social network that might allow her to travel abroad. Rather, Rubi sought to make sex work safer for other trans people in her community, but she was murdered in La Romana on June 4, 2017.[49]

The Art of Rage

"Art is going to save this ship," says Isabel Spencer in chapter 5 of this text. Her vision for radical engagement as a queer artist based in Santo Domingo looks like the work she continues to pursue: public arts education, community workshops and street theater, working with trans artists, and event curating her own performances of daily rituals via social media. Likewise Michelle Ricardo's poetry adamantly voices a resistance to the status quo, just as the manifesto of Las Maleducadas makes space for the artists to hold hope and assert the kind of society that they want. "Surrealism appears to me in its essentials to be a sort of rage. . . . [A rage] against the existing state of things. A rage against life as it is," determined French philosopher Georges Bataille at the end of his life.[50] Rage drives the women I know in Santo Domingo to drink, to withdraw from their social networks for stints, to seek another life abroad. For decades, feminist rage has driven them to show up in the street, for protest after protest. Feminist rage also helped me to identify the people in Santo Domingo with whom I wanted to spend my time and energy. A counterbalance to rage is feminist community through participation in protest in Santo Domingo. Decades of feminist organizing is being documented by photographers like Lorena Espinoza Peña, who regularly shares her work on Facebook, designating the space as an immense public visual archive.

Like the women to whom I dedicate this work, I understand myself to be caught within ideological frameworks of race and gender and the scopic regimes that sustain them, which are driven by neoliberal capital. Not despite but because of these challenges we continue to produce art, media, and visual culture that represents the diverse reality of Dominican women's transnational lives and the ever-evolving ways that they exist in Santo Domingo. Gabriela Speranza argues that "Surrealism seems to be the seed, indeed, of a wandering and uprooted art, eager to conjure up the intensity of life through the generative grace of chance, ready to turn the negative excess of the world's pain into affirmative excess and to dissolve political boundaries along the way."[51] Dominican women I got to know in Santo Domingo regularly resist the many mainstream cultural productions that obfuscate Dominican anti-blackness, anti-Haitianism, sexism,

Figure 13. Dressed in green for the Marcha Verde, feminist activists connect the dots between government corruption, lack of accountability, and high rates of femicide in the Dominican Republic. Photo by Lorena Espinoza Peña.

homophobia, and violence that they contend with daily; they repeatedly show up in protest and mobilize their communities online—with rage. They do not want to move away, nor did they want to feel unsafe and unheard at home in the Dominican Republic.

Curiouser and Curiouser

In the introduction to *Being La Dominicana*, I provided a framework of analysis for the study of mixed-race blackness in the Caribbean, engaging with the fields of critical mixed race studies and visual cultural studies to better theorize what it is we *see* when we are seeing mixed race and how seeing mixed race intersects with constructions of gender. I began my project with an exploration of an imagined Dominican woman that has cultural currency in the minds of foreign tourists and Dominicans of different classes. I also centered particular details about the spaces that Dominican women in Santo Domingo maneuver, the visual culture they navigate, their own perceptions and critiques of Dominican society today, and how transnational Dominican culture informs who they are and how they see themselves—including various "controlling images" of la dominicana. With a transnational feminist lens and ethnographic approach to cultural studies research I sought to represent Dominican women as experts of their own lives.

I have also demonstrated the usefulness of reading those Dominican visual cultural productions that I have highlighted as surrealist, or even *Afro*-Surrealist. Terri Frances beautifully employs the concept of the "Afro-Surreal" in her categorization of African American artist Romare Bearden's work. Frances names the way that Bearden's work decidedly "leave[s] the viewer tugging between two worlds, two ways of seeing."⁵² Dominican women's visual culture likewise leads us to this unique practice of seeing from multiple worlds. As a visual studies scholar I know well that different people can look at the same image and see entirely different things. As I have sought to demonstrate here, this is equally true of mixed-race bodies. My research has required that I read racial discourse and its intersections with a gendered analysis at multiple levels across cultural contexts, while looking from multiple perspectives.

Thankfully, an eye for surrealism in reading Dominican life leads us to pay greater attention to that which is deemed "irrational" in making meaning around race, as well as a constant awareness of death (*duende*) for Dominican women. By accounting for some of the more elusive aspects of being racially mixed that inform their experiences and transnational discourse about who they are presumed to be, I have revealed some of the many unique challenges they face because of their identities. Placing Dominican women's voices in juxtaposition as I have done here—across class and color hierarchies, though within the relatively privileged terrain that those I spoke with inhabit—I have been able to make more visible those details that have a tendency to disappear. Unwittingly, I have also accounted for the ways that light-skinned or white Dominican women understand themselves in terms of race and gender in stark relief to how Dominican women who are brown-skinned or identify as Afro-Dominican narrate their experiences. It is true that, as Harryette Mullen argued in the realm of photography, the effort to "enhance by contrast" is an essential tool for seeing racialized bodies.[53] As I have demonstrated throughout this text, dichotomous readings of race and color are critical to present-day acts of seeing in transnational contexts of racial mixture and racial ambiguity.

While it is no surprise that dark-skinned Dominican women share entirely different experiences of race in Santo Domingo or while traveling abroad than fair-skinned Dominican women, it is critical to hear Dominican women tell their own stories.[54] In this case, I have shown that such an evaluation demands that we also read the newly available technology of the cellphone, with its built-in lens, as altering how Dominican women view and visually archive their own worlds. Readers of *Being La Dominicana* will have seen the importance of an in-depth engagement with the visual culture of a transnational social media landscape that allows for constant visual engagement and self-fashioning among Dominican youth and continues a legacy of Dominican visual culture that had long been occurring offline.

The visual culture productions of artist Rita Indiana and her "ritaindianístico pastiche" that I explore in chapter 3 are just one example of the ways that Dominican sampling of cultural referents can work like a Surrealist's collection of found objects, problematized as a colonial habit of cultural appropriation. Ultimately, readers are left to determine whether my own scholarship—a curation of cultural representations in its own right—plays to this kind of presentation of Dominican culture as foreign and thus exotic.[55] Although *Being La Dominicana* draws on a vibrant community of students, activists, artists, and scholars accustomed to scholars from abroad in its midst, I have no illusions about my position as privileged outsider each time I return to Santo Domingo. For as anthropologist Margery Wolf writes, "No matter how careful, I fear all of us who do research must be prepared to be the resented Other to the 'objects of our own study.'"[56]

Being able to see the meaning of the Dominican muñeca sin rostro required that I interpret the figurine's ambiguity in the Dominican context, not when carried off into the diaspora. The mixed-race-ness of this "doll without a face" invariably requires a second glance with which to discern how one's narrative eye is interpreting or even recognizing Dominican women's racial meaning. I have argued in this concluding chapter that the same is true for how adolescent innocence is selectively interpreted. Combining visual culture analyses with ethnography has proven effective to better acknowledge the impact of narrative and visual culture on the lives and identities of young women in Santo Domingo.[57] At the same time, my work required a flexible methodology to study racial ambiguity because it is possible to visually signify multiple racial identities at once. There remain innumerable ways that I might have looked at this particular "snapshot," and more angles than I can count from which to approach the concerns of Dominican women in the contemporary moment.

My experiences living in Santo Domingo repeatedly confirmed for me that "some kinds of cultural meanings may only be accurately understood and reported by one who has learned them without realizing it, but much of the cultural union may be as easily or even more easily picked apart by a careful analyst who is not of the culture."[58] Though there are many things I will never fully understand as an outsider, at various moments I observed things about my Dominican peers that they had not always recognized in their own lives: a common gesture, a way of seeing a particular situation, certain skills they used in navigating Dominican society that I was never able to master. I have also been shaped ideologically by Dominican society and culture.[59] I understand and identify with an acute sense of loss that comes with diasporic identity and experience; I have chosen to leave and enjoy the privilege and freedom of return, albeit with transnational longings. I return to my conversations with Dominican women over the span of many years—reaching out to them to share the work I have produced about them—because it is part of my feminist research methodology and one of the ways I live a transnational life. This project remains a testament to that effort, and assembling the book has meant asking for support, fact checking, and securing images and translations from those who were a part of a moment in which we all lived in Santo Domingo. Warm responses to my inquiries via Facebook, WhatsApp, and email to this day are evidence of solidarities built and how I, too, continue to exist within the perimeter of their transnational networks. Through this work I engaged with and built solidarity among Dominican women across borders, in transnational feminist collaboration founded in trust-building and resource-sharing.[60] I spent time building relationships within the community of people I would learn from and eventually interview for my project and it is these relationships that made it possible for me to produce this particular view of Dominican society from the perspective of those artists and activists, plugged into progressive global networks and frequently collaborating with local NGOs for funding and employment opportunities.

At the conclusion of writing this text I have arrived at a greater under-standing of the back and forth of transnational migration among Dominican women that shape the transnational culture of Santo Domingo. While the social moment that I sought to capture has already disappeared into a distant past, Santo Domingo's youth culture is in fact relatively well-archived by what was a decade ago "new digital media." The many cultural productions I have witnessed during my research reflect the expert training and skill of generations of Dominican artists on the island who ought to be more broadly recognized for their resistance to dominant cultural tropes and efforts to define themselves in new ways. A next generation of Dominican women are not leaving la isla, and many have opted to return after growing up in the United States or studying abroad. There is an important see/saw here as well, at the point at which the dichotomous relationship between the Dominican Republic and the United States continues to shift.

In the academy we might think more creatively about where the archives of Dominican studies are located and consider how the preservation of digital archives and support of this work would benefit students and researchers in the Dominican Republic and its diaspora. There are those that are hard to access and there are others already available to us in the palm of our hand; Facebook is just one of those spaces. I am eager to see what a next wave of Dominican women in Santo Domingo will produce, how we might better highlight their work, and how they will continue to use technological tools to represent themselves to transnational audiences. Dominican feminist activ-ist Magaly Pineda at the advent of new technology began asking questions about the ways these advancements might be used to bridge gender and labor divides for Dominican women. Today, access to smartphones plus new apps for some have multiplied exponentially opportunities for self-definition, and artistic production. Theories of digital humanities and transnational access will be as important as feminist theories of democracy to coming generations of Dominicans for whom online audiences are far less "virtual" the more they become the norm in pandemic times.

Notes

Introduction

1. Also known as "la muñeca Limé" for creator Liliana Mera Limé, the doll now comes in a range of styles that reflect regional and market preferences. It was first manufactured in the 1980s in the artisan community of Higuerito, in the town of Moca, in the region of Espaillat. Elaborate versions of the doll (now collectibles) were once crafted out of brightly colored modeling clay by the company Gifina.

2. Like Thompson and many other scholars theorizing blackness in the diaspora, I do not capitalize the term. However, when I am specifically referring to African American Blackness in this text I capitalize it, as is now conventional in the United States.

3. J. Scott, *A Common Wind*.

4. See ibid.

5. Grewal, *Transnational America*; "connectivities" is Grewal's concept.

6. The paradox Manley identifies, however, is that this era of the Dominican feminist movement relied on an "understanding of women's innate abilities as maternal public figures" and reinforced a level of paternalism in Dominican society that women contend with today. Manley, *Paradox of Paternalism*, 4–5.

7. Moya Pons, *Dominican Republic*, 402.

8. Cabezas, *Economies of Desire*, 3.

9. After the violent "Guerra de Abril" of 1965, US forces finally left the country, but thereafter financed many of the projects advanced by Joaquin Balaguer, the president they had selected over the democratically elected Juan Bosch.

10. Outside of Latin American and Caribbean countries, Austria, Canada, China, Germany, France, Israel, Italy, Japan, Korea, Morocco, the Netherlands, Qatar, Spain, Switzerland, Turkey, the UK, and the US all have embassies based in the Dominican Republic, suggesting their close ties with the small country.

11. Shohat, *Talking Visions*; Hoffnung-Garskof, *A Tale of Two Cities*.

12. Canclini, *Hybrid Cultures*.

13. Andújar Persinal, *Meditaciones de cultura*, 27.

14. Garcia Peña, "'Translating Blackness,'" 11.

15. Ibid.

16. Johnson, *Appropriating Blackness*, 7.

17. Ibid., 209.

18. For examples, see Toi Derricotte's *The Black Notebooks*, Danzy Senna's *Symptomatic*, Michelle Cliff's *No Telephone to Heaven*, as well as visual artist Adrienne Piper's writings and work, and my use of Nella Larsen's *Passing* in chapter 5.

19. Trinh, "Not You, Like You"; many women of color feminist scholars have written about this experience of being simultaneously insider and outsider in the communities they write about, often because their formal education has distanced them from their communities of origin, while institutions of higher learning have trained them to be researchers of their own people. See Cotera, *Native Speakers*; also, Chowdhury, *Transnationalism Reversed* and Visweswaran, *Fictions of Feminist Ethnography*.

20. Olumide, *Raiding the Gene Pool*.

21. See García Peña, *Borders of Dominicanidad*, 3. Unlike García Peña, the focus of my research does not interrogate an expansive notion of *dominicanidad* but rather what form Dominican women's identities take in Santo Domingo.

22. I am inspired by Jasmine Mitchell to take this approach. See *Imagining the Mulatta: Blackness in U.S. and Brazilian Media*.

23. Taylor, *The Archive and the Repertoire*, 271.

24. Ibid.

25. Carlos Andújar Persinal writes on Dominican popular culture and its significance in *Meditaciones de cultura*, 27.

26. Although the public university is flooded with research projects, theses, and monographs produced by female students (who are in the majority) and their different take on the history of the nation, such alternate tellings of Dominican history though submitted for degree rarely see publication.

27. Ferguson, *Aberrations in Black*, 117.

28. Mohanty, "*Under Western Eyes* Revisited."

29. Chowdhury, "Introduction," *Transnationalism Reversed*.

30. Falcón, "Transnational Feminism as a Paradigm for Decolonizing the Practice of Research," 175–176.

31. Swarr and Nagar, *Critical Transnational Feminist Praxis*, 12.

32. I anonymize most interviewees across the text, a commitment I made to them that impacted how freely they spoke with me. The Dominican actors and artists I interviewed, however, allowed me to include their full names in order to further contextualize them by connecting them to existing media archives that precede them.

33. Anzaldúa, *Borderlands/La Frontera*, 91.

34. Carby, "Belonging to Britain," 15.

35. Thompson, *An Eye for the Tropics*, 11.

36. Grandin, "Can the Subaltern Be Seen?," 85.

37. Thompson, *An Eye for the Tropics*, 12.

38. In her sociological study, Candelario reveals these relational hierarchies of color among Dominicans in diaspora. See *Black Behind the Ears*, 199.

39. Charles, "Poor and Working Class Haitian Women's Discourses on the Use of their Bodies," 178–179.

40. Thompson, *Shine*, 11.

41. Enloe, *Bananas, Beaches, and Bases*.

42. Thompson, *An Eye for the Tropics*, 6–7.

43. As I remember it, speaking wtih Christina Sharpe at the University of Michigan in 2010 sparked my thinking on how we draw on prior knowledge (a "narrative eye") in order to see mixed race.

44. Beltrán, *Latina/o Stars in U.S. Eyes*, 8.

45. Somerville, *Queering the Colorline*, 5.

46. Beyoncé continues to be an excellent example of the marketability of the shape-shifter (though generally not identified as "mixed race," but French Creole). See *Rivas*, "Beyoncé Is the Whitest She's Ever Been in New Album Promo."

47. Omi and Winant, *Racial Formation in the United States*, 69.

48. Sontag, *On Photography*, 85.

49. Ibid.

50. Bryson, "The Gaze in the Expanded Field," 93.

51. See Wallace and Smith, *Pictures and Progress*.

52. This is inspired by Nicole Fleetwood's engagement with Christian Metz's useful concept of "scopic regimes" that had been taken up by Martin Jay in "Scopic Regimes of Visuality."

53. Fusco, "Racial Time, Racial Marks," 22.

54. I explore this idea in more detail in "Spinning the Zoetrope."

55. Jasbir Puar asks, "What does it mean to be examining, absorbing, feeling, reflecting on, and writing about the archive as it is being produced, rushing at us— literally, to entertain an unfolding archive?" *Terrorist Assemblages*, xix.

56. Horn, *Masculinity after Trujillo*.

57. Fernandez's commitment to realizing construction projects that reshaped the landscape, investing in the image of a more modern city, harkens back to the era in which "Ciudad Trujillo" (as the capital was once called) was constructed.

58. Initially, I asked young women about what they were watching, listening to, and influenced by. I self-consciously excluded *telenovelas* from my study of Dominican women, while recognizing they do have a broad social influence because of their prevalence in Dominican households each and every weeknight. However, the majority of the young women I spoke with were watching American movies and television shows shared online via MegaUpload rather than local programming.

59. Levitt writes about "social remittances" in *Transnational Villagers*. See also Hoffnung-Garskof, *A Tale of Two Cities*, 77. Immigration numbers dramatically increased in the early 1960, reaching more than 10,000 Dominican immigrants to the United States per year into the 1970s. Fifty-eight of the seventy Dominican women

who completed my initial online reported that they were in contact with Dominicans in the United States. Other locations where they had family or friends in order of popularity: Spain, Puerto Rico, Italy, other parts of Latin America, Europe, Japan, and Korea.

60. Suki, *Financial Institutions and the Remittances Market in the Dominican Republic*.

61. Shohat and Stam, *Unthinking Eurocentrism*.

62. For more on baseball as a national project in the Dominican Republic see Yoder, "Dominican Baseball and Latin American Pluralism, 1969–1974."

63. See, for example, Mark Padilla's book *Caribbean Pleasure Industry*.

64. There is no term equivalent to "sanky panky" for Dominican women's engagement with this economy or satirical representation of the prostitution of women and girls. The 2014 film *Sand Dollars* does suggest the tragedy of transactional romantic relationships between women, although it is based on a story written about two men.

65. Duggan, *Twilight of Equality*; Harvey, *A Brief History of Neoliberalism*. See also Martinez and Garcia's "What Is Neoliberalism?"

66. Valdivia, "The Gendered Face of Latinidad," 53.

67. Kempadoo, "Theorizing Sexual Relations in the Caribbean," 160; Kempadoo, "Women of Color and the Global Sex Trade," 33.

68. Nixon, *Resisting Paradise*, 14.

69. Tourists' and expats' treatment of Dominican women as sex objects, potential romantic partners, or simply purchasable goods also impacts Dominican men's relationships with and treatment of Dominican women and girls. It is commonly understood that men in Dominican society will marry, start a family, and then have a girlfriend on the side—often repeatedly moving on to younger women. It exists as a trope in popular culture and is much talked about in daily life.

70. hooks, *Black Looks*; Valdivia, "The Gendered Face of Latinidad," 53.

71. Suero, "La cuestión mulata."

72. Cocco de Filippis, *Documents of Dissidence*, 143.

73. Galván, "Power, Racism, and Identity"; Kempadoo, "Theorizing Sexual Relations in the Caribbean."

74. Hunter articulates, "It is difficult to distinguish between our own innocent preferences for skin tones and the socially constructed hierarchy of skin tones informed by racism. Many have internalized this racism so deeply that they can no longer recognize colorism and racism for what they are, and instead see them simply as individual tastes," *Race, Gender, and the Politics of Skin Tone*, 89. See also EFE Newswire, "Documental revela obsesión de dominicanas por pelo liso," 1D.

75. Fiol-Mata, *Queer Mother for the Nation*, 13.

76. Mayes, *Mulatto Republic*, 3. For a precise historiography of Dominican anti-Haitianism, see Mayes's impressive *Mulatto Republic*.

77. Ricourt, *Dominican Racial Imaginary*, 5.

78. Toni Morrison captures this so eloquently in her first novel, *The Bluest Eye*.

79. Bost, *Mulattas and Mestizas*, 16.

80. Following the Haitian Revolution (1791–1804), Haiti was no longer perceived as the "Pearl of the Caribbean" for its excess of wealth due to the peak production of sugar. Dominicans feared Haitian occupation, which indeed occurred from 1822 to 1844, ending slavery. The Spanish feared the Haitian Revolution would be an example to Cubans who fought the Ten Years' War for independence (1868–1878). See Torres-Saillant, "Tribulations of Blackness."

81. Deive, *¿Y tu abuela dónde está?*, 317; Sagás, "A Case of Mistaken Identity."

82. Garcia Peña, *Borders of Dominicanidad*, 159.

83. Horn, *Masculinity after Trujillo*, 39; Pierre, "Fobias nacionalists y los domínico-haitianos," 79; Valdez, "Genero, discriminación racial y ciudadanía," 236–237.

84. Pierre, "Fobias nacionalists y los domínico-haitianos," 79–80.

85. Valdez, "Genero, discriminación racial y ciudadanía."

86. Deserving of much more than a footnote is Cardi B's racial malleability and the ways that she and Trinidadian American Nicki Minaj have both presented their race and gender in alignment with a particularly marketable mixed-race body, so much so that there are images on the internet in which discerning one woman from the other is difficult.

87. Simmons, *Reconstructing Racial Identity*, 119.

88. See *Memoria del Foro*.

89. Albert Batista, *Los africanos y nuestra isla*, 41.

90. See not only Candelario's work, but also Edwidge Danticat's *Farming of the Bones*; the expression continues to have social significance, and turned up in my interviews and day-to-day conversations.

91. Candelario, *Black Behind the Ears*, 94.

92. Candelario writes, regarding Dominican women's transformation of hair, that "the ability to invest in self-care and self-beautification is an expression of a sense of entitlement to economic, emotional, and social well-being and an effort at its attainment," ibid., 254.

93. Johnson, *Appropriating Blackness*, 3.

94. Barron, "Frank Báez on What It Means to Be a Dominican Writer and Poet."

95. Fort and Arcq, "Introduction," 27.

96. Miller, "Afrosurreal Manifesto," 116.

97. Initially, I was also able to produce and circulate an online survey on stereotypes completed by seventy self-selecting women in Santo Domingo, which expanded my vocabulary and understanding and led me to interviewees.

98. I conducted only one formal interview with a male interviewee, "Rafael," for the section on student activism at La UASD in chapter 1.

99. Out of seventy responses to the survey question, "What are the physical characteristics you most identify with the Dominican woman?": forty-one replied "well put together"; forty-four—"*morena*"; twenty-eight—"sexy"; and twenty-nine—"*pelo malo*."

100. I handed out flyers on university campuses in Santo Domingo and asked friends and acquaintances to refer their friends to my survey and interviews.

101. See Alexander, "'Coming Out Blackened and Whole'" on black women's processes of joining different parts of themselves together in a text; the postmodern moment is reflected in Shohat's *Talking Visions*, for example; Jameson's "postmodern pastiche" likewise draws on diverse signifiers to create something pleasing in sensory ways (*Marxism and Form*).

102. Taylor, *The Archive and the Repertoire*, 271.

103. Grewal and Kaplan (*Scattered Hegemonies*) call on feminist scholars to complicate ideological constructions that uphold the cultural hegemony of the West, and do away with concepts such as "hybridity." They argue that an investment in these types of ideological constructions reinforce powerful native/Other, us/them, and center/periphery dichotomies; they call for a transnational feminism that goes beyond a race-gender-class triad, in order to resist what they identify as a global-local monolithic dichotomy that inevitably subordinates the local.

104. Ethnographic notes, November 24, 2011.

105. Caldwell, *Negras in Brazil*, xxi; Ulysse, *Downtown Ladies;* Collins, *Black Feminist Thought*.

106. Caldwell, *Negras in Brazil*, xxi.

107. Paul Gilroy quotes Gramsci (selections from the chapter "The Study of Philosophy" in *Prison Notebooks*) in his use of the concept of the "critical self-inventory": "The starting-point of critical elaboration is the consciousness of what one really is, and is 'knowing thyself' as a product of the historical process to date, which has deposited in you an infinity of traces, without leaving an inventory." See Gilroy, *Small Acts*, 69.

108. Grewal and Kaplan, *Scattered Hegemonies;* see also Swarr and Nagar, *Critical Transnational Feminist Praxis*.

109. Chowdhury and Philipose, *Dissident Friendships*, 3.

Chapter 1. Sites of Identity

1. Posted on Facebook May 12, 2014.

2. Willis, *Picturing Us*, 17.

3. In Puerto Rico *jíbara* may be used to refer to an Indigenous woman from the countryside, but can be derogatory and suggest someone is ignorant or "backward." However, in some places the term has been reclaimed and politicized. In the DR, it may be used to refer to descendants of enslaved people who escaped by hiding in the mountains (*cimarrones*) and who are seen as untouched by modernity.

4. The language used in posts is often abbreviated text, as is common in text messaging.

5. Thompson, *Shine*.

6. Ibid., 5.

7. Ibid., 23. Here she is citing Mimi Schiller. Additionally, the aim was to depict societies in which white people could imagine themselves and thus consider relocating to the islands.

8. Ibid., 5. Postcolonial images have also been used to justify occupation and military interventions; see Renda, *Taking Haiti*; Wexler, *Tender Violence*.

9. Ibid., 17. Here she cites William Gilpin.

10. There is much to be written about the influence of Mexican muralism on the visual culture of Latin American urban landcapes that might offer insights into today's neoliberal efforts to rebrand and beautify neighborhoods in racially segregated cities around the world.

11. D. Hernandez, "We're All Racial Justice Media Makers Now." She goes on to write, "I hope to see you all on Facebook."

12. My Facebook friends from the DR all added me as friends online during the course of my research and I have asked their permission to write about any information drawn from their posts.

13. Chon, "The Role of Destination Image in Tourism." Chon examines how the image-based fantasy of the tourist destination motivates the individual traveler.

14. Rosemont and Kelley, *Black, Brown, and Beige*, 4.

15. Shohat, *Talking Visions*, 27.

16. Hall, "What Is This 'Black' in Black Popular Culture," 32.

17. Ibid.

18. Shohat and Stam, Unthinking *Eurocentrism*; Charles, "Poor and Working Class Haitian Women's Discourses on the Use of Their Bodies," 170.

19. Lionnet and Shih, *Minor Transnationalism*, 7.

20. Willis and Williams, *The Black Female Body*, 22.

21. Willis offers a methodology for engaging with vernacular images: "imaginatively retitling" a photograph allows her to reconstruct the lived experience of those captured in it and ask questions of their lives that which falls outside the frame. Willis, *Picturing Us*, 22.

22. Fusco, "Racial Time, Racial Marks," 13.

23. Campt, *Image Matters*, 7.

24. Yosaira's Facebook posts. Translations are my own.

25. Ibid.

26. Ibid.

27. Ibid.

28. Ibid.

29. Skype chat, June 1, 2011.

30. Quoted in Howard, "Doom and Glory of Knowing Who You Are," 89.

31. I interviewed the two friends at my apartment in Los Jardines del Norte. We shared lunch with a friend of mine visiting from the United States. Conversation took place mainly in English.

32. Mejía-Ricart, *Historia de la Universidad Dominicana*.

33. La UASD also serves a greater number of poor and working-class Haitian students than other universities in the capital; after the 2010 earthquake in Haiti, the university waived many fees for Haitian students. In the past, la UASD has provided fellowships for Haitian students.

34. Quiroga, "Feminización universitaria en la República Dominicana: 1977–2001." In 2002, women were 62.6 percent of graduates.

35. Moya Pons, *The Dominican Republic*, 395.

36. Muñiz, *Ladrones al domicilio*.

37. See discussion of *progreso* in Hoffnung-Garskof, *A Tale of Two Cities*.

38. Canclini, *Hybrid Cultures*, xxix.

39. Ibid.

40. Their use of the term "Gringolandia" draws on to the derogatory term "gringo" used throughout Latin America for white people and foreigners more broadly.

41. See, for example, the campaign by past president Hipólito Mejía (2000–2004), a PLD candidate in 2011. Nelson Peralta, "Llegó Papá: Slogan que aterra al PLD . . . ," *Caribbean Digital*, September 4, 2011, https://caribbeandigital.net/llego-papa -%e2%80%9cslogan-que-aterra-al-pld-%e2%80%9d/.

42. Fukuyama, *The End of History and the Last Man*, xiv.

43. Ibid., xv.

44. The comic strip *Boque Chivo*, by the late Harold Priego, was also a popular form of eliciting dialogue by presenting images. In September 2010, enlarged comic strips from Priego's series were displayed along the outside wall of the Parque Independencia so that *capitaleñxs* could view them strolling by or driving past.

45. Theater shaped a generation of Dominican intellectuals. A handful of Dominican scholars have written about this era since the 1960s. See the work of Raj Chetty.

46. The caption to the photo reads: "La crisis de la UASD tuvo un respiro ayer con el reinició de las clases del curso de verano pero persiguió la discusión en turno a las causas y las soluciones para los problemas permanentes que afectan esa institución. En la foto uno de los murales con la position de un grupo estudi-antil es desplegado en las pasillas del alma mater antes de la mirada indiferente de varios estudiantes."

47. These conflicts have continued over decades and throughout my writing of this text. In June 2011, summer classes came to a halt abruptly in the second week of the term because of a lack of funds to pay teacher salaries.

48. Cabral, "Protesta-Dominicana."

49. See Quinn, "Dominican Pride and Shame."

50. Riggs, *Ethnic Notions*.

51. The leap from 2010's gay pride events and 2013's was significant. Visually, the difference looked like 200 participants for Pride 2010, and as many as 1,500 with NGO support in 2013. See Quinn, "Dominican Pride and Shame."

52. Afro-Dominican lesbian feminist activism led by the now disbanded Tres Ga-tas, for example, was able to democratize through its use of social media to circulate information about LGBTQ+ rights; for more on this topic see Quinn, "Dominican Pride and Shame."

53. "Del manifiesto del placer al beso micropolítico."

54. Chetty, "'La calle es libre.'"

55. Ibid.

56. Email excerpt. Translation is my own.

57. Quoted in Rodríguez Calderón, "El besatón."

58. Pérez, "La Iglesia patriarchal dominicana."

59. Espinosa Miñoso, "Homogeneidad, proyecto de nación y homophobia," 367.

60. This has changed over just the last few years—I now receive compliments from Dominicans on my "pajón [big hair]."

61. Espinosa Miñoso, "Homogeneidad, proyecto de nación y homophobia," 362.

Chapter 2. Me Quedo con la Greña

1. See Candelario, *Black Behind the Ears*.

2. In her "Solo en Santo Domingo . . ." blog post on November 29, 2011, Carolina Contreras describes having this same conversation with a taxi driver and they calculate it out, estimating that his wife, who goes to the salon twice a week, as many women do, is spending around RD$40,000 or over US$1,000 each year. https://www.missrizos.com/2011/11/29/solo-en-santo-domingo/.

3. The plastic surgery industry is also booming in Santo Domingo.

4. In 2012, anthropologist Gerald R. Murray and sociologist Marina Ortiz published *Pelo bueno/pelo malo*, a controversial book about Dominican beauty salons, funded by El Fondo para el Financiamiento de la Microempresa [The Fund for Small Business Financing] or "Fondomicro" in Santo Domingo. While it mistakenly argues that there is no longer a pigmentocracy or "hair-ocracy" in the DR, it does provide a useful study of the economy of beauty salons.

5. The amount of time and money spent by Dominican women in these women-owned small businesses is worthy of study, as Ginetta Candelario and others have shown. Women's investment in beauty salons as small business owners is promoted in an advertisement/short film for the savings and loan bank ADOPEM entitled *Magia* [Magic], directed by Sarah De la Cruz. https://www.youtube.com/watch?v=98gx14buZiU.

6. The results of the competition also reveal the degree to which Dominicans are connected to tools of digital communication. Heredia would later fall from grace after her involvement in a hit and run accident and other run-ins with the police.

7. This interview took place in June 2010 in Spanish. Translations are my own.

8. See the castas paintings that cataloged race and racial mixture in New Spain.

9. See DaCosta, *Making Multiracials*; Willis and Williams, *The Black Female Body*; Root, *The Multiracial Experience*.

10. African American scholar Henry Louis Gates Jr. has been extremely vocal about his misinterpretation of Dominican racial identity, arguing that Dominicans do not recognize that they are black; see Roth, "A Single Shade of 'Negro.'"

11. The 2007 *Miami Herald* multimedia series on "A Rising Voice: Afro-Latin Americans" is one example of an early wave of discourse on blackness in US Latinx and transnational Latin American communities.

12. Mercer, "Diaspora Aesthetics and Visual Culture," 156.

13. Reyes Bonilla, "Primero puta que pájara," 367.

14. Doble T, El Crok, y Los Pepes, "Pa' manga mi visa."

15. Young Dominican women who have been abroad have a different sense of independence, Hoffnung-Garskof (*A Tale of Two Cities*) has written. Chíqui Viciosa describes this as well, in "Discovering Myself: Un Testimonio."

16. In 2006, the language school I attended had produced a full page of common *piropos* in translation, so that foreign students might be able to recognize what was being shouted at them on the street each day.

17. Trinh, "Not You/Like You."

18. Via Instagram, I have kept in contact with Dulcina (@downtowntropico) who went from Chavón to study at Parson's School of Design not long after our interview. A decade later, Dulcina self-identifies as a queer femme "Dominicanyork" with a career in the arts/museum field globally, working remotely from Baltimore, MD.

19. This contrasts Yessica's experience in which she remarks on how much more freedom women have; she does not see obligatory trips to the salon as oppressive.

20. Often derogatorily referred to as "*hijos de mamí y papí,*" to signify their dependence on their parents.

21. Another panelist, after "going natural," was one day handed money by an older Dominican man she did not know. He wanted to pay for her to go to the salon because he preferred her hair straightened. These examples illustrate just a few of the ways mainstream beauty aesthetics are upheld and how Dominican men to feel entitled to exert their will over women.

22. Meaning "hair," "mop," or "entanglement," which perhaps better translates into "nappiness" and is often used as a derogatory term.

23. In a March 2020 visit to Santo Domingo I could see natural hairstyles, which had first taken off among edgy young people, had become ubiquitous among Dominicans of all different class backgrounds and across generations.

24. O'Hearn, *Half + Half*; Zack, *American Mixed Race*.

25. Hoffnung-Garskof explores this construction in his book *A Tale of Two Cities*.

26. Vargas, "Little New York."

27. Mejía, "PN 'pela a caco' a joven barbero 'por greñú.'"

28. She tells me that although her interactions that day happened in English, she remembers them in Spanish.

29. The *tiguere* and the concept of *tigueraje* are significant in Dominican society as a way of naming a uniquely Dominican form of masculinity: somewhat slick and opportunist and from the street; ethnomusicologist Sydney Hutchinson explores this performance of gender among Dominican musicians in *Tigers of a Different Stripe*.

30. Ricardo, "Negra Caribeña." The video is a production of the transnational hip-hop group Quilombo arte.

31. Michelle Ricardo, "Negra Caribeña Soy," performed in 2010 at La Espiral, in the Colonial Zone in Santo Domingo. Translations are my own.

32. Murray and Ortiz's book, *Pelo bueno/pelo malo*, is a prime example of this: they argue that Dominican women's investment in straightening their hair has nothing to do with living within a white supremacist culture in which white bodies are more valued, but rather it takes women's explanation of wanting to be "beautiful" at face value.

33. This reflects my translation (with assistance from Dominican friends) of the following comment made online: "Muy chulo, pero creo que 'la isla' aún no está del todo preparada para la profundidad de esta letra. Creo que por eso se fue Rita Indiana. Pero sigue adelante que si no es allá será por aquí :))[*sic*]."

34. In Santo Domingo, one can see a wide selection of skin "brighteners" (bleaches) on store shelves positioned beside products used for straightening hair.

Chapter 3. Whiteness, Transformative Bodies, and the Queer Dominicanidad of Rita Indiana

This chapter includes an English revision of my previously published essay "El Rostro negro dominicano y la quisqueya queer de Rita Indiana Hernández."

1. Horn, *Masculinity after Trujillo*, 28.

2. Hutchinson, *Tigers of a Different Stripe*, 174; Vera-Rojas, "¡Se armó el juidero!," 209.

3. Hernández, Interview with Moreno-Anderson and Ríos Avila.

4. Horn, *Masculinity after Trujillo*, 113.

5. Ibid., 106.

6. Johnson, *Appropriating Blackness*.

7. Zalman, "The Art of Window Display," 69.

8. Rabinovich, *Surrealism and the Sacred*, 167.

9. Hernández, Interview.

10. Reber points to this in "Visual Storytelling."

11. Gefin, "Collage Theory, Reception, and the Cutups of William Burroughs."

12. Gefin points to the theorization I have employed here from Jameson, *Marxism and Form*, 20–21.

13. Zalman, "The Art of Window Display," 75.

14. Ibid.

15. Rmessina, "Rita Indiana Says: Death to el Feisbu," *Remezcla.com*, https://remezcla .com/culture/rita-indiana-facebook-maldito-feisbu/.

16. Hernandez, Interview, at minute mark 3:11.

17. Díaz, *Diez años blogueando música*.

18. Hernández, Interview.

19. Hutchinson writes about the many ways that music shapes the written work of Rita Indiana in *Tigers of a Different Stripe*; see also Maillo-Pozo, "La comunión entre música y literatura en la strategic de Chochueca," 344.

20. Hernández, Interview.

21. Musician José Duluc finished the performance and Rita Indiana only returned later for one more song.

22. In a biographical interview I conducted with Xiomara Fortuna, she said her parents feared she would be an artist because they likened it to becoming a prostitute. Actress Yasamin Yarmal articulates this same sentiment in Mariam Ghani's documentary *What We Left Unfinished* (2019) about film in Communist-era Afghanistan.

23. Gopinath, *Impossible Desires*, 61.

24. I use the term "dominicanidad" in this instance to get at a much broader construction of national identity that extends beyond the island. See García Peña, *Borders of Dominicanidad*, 3.

25. Horn, *Masculinity after Trujillo*.

26. "La polifacética Rita Indiana condensa en 'Papi' lo mejor y lo peor de la cultura caribeña."

27. Ramírez, *Colonial Phantoms*, 182.

28. Reyes Bonilla notes in "Primero puta que pájara" that this was common in the 1980s and 1990s on *El show de medio día*. During the internationally televised 2012 Casandras Awards in Santo Domingo, a "living Barbie doll" on the red carpet (a live woman in a pink plastic box) and an effeminant interior designer dressed in pink were the staged comic relief during the program.

29. Pérez, "La Iglesia patriarchal dominicana."

30. Another example of living with Dominican contradiction that comes to mind is a march against the exploits of Barrick Gold in 2010 that was simultaneously a nature hike. The trail through nature that young people sought to protect turned out to be littered with nine miles of trash left behind by Dominican students.

31. Reyes Bonilla, "Primero puta que pájara," 376.

32. In the documentary film *Cimarrón Spirit* (dir. Durán, 2015), we captured how in the rural community of Elias Piña the threat of violence from the masked figures *Los Negros* was used to instilled fear in young children to coerce their good behavior.

33. Reyes Bonilla, "Primero puta que pájara," 379.

34. Puar, *Terrorist Assemblages*, 32.

35. Hernández, Interview.

36. See "Rita Indiana Talks about Being a Lesbian, Coming Out, Family Acceptance, and Marriage Equality."

37. Hernández, Interview.

38. M. J. Alexander, *Pedagogies of Crossing*, 23.

39. Concept and directing, Noelia Quintero Herencia; director of photography, Sonnel Velázquez; art direction, Gisella Madera; editing, Gabriel Coss.

40. Reyes, "Rita Indiana y Los Misterios—*El juidero.*"

41. Villanueva, "Rita Indiana estrena video internacionalmente."

42. Quintero holds an MA in Film Studies from New York University and a PhD in Digital Visual Culture from Universitat Oberta de Catalunya in Barcelona.

43. María Teresa Vera-Rojas expertly interprets the lyrics of "El juidero," "La hora de volvé,'" and "Maldito feisbú" but does not reflect on the visual images. Vera-Rojas, "¡Se armó el juidero!," 210.

44. Author's notes from talk at the Contemporary Art Museum Houston, October 24, 2018.

45. See Liberato, *Joaquín Balaguer, Memory, and Diaspora*.

46. Hutchinson, *Tigers of a Different Stripe*, 191, 193.

47. Ibid., 190.

48. Rivera-Velazquez, "The Importance of Being Rita Indiana-Hernandez," 206.

49. Ibid., 223.

50. Hernández, Interview.

51. Ibid. She names musician Luis Días as one of her inspirations. Singer-songwriter Xiomara Fortuna and poet Frank Báez are also masters of this art; Josefina Baez's book *Dominicanish* and social media work reflect this practice.

52. Ibid.

53. Hutchinson, *Tigers of a Different Stripe*, 176.

54. Vera-Rojas, "¡Se armó el juidero!," 211–212; translation my own.

55. Hernández, Interview.

56. Zalman, "The Art of Window Display," 67.

57. Quinn, "Spinning the Zoetrope."

58. Harrison-Kahan, "Her 'Nig,'" 117.

59. See Kathleen Pfeiffer for the use of the term "racial vacillation" in "Individualism, Success, and American Identity in *The Autobiography of an Ex-Colored Man*."

60. It is not unlike the internal stream of consciousness of characters Lorca wrote in *La Casa de Bernada Alba* just seven years later.

61. Larsen, *Passing*, 29.

62. Butler, *Bodies That Matter*, 172.

63. Ibid.

64. Garcia Peña, *Borders of Dominicanidad*, 165.

65. Dominican comedian, poet, and film actress Cheddy García famously performed in blackface as an Afro-Cuban rural caricature on *Freddy y Punto*, a talk show hosted by conservative Freddy Berais Goica. See García, *La negrita carida*.

66. Leonardo, "Da' pa' lo' do.'"

67. Wade, "Racial Identity and Nationalism," 848.

68. Somerville, *Queering the Color Line*, 6.

69. Brugal, "Rita Indiana y Todo sus Misterios," 25.

70. Indiana, "Magia negra."

71. Guilamo, "Dominican Funnies, Not So Funny," 68.

72. Lorgia García Peña in her important text, *Borders of Dominicanidad*, theorizes a "rayano consciousness" that captures the significance of the border space to Dominican identity broadly.

73. "Gente UEPA: Engel Leonardo."

74. The symbol was designed for Los Misterios by one Eddy Núñez, according to Hutchinson, *Tigers of a Different Stripe*, 186.

75. Marouan, *Witches, Goddesses, and Angry Spirits*, 43.

76. Additionally, the music video opens and closes with the image of a single imposing acacia tree. The wide shot establishes a familiar if somewhat generic image of the "tree of life," now a common symbol for the continent of Africa. See Ross, "The Dangers of a Single Book Cover."

77. Dayan, "Erzulie," 16.

78. Ibid., 6.

79. Marouan, *Witches, Goddesses, and Angry Spirits*, 41.

80. Dayan, "Erzulie," 6.

81. Hutchinson, *Tigers of a Different Stripe*, 187.

82. Lott, "Love and Theft," 25.

83. Johnson, *Appropriating Blackness*, 7.

84. Palacios, "Actos peatonales, actos de consumo," 568; Martinez-San Miguel, "Más allá de la homonormatividad."

85. Brugal, "Rita Indiana y Todo sus Misterios," 26.

86. Marouan, *Witches, Goddesses, and Angry Spirits*, 44.

87. Alamo, "Interview: Rita Indiana Hernández."

88. Fiol-Mata, *Queer Mother for the Nation*, 19.

89. Brugal, "Rita Indiana y Todo sus Misterios," 22.

90. Lott, "Love and Theft," 25; Wade, "Racial Identity and Nationalism," 849.

91. Indiana, "Bowie, estrella negra."

92. Ibid. Translations are my own.

93. In the 1983 interview clip that Rita Indiana references, Bowie challenges VJ Mark Goldman about why there are so few Black artists on Music Television (MTV) and those few are on only at dawn; Goldman responds that more Black artists might scare away white audiences. See Goodman and Bowie, "David Bowie Criticizes MTV for Not Playing Videos by Black Artists."

94. Indiana, "Bowie, estrella negra."

Chapter 4. A Thorn in Her Foot

1. Quoted in Spickard, "The Subject Is Mixed Race," 93.

2. Our conversation took place in Spanish. At times the terms she used in Dominican Spanish are much more illustrative of what she is trying to say so I leave them in the original with my own translations in brackets.

3. We meet for an interview in March 2010, in the back of The Cafetera on El Conde.

4. "The Jerk" is an example of one such transnational cultural trend that could be seen all over the DR that year, thanks to the music video "You're a Jerk" (2009) by the LA-based hip-hop group The New Boys, along with the fleeting fashion trend of brightly colored skinny jeans on men.

5. Silvio Torres-Saillant writes about "intellectual *tigueraje*."

6. Carby, "Becoming Modern Racialized Subjects," 625.

7. "Miss Republica Dominicana Universo," Facebook, April 14, 2012, https://www.facebook.com/media/set/?set=a.303597246373462.73084.135540866512435&type=3.

Chapter 5. The Camera Obscura

1. The scene evokes French impressionist painter Edgar Degas's iconic dancer and bather images or, more recently, a popular series of photographs circulated online of ballet dancer Misty Copeland, in which she inserts her brown body into tableaux vivants of these French masterpieces.

2. Fusco, "Racial Time, Racial Marks," 19.

3. Willis and Williams, *The Black Female Body*, 1.

4. The Dominican theater collective first debuted the play in 2012 and has produced it numerous times since, with different casts.

5. Oxford, "Cultural and Literary Ethos as Represented in García Lorca's *La Casa de Bernarda Alba*," 108–109.

6. A colleague mentioned to me that she had taught the play in Ghana; the 1982 film production by Mexican filmmaker Gustavo Alatriste aired on Spanish television and is easily accessible on YouTube; see Pedro Ruffo's blog post about the all-male cast in Saõ Paolo, Brazil; the all–East Asian women's production in 2007, with the National Asian American Theater Company in New York is available at http://www.naatco.org/2007-bernarda/.

7. Butler, "Endangered/Endangering," 16.

8. Fleetwood, *Troubling Vision*, 7; Hall, "Cultural Identity and Cinematic Representation."

9. Muñoz, "Feeling Brown," 70.

10. A narrow reading of the text, one that does not account for race, also overlooks Lorca's real-world transnational influences and what he was capable of imagining for his cast.

11. Butler, "Endangered/Endangering," 16.

12. Fleetwood, *Troubling Vision*, 7.

13. N. M. Scott, "Sight and Insight in *La Casa de Bernarda Alba*," 302.

14. Bryson, "The Gaze in the Expanded Field," 91–92.

15. Oxford, "Cultural and Literary Ethos as Represented in García Lorca's *La Casa de Bernarda Alba*," 112n2.

16. Soufas, *The Subject in Question*, 211.

17. Maurer, "Introduction," ix.

18. Ibid.

19. Betances, "Una visión femenina."

20. Audiences in Santo Domingo have likely seen *Bernarda Alba* many times as a live production, typically cast with fair-skinned Dominicans; or they have seen the 1987 Spanish film adaption or 1982 Mexican version on YouTube or Dominican TV. Las Maleducadas have since performed it in multiple runs at least fifteen times.

21. Soufas, *The Subject in Question*, 233.

22. N. M. Scott, "Sight and Insight in *La Casa de Bernarda Alba*," 298.

23. Fusco, "Racial Time, Racial Marks," 19.

24. Knapp, "Federico García Lorca's *The House of Bernarda Alba*," 385.

25. Fleetwood, *Troubling Vision*, 17.

26. Ibid. See also Wallace and Smith, *Pictures and Progress*.

27. Fleetwood, *Troubling Vision*, 17.

28. Ibid.

29. Suero, "La maleducada."

30. In 2015 she won the Dominican Republic's top arts and cultures award, the Soberano, for her direction of the play *Hasta el abismo*. https://www.conectate.com .do/articulo/nominados-ganadores-premios-soberano/.

31. All translations are my own.

32. Yaneris's centrally located apartment in Gazcue was a hub for local activists from 2010 to 2018, as well as an Airbnb for researchers from abroad and Dominican activists making short-term visits back to the island.

33. "'La casa de Bernarda Alba' regresa a escena en Casa de Teatro"; Guerrero, "Vuelve a escena la obra de teatro *La casa de Bernarda Alba*."

34. Betances, "Una visión femenina."

35. Gabriele, "Of Mothers and Freedom," 191.

36. Quoted in Betances, "Una visión femenina."

37. It is not surprising then that Isabel posted the following statement (in Spanish) on Facebook page of Teatro Maleducadas on October 12, 2015, as education in the arts faced ongoing attack: "All these women we see here are great actresses, tireless fighters on the job who are of unquestionable professionalism. All are graduated from the National School of Art Dramatico (ENAD) Rep. Dom. Thanks to the existence of the school and the training of teachers and staff who work there, actresses of this caliber committed to their art exist. It is unfortunate that our school the school we formed is going through this difficult time and that our teachers who have enabled generation after generation to keep alive the flame of theater despite the precarious conditions in which they work and nevertheless keep fighting. It is also unfortunate that a group of *barbaros*, those "cheap politicians" who have nothing to do with art want to spoil this wonderful effort. I hope the fire of the fight never ceases in what keeps us alive here and now!"

38. Posted on Facebook January 3, 2013, https://www.facebook.com/notes/teatro -maleducadas/manifiesto-grupo-de-teatro-maleducadas-/141538562667317.

39. Rosemont and Kelley, *Black, Brown, and Beige*, 3–4.

40. Previously known as the Casandra, the Soberano is an award honoring Dominican artistic production in the country and in the diaspora.

41. See Johanna's talent in a video spot for promotion of *Hasta el abismo*. https:// www.facebook.com/grupodeteatromaleducadas/videos/1190721124415717/.

42. These color categories were delineated further on identity cards, according to Bienvenida Mendoza in Casa por la Identidad de las Mujeres Afro, *Memoria del foro "Por una sociedad libre de prejuicio*," 5.

43. Chávez, *Queer Migration Politics*, 27.

44. This interview took place in Spanish on July 11, 2016. Translations are my own.

45. Knapp, "Federico García Lorca's *The House of Bernarda Alba*," 385.

46. Gabriele, "Of Mothers and Freedom," 190.

47. Knapp, "Federico García Lorca's *The House of Bernarda Alba*," 388.

48. Hart, "The Bear and the Dawn," 65.

49. García Lorca, *The House of Bernarda Alba*, 4.

50. Knapp, "Federico García Lorca's *The House of Bernarda Alba*," 383.

51. Oxford, "Cultural and Literary Ethos as Represented in García Lorca's *La Casa de Bernarda Alba*," 102.

52. Knapp, "Federico García Lorca's *The House of Bernarda Alba*," 383.

53. García Lorca, *The House of Bernarda Alba*, 56.

54. Ibid., 18.

55. Ibid., 55.

56. Knapp, "Federico García Lorca's *The House of Bernarda Alba*," 392.

57. Wallace and Smith, *Pictures and Progress*, 147.

58. Soufas, *The Subject in Question* 234.

59. García Lorca, *The House of Bernarda Alba*, 34.

60. In the Mexican film version Martirio damages the image in her possession, stabbing holes through the eyes of the photo as if halting the gaze from the photograph.

61. Sontag, *On Photography*, 167.

62. Hart, "The Bear and the Dawn," 64.

63. García Lorca, *The House of Bernarda Alba*, 49.

64. Ibid., 34–35.

65. Ibid., 45.

66. Ibid., 17.

67. Oxford, "Cultural and Literary Ethos as Represented in García Lorca's *La Casa de Bernarda Alba*," 107.

68. Interview with Spencer, July 2014.

69. Horn, *Masculinity after Trujillo*.

70. Maurer, "Introduction," xix.

71. Soufas, *The Subject in Question*, 207.

72. Hart, "The Bear and the Dawn," 68; Soufas, *The Subject in Question*, 206.

Chapter 6. Feminist Rage and the Right to Life for Women in the Dominican Republic

1. Thornton and Ubiera, "Caribbean Exceptions," 415.

2. CIPAF, *Que Haceres*, 11.

3. Cox, *Shapeshifters*, 28.

4. Ibid., 25.

5. Lorde, "Uses of Anger," 128.

6. Harrison, *Outsider Within*, 193.

7. Pineda, García, and Faxas, "Mujer, mito y realidad," 123, 127.

8. Moya and García, *Reclaiming Identity*, 8.

9. Lorde, "Uses of Anger," 131.

10. Horn, *Masculinity after Trujillo*, 46.

11. "Como si importa."

12. Manley, "Revitalizing Feminism in the Dominican Republic."

13. Amaury Rodriguez's article for NACLA captures the moment but may have overlooked decades of feminist organizing in the streets that fueled this "heterogeneous movement." "A 'Green Tide' Engulfs the D.R."

14. Las Hermanas Mirabal are also known as las mariposas (the butterflies), in reference to Julia Álvarez's novel *In the Time of the Butterflies*, about the sisters and their death. "Las mariposas: Símbolo de las Hermanas Mirabal," *Hoy*, December 3, 2009, https://hoy.com.do/las-mariposas-simbolo-de-lashermanas-mirabal/.

15. As the camera pans across the protesters, it freeze-frames on notable generals and male historical figures to give us their names as they protest in the streets and face police violence, also demonstrating the significance of the historic moment and its transnational ties. For example, we see Pericles Franco from Chile protesting in the streets of the capital city.

16. This is a racialized distinction that eighteen-year-old Ambar articulated in chapter 3.

17. According to Leiter, he objected to Rodriguez in the role because she was an alcoholic. Rodriguez had in fact recently completed a seventeen-day sentence in jail for disobeying a judge's order after a DUI. Miguel Cruz Tejada, "Fundación demandaría película *Trópico de Sangre* y a Michelle Rodríguez," *El Diario*, July 9, 2008, https://www.diariolibre.com/revista/fundacin-demandara-pelcula-trpico-de -sangre-y-a-michelle-rodrguez-NCDL23825.

18. "Filmará Michelle Rodríguez en República Dominicana."

19. Jovovich, "Michelle Rodriguez,"116. Her feeling of being an "outsider" aligns with the narratives of mixed-race identity of the 1990s, when she was growing up. In the 2000s, there was a shift in US ideologies, marked I would argue by Danzy Senna's essay "Mulatto Millennium," in which mixed race becomes in fashion and marketable in new ways as part of a "Generation E. A." (Ethnically Ambiguous).

20. Jovovich, "Michelle Rodriguez," 117. Interestingly, the black-and-white portrait of Rodriguez smoking a cigarette that accompanies her interview appears to be a riff on the iconic image of the black Caribbean woman smoking a cigar—but more feminized, slender, and whitened.

21. Quoted in ibid., 116.

22. Vilkomerson, "Michelle Rodriguez Talks Movies, Female Empowerment, and Sex."

23. Rivera, "Michelle Rodriguez Answers Six 'Fast & Furious' Questions for *New York Daily News* Viva."

24. Vilkomerson, "Michelle Rodriguez Talks Movies, Female Empowerment, and Sex."

25. Clarke, "Lesbianism as an Act of Resistance," 129.

26. Jovovich, "Michelle Rodriguez," 117.

27. Notably, the term "morena" uttered by Trujillo is translated in the film's English subtitles as "mulatto."

28. Mayes, *The Mulatto Republic*, 1.

29. Tineo Durán, *Imaginarios de género en juventudes dominicanas*, 155.

30. At the 1981 convening of Encuentros Feministas Latinoamericanas y del Caribe, Dominican feminist activists had determined that the anniversary of the death of the Mirabal sisters should be recognized annually and they fought for this recognition.

31. CIPAF, *Que Haceres*, 2.

32. It is the same space that Amalia Cabeza observes in her writing on sex work in the Dominican Republic in the 1990s.

33. At the opposite end of El Conde there is another café where you can sit and watch young Dominican men introduce themselves to gay male tourists, many of whom are African American.

34. Freehill, "Análisis geográfico de violencia contra la mujer en República Dominicana."

35. United Nations, "Gender Equity Observatory for Latin America and the Caribbean."

36. "Take Five: Fighting Femicide in Latin America."

37. Ibid.

38. Ibid. The sentence translates as "Violence against women emerges as a key social concern worsened by the silence of victims and the indifference and or complicity of the authorities and society."

39. Manley, "Revitalizing Feminism in the Dominican Republic," 19.

40. Morgan, *Sisterhood Is Global*, 291.

41. Human Rights Watch, "Interview Defying Dominican Republic's Abortion Law."

42. Sedgh et al., "Abortion Incidence between 1990 and 2014."

43. Human Rights Watch, "It's Your Decision, It's Your Life."

44. See Morrison, *The Bluest Eye*.

45. Roberts, *Killing the Black Body*, 303.

46. Photojournalist and filmmaker Tatiana Hernandez Geara's striking photograph is included inside the Human Rights Watch report and on its website at https://www .hrw.org/news/2018/11/19/dominican-republic-abortion-ban-endangers-health.

47. Warren, "The Poor Girl and the Rich Boy."

48. Rojas, "Emely Peguero."

49. Amnesty International recently published the report online, "If They Can Have Her, Why Can't We?"

50. Richardson, "Introduction," in Bataille, *The Absence of Myth*, 24. Richardson attributes Bataille's thinking on Surrealism as rage against the influence of Hegel's master-and-slave dialectic.

51. Speranza, "Wanderers," 195.

52. Francis, "Introduction," 96.

53. Mullen quoted in Wexler, *Tender Violence*, 84.

54. See also E. M. Martinez's collection of essays both fiction and nonfiction, *Daring to Write*.

55. Thornton and Ubiera, "Caribbean Exceptions," 420.

56. Wolf, *A Thrice-Told Tale*, 13.

57. See Smith, *American Archives*; Shohat, *Talking Visions*; Trinh, *Woman, Native, Other*.

58. Wolf, *A Thrice-Told Tale*, 5.

59. Simmons, *Reconstructing Racial Identity and the African Past in the Dominican Republic*, 7.

60. Swarr and Nagar, *Critical Transnational Feminist Praxis*.

Works Cited

Alamo, Hector Luis. "Interview: Rita Indiana Hernández." *Gozamos.com*, December 22, 2013. https://gozamos.com/2013/12/interview-rita-indiana-hernandez/.

Albert Batista, Celsa. *Los africanos y nuestra isla (historia, cultura e identidad)*. 1987. Reprint, Santo Domingo : Ediciones Libería La Trinitaria, 2010.

Alexander, Elizabeth. "'Coming Out Blackened and Whole': Fragmentation and Reintegration in Audre Lorde's *Zami* and *The Cancer Journals*." *American Literary History* 6, no. 4 (Winter 1994): 695–715.

Alexander, M. Jacqui. *Pedagogies of Crossing: Meditations on Feminism, Sexual Politics, Memory, and the Sacred*. Durham, NC: Duke University Press, 2005.

Alexander, Meena. "Alphabets of Flesh." In *Talking Visions: Multicultural Feminism in Transnational Age*, edited by Ella Shohat. New York: New Museum of Contemporary Art; Cambridge, MA: MIT Press, 1998.

Álvarez, Julia. "A White Woman of Color." In *Half and Half: Writers on Growing Up Biracial and Bicultural*, edited by Claudine Chiawei O'Hearn. New York: Pantheon, 1998.

Amnesty International. "'If They Can Have Her, Why Can't We?': Gender-Based Torture and Other Ill-Treatment of Women Engaged in Sex Work in the Dominican Republic." *Amnesty.org*, 2019. https://www.amnestyusa.org/wp-content/uploads/2019/03/If-they-can-have-her-why-cant-we.pdf.

Andújar Persinal, Carlos. *Meditaciones de cultura: Laberintos de la dominicanidad*. Vol. 152. Santo Domingo: Archivo General de la Nación, 2012.

Anzaldúa, Gloria. *Borderlands/La Frontera*. 3rd ed. San Francisco: Aunt Lute Books, 2007.

Aparicio, Frances R., and Susana Chavelez-Silverman. *Tropicalizations: Transcultural Representations of Latinidad*. Lebanon, NH: University Press of New England, 1997.

Badenes, José I. "All About Mothers: Sacred Violence in Federico García Lorca's *The House of Bernarda Alba* and Tennessee Williams's *Suddenly, Last Summer.*" *Text and Presentation* (2012): 125–135.

Báez, Josefina. *Dominicanish: A Performance Text.* New York: Josefina Báez, 2000.

Barron, Michael. "Frank Báez on What It Means to Be a Dominican Writer and Poet." *Culture Trip* (blog), July 12, 2017. https://theculturetrip.com/caribbean/dominican -republic/articles/frank-baez-on-what-it-means-to-be-a-dominican-writer-and -poet/.

Bataille, Georges. *The Absence of Myth: Writings on Surrealism.* Ed. and trans. Michael Richardson. London: Verso, 1994.

Beltrán, Mary C. *Latina/o Stars in U.S. Eyes: The Making and Meanings of Film and TV Stardom.* Urbana: University of Illinois Press, 2009.

Betances, Rosanna Cruz. "Una visión feminina." *Listín Diario,* June 27, 2013. https:// listindiario.com/entretenimiento/2013/06/27/282257/una-vision-femenina.

Bost, Suzanne. *Mulattas and Mestizas: Representing Mixed Identities in the Americas, 1850–2000.* Athens: University of Georgia Press, 2003.

Brennan, Denise. *What's Love Got to Do with It?: Transnational Desires and Sex Tourism in the Dominiccan Republic.* Durham, NC: Duke University Press, 2004.

Brugal, Carmen Imbert. "Rita Indiana y Todo sus Misterios." *Mujer Unica* 179 (August 2009): 20–27.

Bryson, Norman. "The Gaze in the Expanded Field." In *Vision and Visuality,* edited by Hal Foster. New York: Dia Art Foundation, 1988.

Butler, Judith. *Bodies That Matter: On the Discursive Limits of "Sex."* New York: Routledge, 1993.

———. "Endangered/Endangering: Schematic Racism and White Paranoia." In *Reading Rodney King/Reading Urban Uprising,* edited by Robert Gooding-Williams. New York: Routledge, 1993.

———. "Performative Acts and Gender Constitution: An Essay in Phenomenology and Feminist Theory." *Theatre Journal* 40, no. 4 (December 1988): 519–531.

Cabezas, Amalia. *Economies of Desire: Sex and Tourism in Cuba and the Dominican Republic.* Philadelphia: Temple University Press, 2009.

Cabral, José María, dir. "Protesta-Dominicana." *YouTube,* July 2, 2010. Video, 3:47. http://youtu.be/OxNRlqaJt-4.

Caldwell, Kia Lilly. *Negras in Brazil: Re-envisioning Black Women, Citizenship, and the Politics of Identity.* New Brunswick, NJ: Rutgers University Press, 2007.

Campt, Tina. *Image Matters: Archive, Photography, and the African Diaspora in Europe.* Durham, NC: Duke University Press, 2012.

Canclini, Nestor Garcia. *Hybrid Cultures: Strategies for Entering and Leaving Modernity.* Minneapolis: University of Minnesota Press, 1995.

Candelario, Ginetta E. B. *Black Behind the Ears: Dominican Racial Identity from Museums to Beauty Shops.* Durham, NC: Duke University Press, 2007.

Candelario, Ginetta E. B., ed. *Miradas descencadenantes: Los estudios de género en la República Dominicana al inicio del Tercer Milenio*. Santo Domingo: Centro de Estudios de Género, INTEC, 2005.

Candelario, Ginetta, April Mayes, and Elizabeth Manley, eds. *Cien años de feminismos dominicanos: Una colección de documentos y escrituras claves en la formación y evolución del pensamiento y el movimiento feminista en la República Dominciana, 1865–1965*. Santo Domingo: Archivo General de la Nación, 2016.

Carby, Hazel V. "Becoming Modern Racialized Subjects." *Cultural Studies* 23, no. 4 (2009): 624–657.

———. "Belonging to Britain." CLR James Lecture, University of Michigan, Ann Arbor, MI, September 25, 2008.

Carroll, Lewis. *Alice's Adventures in Wonderland*. Gutenberg e-Book, June 25, 2008. http://www.gutenberg.org/files/11/11-h/11-h.htm.

Casa por la Identidad de las Mujeres Afro. *Memoria del foro "Por una sociedad libre de prejuicio."* Santo Domingo: Editora Búho, 1997.

Centro de Investigación para la Acción Femenina (CIPAF). *Que Haceres* 31, no. 2 (November 2011).

Charles, Carolle. "Poor and Working Class Haitian Women's Discourses on the Use of Their Bodies." In *The Culture of Gender and Sexuality in the Caribbean*, edited by Linden Lewis. Gainesville: University Press of Florida, 2003.

Chávez, Karma R. *Queer Migration Politics: Activist Rhetoric and Coalitional Possibilities*. Chicago: University of Illinois Press, 2013.

Chesaniuk, Marie. "Duende in the Works of Federico García Lorca." Paper presented to Proceedings of the National Conference on Undergraduate Research (NCUR), UNC Asheville, April 6–8, 2006. http://www.ncur20.com/presentations/5/561/paper .pdf.

Chetty, Raj. "'La calle es libre': Race, Recognition, and Dominican Street Theater." *Afro-Hispanic Review* 32, no. 2 (2013): 41–56.

Chon, Kye-Sung. "The Role of Destination Image in Tourism: A Review and Discussion." *Tourism Review* 45, no. 2 (1990): 2–9.

Clarke, Cheryl. "Lesbianism as an Act of Resistance." In *This Bridge Called My Back: Writings by Radical Women of Color*, edited by Cherríe Moraga and Gloria Anzaldúa. Watertown, MA: Persephone Press, 1981.

Cliff, Michelle. *No Telephone to Heaven*. New York: Vintage Books, 1989.

Cocco de Filippis, Daisy. *Documents of Dissidence: Selected Writings by Dominican Women*. New York: CUNY Academic Works, 2000.

Collins, Patricia Hill. "Mammies, Matriarchs, and Other Controlling Images." In *Black Feminist Thought: Knowledge, Consciousness, and the Politics of Empowerment*. New York: Routledge, 2008.

"Como si importa." *Diario Libre*, March 21, 2012. http://www.diariolibre.com/de-stacada/2012/03/21/i328561_feminicidios-machismo-violencia-de-genero.html.

Cotera, María Eugenia. *Native Speakers: Ella Deloria, Zora Neale Hurston, Jovita Gonzalez, and the Poetics of Culture.* Austin: University of Texas Press, 2010.

Cox, Aimee Meredith. *Shapeshifters: Black Girls and the Choreography of Citizenship.* Durham, NC: Duke University Press, 2015.

Cruz Betances, Roxanna. "Una visión femenina." *Listindiario.com,* June 27, 2013. https://listindiario.com/entretenimiento/2013/06/27/282257/una-vision-femenina.

Curiel, Ochy. "Decolonizando el feminismo." *Feministas.org,* August 14, 2011. http://www.feministas.org/IMG/pdf/Ochy_Curiel.pdf.

———. "Identidades esencialistas o construcción de identidades políticas: El dilema de las feministas negras." *Otras Miradas* 2, no. 2 (December 2002): 96–113. https://www.redalyc.org/pdf/183/18320204.pdf.

DaCosta, Kimberly McClain. *Making Multiracials: State, Family, and Market in the Redrawing of the Color Line.* Stanford, CA: Stanford University Press, 2007.

Daly, Guilamo. "Dominican Funnies, Not So Funny: The Representation of Haitians in Dominican Newspaper Comic Strips, after the 2010 Earthquake." *Journal of Pan African Studies* 5, no. 9 (March 2013): 63–68.

Dayan, Joan. "Erzulie: A Women's History of Haiti." *Research in African Literatures* 25, no. 2, Special Issue: Caribbean Literature (Summer 1994): 5–31.

Deive, Carlos Esteban. *¿Y tu abuela dónde está?: El negro en la historia y la cultura dominicanas.* Santo Domingo: Editora Nacional, 2013.

de la Cadena, Marisol. *Indigenous Mestizos: The Politics of Race and Culture in Cuzco, Peru, 1919–1991.* Durham, NC: Duke University Press, 2000.

De la Cruz, Sarah. "ADOPEM: Magia [Magic]." Ad for Banco de Ahorro y Credito Adopem. Video, 1:04. http://vimeo.com/40456810.

Delancer, Juan, dir. *Tropico de sangre.* Kamasi Films, 2010.

"Del manifiesto del placer al beso micropolítico." *Nuestro Tiempo,* April 15, 2015. http://nuestrotiempo.com.do/2015/08/del-manifiesto-del-placer-al-beso-micropolitico.

de Moya, E. Antonio. "Power Games and Totalitarian Masculinity in the Dominican Republic." In *Interrogating Caribbean Masculinities: Theoretical and Empirical Analyses,* edited by Rhoda E. Reddock. Kingston, Jamaica: University of the West Indies Press, 2004.

Derby, Lauren H. *The Dictator's Seduction: Politics and the Popular Imagination in the Era of Trujillo.* Durham, NC: Duke University Press, 2009.

Derricotte, Toi. *The Black Notebooks: An Interior Journey.* New York: W. W. Norton, 1999.

Díaz, Rossy. *Diez años blogueando música.* Santo Domingo: Luna Insomne Editores, 2018.

Doble T, El Crok, y Los Pepes. "Pa' manga mi visa." *YouTube,* January 24, 2011. Video, 3:15. https://www.youtube.com/watch?v=F3Nver8B7nE.

Duggan, Lisa. *The Twilight of Equality: Neoliberalism, Cultural Politics, and the Attack on Democracy.* Boston: Beacon Press, 2004.

Durán, Rubén, dir. *Cimarrón Spirit.* Cab 95 Films, in collaboration with Cosmic Light Productions, 2015.

EFE Newswire. "Documental revela obsesión de dominicanas por pelo liso." *Hoy*, May 15, 2008, 1D.

Engel, Leonardo, dir. "Da' pa lo do." *YouTube*, October 19, 2011. Video, 4:24. https://www.youtube.com/watch?v=Y72XAybPTnU.

Enloe, Cynthia. *Bananas, Beaches, and Bases: Making Feminist Sense of International Politics*. Berkeley: University of California Press, 2001.

Espinosa Miñoso, Yuderkys. "Homogeneidad, proyecto de nación y homophobia." In *Desde la orilla: Hacia una nacionalidad sin desalojos*, edited by Silvio Torres-Saillant, Ramona Hernández, and Blas Jiménez. Santo Domingo: Ediciones Librería La Trinitaria, 2004.

Falcón, Sylvanna M. *Power Interrupted: Anti-Racist and Feminist Activism Inside the United Nations*. Seattle: University of Washington Press, 2016.

———. "Transnational Feminism as a Paradigm for Decolonizing the Practice of Research: Identifying Feminist Principles and Methodology Criteria for US-Based Scholars." *Frontiers: A Journal of Women Studies* 37, no. 1 (2016): 174–194.

Ferguson, Roderick. *Aberrations in Black: Toward a Queer of Color Critique*. Minneapolis: University of Minnesota Press, 2003.

"Filmará Michelle Rodríguez en República Dominicana." *El Universal*, July 4, 2008. https://archivo.eluniversal.com.mx/notas/520110.html.

Fiol-Matta, Licia. *Queer Mother for the Nation: The State and Gabriela Mistral*. Minneapolis: University of Minnesota Press, 2002.

Fleetwood, Nicole R. *Troubling Vision: Performance, Visuality, and Blackness*. Chicago: University of Chicago Press, 2011.

Flores, Juan. *The Diaspora Strikes Back: Cultural Challenges of Circular Migration and Transnational Communities*. New York: Routledge, 2008.

Fort, Ilene Susan, and Tere Arcq. "Introduction." In *Wonderland: Las aventuras surrealistas de mujeres artistas en Mexico y Estados Unidos*. Munich: Prestel Publishing, 2012.

Francis, Terri. "Introduction: The No-Theory Chant of Afrosurrealism." *Black Camera* 5, no. 1 (Fall 2013): 95–111.

Freehill, Jeremy. "Análisis geográfico de violencia contra la mujer en República Dominicana." United Nations Population Fund, August 15, 2011.

Fukuyama, Francis. *The End of History and the Last Man*. New York: Free Press, 2006.

Fusco, Coco. "Racial Time, Racial Marks." In *Only Skin Deep: Changing Visions of the American Self*, edited by Coco Fusco and Brian Wallis. New York: Harry M. Abrams, 2003.

Gabriele, John P. "Of Mothers and Freedom: Adela's Struggle for Selfhood in *La Casa de Bernarda Alba*." *Symposium* 47, no. 3 (1993): 188–199.

Gairola, Rahul K. "Digital Closets: Postmillenial Representations of Queerness in *Kapoor and Sons* and *Aligarh*." In *Queering Digital India: Activisms, Identities, and Subjectivities*, edited by Rohit K. Dasgupta and Debanuj DasGupta. Edinburgh: Edinburgh University Press, 2018.

Galván, Sergia. "Power, Racism, and Identity." In *Connecting Across Cultures and Continents: Black Women Speak Out on Identity, Race, and Development*, edited by Achola O. Pala. New York: United Nations Development Fund for Women, UNIFEM, 1995.

García, Cheddy. *La negrita caridad*. Santo Domingo: Media Byte, 2004.

García Lorca, Federico. *La casa de Bernarda Alba*. Newburyport, MA: Focus Publishing, 2005.

———. *The House of Bernarda Alba*. Oxford: Oxbow, 2009.

García-Peña, Lorgia. *Borders of Dominicanidad: Race, Nation, and Archives of Contradiction*. Durham, NC: Duke University Press, 2016.

———. "Translating 'Blackness': Dominicans Negotiating Race and Belonging." *Black Scholar* 45, no. 2 (2015): 10–20.

Gefin, Laszlo K. "Collage Theory, Reception, and the Cutups of William Burroughs." In *Perspectives on Contemporary Literature: Literature and the Other Arts*, edited by David Hershberg. Lexington: University Press of Kentucky, 2015.

"Gente UEPA: Engel Leonardo." Accessed June 5, 2015. http://uepa.com/article .aspx?id=32449#.VXG79lxViko.

Gilroy, Paul. *Small Acts: Thoughts on the Politics of Black Cultures.* London: Serpent's Tail, 1993.

Goodman, Mark, and David Bowie. "David Bowie Criticizes MTV for Not Playing Videos by Black Artists." *MTV News*, 1983. *YouTube*, January 11, 2016. Video, 4:39. https://www.youtube.com/watch?v=XZGiVzIr8Qg.

Gopinath, Gayatri. *Impossible Desires: Queer Diasporas and South Asian Public Cultures*. Durham, NC: Duke University Press, 2005.

Grandin, Greg. "Can the Subaltern Be Seen? Photography and the Affects of Nationalism." *Hispanic American Historical Review* 84, no. 1 (2004): 83–111.

Gregory, Steven. *The Devil Behind the Mirror: Globalization and Politics in the Dominican Republic*. 2nd ed. Berkeley: University of California Press, 2014.

Grewal, Inderpal. *Transnational America: Feminisms, Diasporas, Neoliberalisms*. Durham, NC: Duke University Press, 2005.

Grewal, Inderpal, and Caren Kaplan, eds. *Scattered Hegemonies: Postmodernity and Transnational Feminist Practices*. Minneapolis: University of Minnesota Press, 1994.

Guerrero, Teresa. "Arriba abajo Isabel Spencer: Nuevas expresiones frescas perfuman el teatro dominicano." *Acento*, November 11, 2012. https://acento.com.do/cultura/ nuevas-expresiones--frescas-perfuman-el-teatro-dominicano-27609.html.

———. "Maleducadas: Colectivo de teatro desde perspectiva feminine." *Acento*, November 16, 2012. https://acento.com.do/cultura/maleducadas-colectivo-de -teatro-desde-perspectiva-femenina-24400.html.

———. "Vuelve a escena la obra de teatro *La casa de Bernarda Alba.*" *Acento*, January 8, 2013. https://acento.com.do/cultura/vuelve-a-escena-la-obra-de-teatro-la-casa-de -bernarda-alba-36397.html.

Halim Chowdhury, Elora. *Transnationalism Reversed: Women Organizing against Gender Violence in Bangladesh*. Albany: SUNY Press, 2011.

Halim Chowdhury, Elora, and Liz Philipose. *Dissident Friendships: Feminism, Imperialism, and Transnational Solidarity*. Chicago: University of Illinois Press, 2016.

Hall, Stuart. "Cultural Identity and Cinematic Representation." In *Stuart Hall: Critical Dialogues in Cultural Studies*, edited by David Morley and Kuan-Hsing Chen. London: Routledge, 1996.

———. "New Ethnicities." In *Stuart Hall: Critical Dialogues in Cultural Studies*, edited by David Morley and Kuan-Hsing Chen. London: Routledge, 1996.

———. "What Is This 'Black' in Black Popular Culture?" In *Black Popular Culture*, edited by Gina Dent and Michele Wallace. Seattle: Bay Press, 1992.

Harrison, Faye V. *Outsider Within: Reworking Anthropology in the Global Age*. Urbana: University of Illinois Press, 2008.

Harrison-Kahan, Lori. "Her 'Nig': Returning the Gaze of Nella Larsen's 'Passing.'" *Modern Language Studies* 32, no. 2 (Autumn 2002): 109–138.

Hart, Stephen M. "The Bear and the Dawn: Versions of 'La Casa de Bernarda Alba.'" *Neolophiliogus* 73, no. 1 (January 1989): 62–68.

Harvey, David. *A Brief History of Neoliberalism*. Oxford: Oxford University Press, 2005.

Hedervary, Claire. "The United Nations: Good Grief, There Are Women Here!" Remarks presented March 8, 1982, at National Women's Day panel. In *Sisterhood Is Global: The International Women's Movement Anthology*, edited by Robin Morgan. New York: Feminist Press, 1996.

Herencia, Noelia Quintero, dir. "El juidero." *YouTube*, April 15, 2020. Video, 4:26. https://www.youtube.com/watch?v=Wf-2tmmcDqo.

Hernandez, Daisy. "We're All Racial Justice Media Makers Now." *Colorlines*, August 13, 2010. https://www.colorlines.com/articles/were-all-racial-justice-media-makers-now.

Hernández, Rita Indiana. *La estrategia de Chochueca*. San Juan, PR: Editorial Isla Negra, 2003.

———. Interview with Marisel Moreno-Anderson and Rubén Ríos Avila, Oral History Archive, Latino Studies, University of Notre Dame, October 9, 2006. *YouTube*, March 24, 2016. Video, 1:22:34. https://www.youtube.com/watch?v=vI4Gj2woZoQ.

———. *Papi*. San Juan, PR: Ediciones Vértigo, 2005.

Hoffnung-Garskof, Jesse. *A Tale of Two Cities: Santo Domingo and New York after 1950*. Princeton, NJ: Princeton University Press, 2007.

hooks, bell. *Black Looks: Race and Representation*. Cambridge, MA: South End Press, 1992.

Horn, Maja. *Masculinity after Trujillo: Globalized Dominican Subjectivities in the Novels of Rita Indiana Hernandez*. Gainesville: University Press of Florida, 2016.

Howard, Jane. "Doom and Glory of Knowing Who You Are." *Life*, May 24, 1963.

Hull, Gloria T., Patricia Bell-Scott, and Barbara Smith, eds. *All the Women Are White, All the Blacks Are Men, But Some of Us Are Brave: Black Women's Studies.* 2nd ed. New York: Feminist Press at CUNY, 2015.

Human Rights Watch. "Interview Defying Dominican Republic's Abortion Law." November 19, 2018. https://www.hrw.org/news/2018/11/19/interview-defying -dominican-republics-abortion-law#.

———. "'It's Your Decision, It's Your Life': The Total Criminalization of Abortion in the Dominican Republic." November 19, 2018. https://www.hrw.org/sites/default/ files/report_pdf/dr1118_web.pdf.

Hunter, Margaret L. *Race, Gender, and the Politics of Skin Tone.* New York: Routledge, 2005.

Hutchinson, Sydney. *Tigers of a Different Stripe: Performing Gender in Dominican Music.* Chicago: University of Chicago Press, 2016.

Indiana, Rita. "Bowie, estrella negra." *El País,* February 1, 2016. https://elpais.com/ elpais/2016/01/29/eps/1454072363_461493.html.

———. "Magia negra." *El País,* October 9, 2013.

Jameson, Fredric. *Marxism and Form: Twentieth-Century Dialectical Theories of Literature.* Princeton, NJ: Princeton University Press, 1972.

Jay, Martin. "Scopic Regimes of Visuality." In *Vision and Visuality,* edited by Hal Foster. New York: Dia Art Foundation, 1988.

Jiménez Román, Miriam, and Juan Flores, eds. *The Afro-Latin@ Reader: History and Culture in the United States.* Durham, NC: Duke University Press, 2010.

Johnson, E. Patrick. *Appropriating Blackness: Performance and the Politics of Authenticity.* Durham, NC: Duke University Press, 2003.

Joseph, May. "Transatlantic Inscriptions: Desire, Diaspora, and Cultural Citizenship." In *Talking Visions: Multicultural Feminism in Transnational Age,* edited by Ella Shohat. Cambridge, MA: MIT Press, 1998.

Jovovich, Milla. "Michelle Rodriguez." *Interview,* January 12, 2015. https://www .interviewmagazine.com/film/michelle-rodriguez.

Khan, Aisha. "What Is a Spanish?: Ambiguity and 'Mixed' Ethnicity in Trinidad." In *Perspectives on the Caribbean: A Reader in Culture, History, and Representation,* edited by Philip W. Scher. Oxford: Blackwell Publishing, 2010.

Kempadoo, Kamala. "Theorizing Sexual Relations in the Caribbean: Prostitution and the Problem of the 'Exotic.'" In *Confronting Power, Theorizing Gender: Interdisciplinary Perspectives in the Caribbean,* edited by Eudine Barriteau. Kingston, Jamaica: University of the West Indies Press, 2003.

———. "Women of Color and the Global Sex Trade: Transnational Feminist Perspectives." *Meridians* 1, no. 2 (Spring, 2001): 28–51.

Knapp, Bettina. "Federico García Lorca's *The House of Bernarda Alba*: A Hermaph-roditic Matriarchate." *Modern Drama* 27, no. 3 (Fall 1984): 382–394.

Larsen, Nella. *Passing.* New York: Penguin Classics, 2003.

"'La casa de Bernarda Alba' regresa a escena en Casa de Teatro." *El Caribe*, January 8, 2013. https://www.elcaribe.com.do/2013/01/08/ldquo-casa-bernarda-albardquo -regresa-escena-casa-teatro/.

"La polifacética Rita Indiana condensa en 'Papi' lo mejor y lo peor de la cultura caribeña." *La Vanguardia*, September 22, 2011. http://www.lavanguardia.com/libros/ 20110922/54219474411/la-polifacetica-rita-indiana-condensa-en-papi-lo-mejor-y -lo-peor-de-la-cultura-caribena.html.

Leonardo, Engel. "Da' pa' lo' do." YouTube, October 18, 2011. Video, 4:24. https:// www.youtube.com/watch?v=Y72XAybPTnU.

Levitt, Peggy. *The Transnational Villagers*. Berkeley: University of California Press, 2001.

Liberato, Ana S. Q. *Joaquín Balaguer, Memory, and Diaspora: The Lasting Political Legacies of an American Protégé*. New York: Lexington Books, 2013.

Lima, Robert. "Missing in Action: Invisible Males in *La Casa de Bernarda Alba*." *Bucknell Review* 45, no. 1 (2001): 136–148.

Lionnet, Françoise, and Shu-mei Shih. *Minor Transnationalism*. Durham, NC: Duke University Press, 2005.

Lorde, Audre. "Uses of Anger: Women Responding to Racism." In *Sister Outsider: Essays and Speeches*. Freedom, CA: Crossing Press, 1984.

Lott, Eric. "Love and Theft: The Racial Unconscious of Blackface Minstrelsy." *Representations* 39 (Summer 1992): 23–50.

Lugones, María C., and Elizabeth Spelman. "Have We Got a Theory for You! Feminist Cultural Theory, Cultural Imperialism, and the Demand for the 'Woman's Voice.'" *Women's Studies International* 6, no. 6 (1983): 573–577.

Maillo Pozo, Sharina. "La comunión entre música y literature en la strategic de Chochueca: En busca de la heterogeneidad Pereira." In *El snide de la música en la narrativa dominicana: Ensayos sobre identidad, nación y performance*, edited by Médar Serrata. Santo Domingo: Instituto de Estudios Caribeños, 2017.

Manley, Elizabeth S. *The Paradox of Paternalism: Women and the Politics of Authoritarianism in the Dominican Republic University*. Gainesville: University Press of Florida, 2018.

———. "Revitalizing Feminism in the Dominican Republic." *NACLA* (North American Congress on Latin America), November 27, 2018. https://nacla.org/ news/2018/11/27/revitalizing-feminism-dominican-republic.

Marouan, Maha. *Witches, Goddesses, and Angry Spirits: The Politics of Spiritual Liberation in African Diaspora Women's Fiction*. Columbus: Ohio State University Press, 2013.

Martínez, Elizabeth, and Arnoldo Garcia. "What Is Neoliberalism?: A Brief Definition for Activists." *CorpWatch.org*, December 5, 2010. http://www.corpwatch.org/article .php?id=376.

Martínez, Erika M. *Daring to Write: Contemporary Narratives by Dominican Women*. Athens: University of Georgia Press, 2016.

Martínez-San Miguel, Yolanda. "Más allá de la homonormatividad: Intimidades alternativas en el Caribe Hispano." *Revista Iberoamericana* 74, no. 225 (2008): 1039–1057.

Maurer, Christopher. "Introduction." In *Selected Verse: Federico García Lorca*, edited by Christopher Maurer. Rev. bilingual ed. Trans. Catherine Brown. New York: Farrar, Straus and Giroux, 2004.

Mayes, April. *The Mulatto Republic: Class, Race, and Dominican National Identity.* Gainesville: University Press of Florida, 2014.

———. "Why Dominican Feminism Moved to the Right: Class, Colour, and Women's Activism in the Dominican Republic, 1880s–1940s." *Gender & History* 20, no. 2 (August 2008): 349–371.

Mbembe, Achille. "Necropolitics." *Public Culture* 15, no. 1 (2003): 11–40.

Mejía, Jorge. "PN 'pela a caco' a joven barbero 'por greñú.'" *El Día*, February 9, 2012. http://www.eldia.com.do/nacionales/2012/2/9/74836/PNpela-a-caco-a-joven -barbero-por-grenu.

Mejía-Ricart, Tirso. *Historia de la Universidad Dominicana.* Santo Domingo: Ciudad Universitaria, 1999.

Mercer, Kobena. "Diaspora Aesthetics and Visual Culture." In *Black Cultural Traffic: Crossroads in Global Performance and Popular Culture*, edited by Harry J. Elam and Kennel A. Jackson. Ann Arbor: University of Michigan Press, 2005.

Miller, D. Scot. "Afrosurreal Manifesto: Black Is the New black—a 21st-Century Manifesto." *Black Camera* 5, no. 1 (2013): 113–117.

Miñoso, Yuderkys Espinosa. "Homogeneidad, proyecto de nación y homophobia." In *Desde la orilla: Hacia una nacionalidad sin desalojos*, edited by Silvio Torres-Saillant, Ramona Hernández, and Blas R. Jiménez. Santo Domingo: Editora Manati, 2004.

Mitchell, Jasmine. *Imagining the Mulatta: Blackness in U.S. and Brazilian Media.* Chicago: University of Illinois Press, 2020.

Moghadam, Valentine M. "Gender and Globalization: Female Labor and Women's Mobilization." *Journal of World-Systems Research* 5, no. 2 (Summer 1999): 367–388.

Mohanty, Chandra Talpade. *Feminism without Borders: Decolonizing Theory, Practicing Solidarity.* Durham, NC: Duke University Press, 2003.

———. "*Under Western Eyes* Revisited: Feminist Solidarity through Anticapitalist Struggles." *Signs: Journal of Women in Culture and Society* 28, no 2 (Winter 2003): 499–535.

Morgan, Robin, ed. *Sisterhood Is Global: The International Women's Movement Anthology.* New York: Feminist Press, 1996.

Morrison, Toni. *The Bluest Eye.* New York : Plume Books, 1994.

Moya, Paula M. L., and Michael R. Hames García. *Reclaiming Identity: Realist Theory and the Predicament of Postmodernism.* Berkeley: University of California Press, 2000.

Moya Pons, Frank. *The Dominican Republic: A National History*. Princeton, NJ: Markus Wiener Publishers, 2010.

Muñiz, Ángel, dir. *Ladrones al domicilio*. Estudio Quitasueño, 2008.

Muñoz, Jose Esteban. "Feeling Brown: Ethnicity and Affect in Ricardo Bracho's *The Sweetest Hangover (and Other STDs)*." *Theatre Journal* 52, no. 1 (March 2000): 67–79.

Murray, Gerald F., and Marina Ortiz. *Pelo bueno/pelo malo: Estudio antropológico de los salones de belleza en la República Dominicana*. Santo Domingo: Fondo para el Financiamiento de la Microempresa (FONDOMICRO), 2012.

Nakamura, Lisa. *Digitizing Race: Visual Cultures of the Internet*. Minneapolis: University of Minnesota Press, 2008.

Narayan, Uma. *Dislocating Cultures: Identities, Traditions, and Third-World Feminism*. New York: Routledge, 1997.

Nixon, Angelique. *Resisting Paradise: Tourism, Diaspora, and Sexuality in Caribbean Culture*. Jackson: University of Mississippi Press, 2015.

O'Hearn, Claudine, ed. *Half + Half: Writers on Growing Up Biracial and Bicultural*. New York: Pantheon, 1998.

Olumide, Jill. *Raiding the Gene Pool: The Social Construction of Mixed Race*. Sterling, VA: Pluto Press, 2002.

Omi, Michael, and Howard Winant. *Racial Formation in the United States: From the 1960s to the 1990s*. New York: Routledge, 1994.

Oxford, Jeffrey. "Cultural and Literary Ethos as Represented in García Lorca's *La Casa de Bernarda Alba*." In *The Woman in Latin America and Spanish Literature: Essays on Iconic Characters*, edited by Eva Paulino Bueno and María Claudia Andre. Jefferson, NC: MacFarland, 2012.

Padilla, Mark. *Caribbean Pleasure Industry: Tourism, Sexuality, and AIDS in the Dominican Republic*. Chicago: University of Chicago Press, 2007.

Palacios, Rita M. "Actos peatonales, actos de consumo: La queerificación del espacio en La estrategia de Chochueca de Rita Indiana Hernández." *Hispania* 97, no. 4 (December 2014): 566–577.

Pérez, Sara. "La Iglesia patriarchal dominicana." In *Desde la orilla: Hacia una nacionalidad sin desalojos*, edited by Silvio Torres Saillant, Ramona Hernanández, and Blas R. Jiménez. Santo Domingo: Editora Manití, 2004.

Pfeiffer, Kathleen. "Individualism, Success, and American Identity in *The Autobiography of an Ex-Colored Man*." *African American Review* 30, no. 3 (1996): 403–419.

Pierre, Sonia. "Fobias nacionalists y los domínico-haitianos." In *Desde la orilla: Hacia una nacionalidad sin desalojos*, edited by Silvio Torres Saillant, Ramona Hernanández, and Blas R. Jiménez. Santo Domingo: Editora Manití, 2004.

Pineda, Magaly, Martha Olga García, and Laura Faxas. "Mujer, mito y realidad." In *Seminario hermanas Mirabal: Diagnóstico, evaluación y recomencaciones modificativas de la condición de la mujer dominicana*. 2nd ed. Santo Domingo: Editora de la Universidad Autónoma de Santo Domingo, 2017.

Polanco, Jacqueline Jiménez. "Dominican Republic LGBT Movement—A Sociopolitical and Cultural Approach." *Global Public Health* (October 11, 2004). Accessed May 5, 2012.

Puar, Jasbir K. *Terrorist Assemblages: Homonationalism in Queer Times*. Durham, NC: Duke University Press, 2007.

Quinn, Rachel Afi. "Dominican Pride and Shame." *Small Axe: A Caribbean Journal of Criticism* 22, no. 2 (2018): 128–143.

———. "El Rostro negro dominicano y la quisqueya queer de Rita Indiana Hernández." In *Nuestro Caribe: Poder, raza y postnacionalismos desde los límites del mapa LGBTQ*, edited by Mabel Cuesta. San Juan and Santo Domingo: Editorial Isla Negra, 2016.

———. "Spinning the Zoetrope." *Latin American & Latinx Visual Culture* 1, no. 3 (July 2019): 44–59.

———. "This Bridge Called the Internet: Black Lesbian Feminist Organizing in Santo Domingo." In *Transatlantic Feminisms: Women and Gender Studies in Africa and the African Diaspora*, edited by Akosua Adomako Ampofo, Cheryl R. Rodriguez, and Dzodzi Tsikata. East Lansing: Michigan State University Press, 2015.

Quiroga, Lucero. "Feminización universitaria en la República Dominicana: 1977–2001." In *Miradas descencadenantes: Los estudios de género en la Republica Dominicana al inicio del Tercer Milenio*, edited by Ginetta E. B. Candelario. Santo Domingo: Centro de Estudios de Género, INTEC, 2005.

Rabinovich, Cecilia. *Surrealism and the Sacred: Power, Eros, and the Occult in Modern Art*. Boulder, CO: Westview Press, 2002.

Ramírez, Dixa. *Colonial Phantoms: Belonging and Refusal in the Dominican Americas, from the 19th Century to the Present*. New York: NYU Press, 2018.

Randall, Margaret. *Our Voices, Our Lives: Stories of Women from Central America and the Caribbean*. Monroe, ME: Common Courage Press, 2002.

Reber, Diedra. "Visual Storytelling: Cinematic Ekphrasis in the Latin American Novel of Globalization." *NOVEL: A Forum on Fiction* 43, no. 1 (Spring 2010): 65–71.

Renda, Mary. *Taking Haiti: Military Occupation and the Culture of U.S. Imperialism, 1915–1940*. Chapel Hill: University of North Carolina Press, 2001.

Reyes, Carlos. "Rita Indiana y Los Misterios—*El juidero*" (Review). *Club Fonograma*, October 2010. https://www.oldfonograma.com/2010/10/rita-indiana-y-los-misterios-el-juidero.html.

Reyes Bonilla, Dulce. "Primero puta que pájara: Sexuality and Dominicanness." In *Desde la orilla: Hacia una nacionalidad sin desalojos*, edited by Silvio Torres-Saillant, Ramona Hernández, and Blas R. Jiménez. Santo Domingo: Ediciones Librería La Trinitária, 2004.

Ricardo, Michelle. "Negra Caribeña." *YouTube*, January 20, 2011. Video, 2:45. https://www.youtube.com/watch?v=Pf3IL5LFmnU.

Ricourt, Milagros. *The Dominican Racial Imaginary: Surveying the Landscape of Race and Nation in Hispaniola.* New Brunswick, NJ: Rutgers University Press, 2016.

Riggs, Marlon, dir. *Ethnic Notions.* California Newsreel, 1986.

"A Rising Voice: Afro-Latin Americans." *Miami Herald*, 2007. http://media.miami herald.com/multimedia/news/afrolatin/index.html.

"Rita Indiana estrena video internacionalmente." F & F Media Corp., October 15, 2010. http://www.ffmediacorp.com/es/Prensa-2/Musica-7/Rita-Indiana-estrena -video-internacionalmente-15-10-10-514.

"Rita Indiana Talks about Being a Lesbian, Coming Out, Family Acceptance, and Marriage Equality." *Noche de Luz, YouTube*, May 11, 2011. Video, 6:19. https://www .youtube.com/watch?v=cNIb6moUPMA.

Rivas, Jorge. "Beyoncé Is the Whitest She's Ever Been in New Album Promo." *Colorlines*, January 19, 2012. https://www.colorlines.com/articles/beyonce-whitest -shes-ever-been-new-album-promo.

Rivera, Zayda. "Michelle Rodriguez Answers Six 'Fast & Furious' Questions for *New York Daily News* Viva." *New York Daily News*, May 28, 2013.

Rivera-Velazquez, Celiany. "The Importance of Being Rita Indiana-Hernandez: Women-Centered Video, Sound, and Performance Interventions within Spanish Caribbean Cultural Studies." In *Globalizing Cultural Studies: Ethnographic Interventions in Theory, Method, and Policy*, edited by Cameron McCarthy, Aisha S. Durham, Laura C. Engel, and Alice A. Filmer. 2nd ed. New York: Peter Lang, 2007.

Roberts, Dorothy. *Killing the Black Body: Race, Reproduction, and the Meaning of Liberty.* New York: Vintage Books, 2017.

Rodriguez, Amaury. "A 'Green Tide' Engulfs the D.R." *NACLA*, June 16, 2017. https:// nacla.org/news/2017/06/19/%E2%80%9Cgreen-tide%E2%80%9D-engulfs-dr.

Rodríguez Calderón, Mirta. "El besatón: Modalidad dominicana de la lucha antihomofóbica." America Latina en Movimiento, June 4, 2010. https://www .alainet.org/es/active/39342.

Rojas, Ana Gabriela. "Emely Peguero: El asesinato de una adolescente embarazada que puso el foco sobre el terrible número de feminicidios en República Dominicana." *BBC Mundo*, October 16, 2017. https://www.bbc.com/mundo/noticias-america -latina-41617665.

Rojas, Enrique. "Baseball Academies Thrive in the Dominican Republic." *ESPN Deportes*, July 15, 2015. https://www.espn.com/blog/onenacion/post/_/id/710/ baseball-academies-thrive-in-the-dominican-republic.

Root, Maria P. P. *The Multiracial Experience: Racial Borders as the New Frontier.* Thousand Oaks, CA: Sage Publications, 1996.

Rosemont, Franklin, and Robin D. G. Kelley, eds. *Black, Brown, and Beige: Surrealist Writings from Africa and the Diaspora.* Austin: University of Texas Press, 2009.

Ross, Elliot. "The Dangers of a Single Book Cover: The Acacia Tree Meme and 'African Literature.'" *Africa Is a Country*, May 7, 2014. https://africasacountry.com/

2014/05/the-dangers-of-a-single-book-cover-the-acacia-tree-meme-and-african
-literature/.

Roth, Wendy D. "A Single Shade of 'Negro': Henry Louis Gates' Depictions of Blackness in the Dominican Republic." *Latin American and Caribbean Ethnic Studies* 8, no. 1 (2013): 95–99.

Rubia Barcia, J. "El realismo 'mágico' de 'La Casa de Bernarda Alba.'" *Revista Hispánica Moderna* 31, no. 1 (January 1965): 385–398.

Sagás, Ernesto. "A Case of Mistaken Identity: Antihaitianismo in Dominican Culture." *Latinamericanist* 29, no. 1 (1993): 1–5.

Scheller, Mimi. "Virtual Islands: Mobilities, Connectivity, and the New Caribbean Spacialities." *Small Axe* (October 2007): 16–33.

Schumann, Rebecka. "Is Michelle Rodriguez Gay? 'Fast and Furious 7' Star Comes Out as Bisexual Following Lesbian Rumors." *International Business Times*, October 3, 2013. https://www.ibtimes.com/michelle-rodriguez-gay-fast-furious-7-star -comes-out-bisexual-following-lesbian-rumors-1414372.

Scott, Julius. *A Common Wind*. New York: Verso Books, 2018.

Scott, Nina M. "Sight and Insight in *La Casa de Bernarda Alba*." *Revista de Estudios Hispánicos* 10, no. 2 (May 1976): 297–308.

Sedgh, Gilda, Jonathan Bearak, Susheela Singh, Akinrinola Bankole, Anna Popinchalk, Bela Ganatra, Clémentine Rossier, Caitlin Gerdts, Özge Tunçalp, Brooke Ronald Johnson Jr., Heidi Bart Johnston, and Leontine Alkema. "Abortion Incidence between 1990 and 2014: Global, Regional, and Subregional Levels and Trends." *The Lancet* 388, no. 10041 (2016): 258–267.

Senna, Danzy. "The Mulatto Millennium." In *Half and Half: Writers on Growing Up Biracial and Bicultural*, edited by Claudine Chiawei O'Hearn. New York: Pantheon, 1998.

———. *Symptomatic*. New York: Riverhead Books, 2004.

Shohat, Ella, ed. *Talking Visions: Multicultural Feminism in a Transnational Age*. Cambridge, MA: MIT Press, 1998.

Shohat, Ella, and Robert Stam. *Unthinking Eurocentrism: Multiculturalism and the Media*. New York: Routledge, 1994.

Sidanius, Jim, Yesilernis Peña, and Mark Sawyer. "Inclusionary Discrimination: Pigmentocracy and Patriotism in the Dominican Republic." *Political Psychology* 22, no. 4 (December 2001): 827–851.

Simmons, Kimberly Eison. *Reconstructing Racial Identity and the African Past in the Dominican Republic*. Gainesville: University Press of Florida, 2009.

Smith, Shawn Michelle. *American Archives: Gender, Race, and Class in Visual Culture*. Princeton, NJ: Princeton University Press, 1999.

Somerville, Siobhan B. *Queering the Color Line: Race and the Invention of Homosexuality in American Culture*. Durham, NC: Duke University Press, 2000.

Sontag, Susan. *On Photography*. New York: Penguin Books, 1977.

Sosa, José Rafael. "Isabel Spencer sorprende como directora teatral: *Casa Bernarda Alba* muestra los talentos de las Maleducadas." *Teatro en la zona y mas*, December

9, 2012. https://teatrolasmascaras.blogspot.com/2012/12/isabel-spencer-sorprende-como-directora.html.

Soufas, C. Christopher. *The Subject in Question: Early Contemporary Spanish Literature and Modernism*. Washington, DC: Catholic University of America Press, 2007.

Speranza, Graciela. "Wanderers: Surrealism and Contemporary Latin American Art and Fiction." In *Surrealism in Latin America: Vivísimo Muerto*, edited by Dawn Ades, Rita Eder, and Graciela Speranza. Los Angeles: Getty Research Institute, 2012.

Spickard, Paul R. "The Subject Is Mixed Race: The Boom in Biracial Biography." In *Rethinking Mixed Race*, edited by David Parker and Miri Song. New York: Pluto Press, 2001.

Suero, Indhira. "La cuestión mulata: A pregunta no es simple ¿si colocan el término mulato en la cédula, se cometería un error oficial?" *Listín Diario*, December 3, 2011.

———. "La maleducada: En República Dominicana es difícil ser negra, mujer, artista e isleña', afirma Isabel Spencer, directora teatral." *Listín Diario*, August 11, 2013.

Suki, Lenora. *Financial Institutions and the Remittances Market in the Dominican Republic*. New York: Earth Institute at Columbia University, 2004.

Swarr, Amanda Lock, and Richa Nagar, eds. *Critical Transnational Feminist Praxis*. Albany: SUNY Press, 2010.

"Take Five: Fighting Femicide in Latin America." *UN Women*, February 15, 2017. http://www.unwomen.org/en/news/stories/2017/2/take-five-adriana-quinones-femicide-in-latin-america.

Taylor, Diana. *The Archive and the Repertoire: Performing Cultural Memory in the Americas*. Durham, NC: Duke University Press, 2003.

Tellerías, Alexéi. "VIVIENDO EN BINARIO: ¿Hashtags en Facebook?" *Tecnología Tuesday*, January 29, 2013. http://listindiario.com/tecnologia/2013/1/28/263896/Hashtags-en-Facebook.

Thompson, Krista A. *An Eye for the Tropics: Tourism, Photography, and Framing the Caribbean Picturesque*. Durham, NC: Duke University Press, 2006.

———. *Shine: The Visual Economy of Light in African Diasporic Aesthetic Practice*. Durham, NC: Duke University Press, 2015.

Thornton, Brendan Jamal, and Diego I. Ubiera. "Caribbean Exceptions: The Problem of Race and Nation in Dominican Studies." *Latin American Research Review* 54, no. 2 (2019): 413–428.

Tineo Durán, Jeannette. *Imaginarios de género en juventudes dominicanas: Aportes para el dabate desde la colonialidad de poder*. Santo Domingo: Instituto Tecnológico de Santo Domingo, 2014.

Torres-Saillant, Silvio. *El tigueraje intelectual*. Santo Domingo: Editora Manatí, 2002.

———. "The Tribulations of Blackness: Stages in Dominican Racial Identity." *Latin American Perspectives* 25, no. 3 (May 1998): 126–146.

Torres-Saillant, Silvio, Ramona Hernández, and Blas R. Jiménez, eds. *Desde la orilla: Hacia una nacionalidad sin desalojos*. Santo Domingo: Editoria Manatí, 2004.

Trinh, T. Minh-Ha. "Not You/Like You: Post-Colonial Women and the Interlocking Questions of Identity and Difference." In "Feminism and the Critique of Colonial

Discourse," ed. Deborah Gordon, *Inscriptions* 3–4 (1988). https://culturalstudies .ucsc.edu/inscriptions/volume-34/trinh-t-minh-ha/.

———. *Woman, Native, Other: Writing Postcoloniality and Feminism.* Bloomington: Indiana University Press, 1989.

Ulysse, Gina Athena. *Downtown Ladies: Informal Commercial Importers, a Haitian Anthropologist, and Self-Making Jamaica.* Chicago: University of Chicago Press, 2007.

United Nations. "Gender Equity Observatory for Latin America and the Caribbean." *Notes for Equality*, no. 17 (July 2015).

———. *Poner fin a la violencia contra la mujer: De las palabras los hecho.* Publication no. S.06.IV.8 (2006). https://www.un.org/womenwatch/daw//public/VAW_Study/ VAW-Spanish.pdf.

Valdez, Claudina. "Genero, discriminación racial y ciudadanía: Un studio en la escuela dominicana." In *Miradas descencadenantes: Los estudios de género en la República Dominicana al inicio del tercer milenio.* Santo Domingo: Centro de Estudios de Género, INTEC, 2005.

Valdivia, Angarhard N. "The Gendered Face of Latinidad: The Global Circulation of Hybridity." In *Circuits of Visibility: Gender and Transnational Media Cultures,* edited by Radha Sarma Hegde. New York: NYU Press, 2011.

Vargas, Melisa. "Little New York." *Monu #7*, October 9, 2007.

Vasconcelos, José. *The Cosmic Race / La Raza Cosmica.* Baltimore: Johns Hopkins University Press, 1997.

Vera-Rojas, María Theresa. "¡Se armó el juidero! Cartografías imprecisas, cuerpos disidentes, sexualidades transgresoras: Hacia una lectura queer de Rita Indiana Hernández." In *Rita Indiana: Archivos,* edited by Fernanda Bustamante Escalona. Santo Domingo: Ediciones Cielonaranja, 2017.

Vicioso, Sherezada "Chiqui." "Discovering Myself: Un Testimonio." In *The Afro-Latin@ Reader,* edited by Miriam Jiménez Román and Juan Flores. Durham, NC: Duke University Press, 2011.

Vilkomerson, Sara. "Michelle Rodriguez Talks Movies, Female Empowerment, and Sex." *Entertainment Weekly*, October 1, 2013.

Visweswaran, Kamala. *Fictions of Feminist Ethnography.* Minneapolis: University of Minnesota Press, 1996.

Wade, Peter. "Racial Identity and Nationalism: A Theoretical View from Latin America." *Ethnic and Racial Studies* 24, no. 5 (September 2001): 845–865.

Wallace, Maurice O., and Shawn Michelle Smith, eds. *Pictures and Progress: Early Photography and the Making of African American Identity.* Durham, NC: Duke University Press, 2012.

Warren, Rossalyn. "The Poor Girl and the Rich Boy—How a Murder Has Left a Country Grappling with Abortion." *BuzzFeed*, May 21, 2018. https://www.buzzfeed news.com/article/rossalyn/abortion-murder-dominican-republic-emely-peguero.

Wexler, Laura. *Tender Violence: Domestic Visions in an Age of U.S. Imperialism*. Chapel Hill: University of North Carolina Press, 2000.

Willis, Deborah, ed. *Picturing Us: African American Identity in Photography*. New York: New Press, 1994.

Willis, Deborah, and Carla Williams. *The Black Female Body: A Photographic History*. Philadelphia: Temple University Press, 2002.

Wolf, Margery. *A Thrice-Told Tale: Feminism, Postmodernism, and Ethnographic Responsibility*. Stanford, CA: Stanford University Press, 1992.

Wright, Michelle M. *Becoming Black: Creating Identity in the African Diaspora*. Durham, NC: Duke University Press, 2004.

Yoder, April. "Dominican Baseball and Latin American Pluralism, 1969–1974." *Oxford Research Encyclopedia of Latin American History*. 29 Sep. 2016.

Zack, Naomi, ed. *American Mixed Race: The Culture of Microdiversity*. Landham, MD: Rowman and Littlefield, 1995.

Zalman, Sandra. "The Art of Window Display: Cross-Promotion at Bonwit Teller and MoMA." In *Architectures of Display: Department Stores and Modern Retail*, edited by Anca I. Lasc, Patricia Lara-Betancourt, and Margaret Maile Petty. New York: Routledge, 2017.

Index

Abreu, Dulcina (interviewee), 61; at Altos de Chavón, 72; on racialized stereotypes, 78–82, 212n18

Adela (character): desire for autonomy, 156, 170, 171–74; desire to be seen, 171–72; fate of, 169, 174; jealousy, 151; as property, 168; "tragic mulatto" narrative, 174. *See also* Galán, Cindy

Afonso, Fran, photos by, 145, 156

African Americans, 12, 98, 198, 203n2, 211n10, appropriating the culture of, 105–6, 117, 134; Dominican impressions of, 78–79, 119, 134; tourism and, 221n33. *See also* Saldaña, Zoe

Afro-Surrealism: Terri Frances on, 198; Wangechi Mutu and, 93–94

Albania (interviewee), 187–89

Alcantara, Amanda, 195–96

Alexander, M. Jacqui, 7

Alice in Wonderland (character), 144, 147, 184

Altos de Chavón (art school), 72, 80

Álvarez, Julia, 13, 118, 178, 220n14

Ambar (interviewee), 100–101, 134–42

ambiguity. *See* gender ambiguity; racial ambiguity

anti-abortion laws, 178, 190–95

Anzaldúa, Gloria, 8

Aparicio, Frances R., 10

artists: and activists, 7, 13, 29, 55–56, 201; Black, 24, 68, 69, 96, 103, 115, 204n18, 216n93; Dominican women, 146, 148, 153, 158–59; murals and graffiti, 45, 52; stereotype of, 73, 74, 97, 101, 214n22; Surrealist, 93, 174, 198; at la UASD, 41. *See also* Altos de Chavón; queerness: of artists; *and names of specific artists*

autonomy, bodily, 190, 192

autonomy, erotic, 103

Balaguer, Joaquin: authoritarian regime of, 49, 88, 96, 203n9; and la UASD, 42, 104

baseball, 18, 206n62

beauty salon, 39, 61–62, 120, 135–38, 211n2, 211nn4–5. *See also* hair style

Bernarda (character): in Dominican context, 157, 162, 165; power of, 156; reputation as concern, 153, 168, 171, 174; as tyrant, 150, 168, 169, 173–74; and whiteness, 167. *See also* Valdez, Karina

Besatón, El, 55–56, 103. *See also* González Gómez, Yaneris

Blackberry, 17, 36–37, 39, 50–51; and Facebook, 54, 85

Black feminism, 7; ethnography, 27–28; Yaneris González Gómez and, 66; Faye Harrison, 175; Dorothy Roberts, 192; Isabel Spencer and, 154, 158; 163

Bost, Suzanne, 20

Bowie, David, 100, 117, 216n93

Brennan, Denise, 18–19

Bryson, Norman, 13–14

RACHEL AFI QUINN is an assistant professor in the Department of Comparative Cultural Studies and the Women's, Gender, & Sexuality Studies Program at the University of Houston.

DISSIDENT FEMINISMS

The University of Illinois Press
is a founding member of the
Association of University Presses.

———————————————————————

Composed in 10.5/13
with Optima LT Std display
by Lisa Connery
at the University of Illinois Press

University of Illinois Press
1325 South Oak Street
Champaign, IL 61820-6903
www.press.uillinois.edu